THE WRITER'S BOOK

The Writer's Book

Edited by HELEN HULL

Presented by THE AUTHORS GUILD

BARNES & NOBLE, INC., NEW YORK

PUBLISHERS • BOOKSELLERS • SINCE 1874

An Everyday Handbook

THE WRITER'S BOOK

Published by Barnes & Noble, Inc.
through Special Arrangement with Harper & Brothers

L. C. Catalogue Card Number: 56-7093

Printed in the United States of America

To Arthur Train

To Will Irwin

Remembering our debt to them

Foreword

The Writer's Book presents an unusual assembly of writers of our time, men and women whose names are among the most distinguished and the most familiar in the profession of writing, as contemporary as television and the secrets of the atom, as well established as the Nobel Award. Here you will find none of the jaded and conventional remarks about the craft of writing. Many of these authors have for the first time looked over their experience in their particular kind of writing and set down some of their conclusions. Of the forty pieces in the book, twenty-eight were written expressly for this volume. The reprinted pieces we have chosen for their pertinence, their illumination of certain problems in writing, and in several cases for their shrewd satire.

The Writer's Book should interest many people; people who like to read books or magazines; people who wonder about television; people who listen to the radio; people who are writing and who hope that someday their names will shine with the brilliance of this list; people who like to listen to good talk from skilled craftsmen. Here is talk which has sincerity and humor, which is practical and profound, stimulating and useful, businesslike and idealistic.

The Writer's Book does not promise to answer all questions about writing or to settle all problems. The contributors include novelists, poets, writers of short stories, article writers, editors, representatives of the important contemporary crafts allied to writing, a drama agent, a statesman, a ghost writer, and a psychoanalyst, a fair sampling of the profession. *The Writer's Book* does promise to interest anyone who likes to read or write.

So many stars billed on one program may suggest that this is a special performance. The Authors Guild presents this *Writer's Book*, and the Table of Contents with its list of authors proves lively interest and belief in the Guild, the writers' section of the Authors League of America. The desire to help the Authors Guild prompted these busy men and women to lay aside their own work and to write these articles for the book. No editor planning an anthology of his favorite pieces could have tempted them with the promise of money, not even with a share of the royalties (if he happened to be thus enlightened). But for this book, which belongs to the Authors Guild, and all the royalties of which go into the Guild's funds, the writers responded with generosity. Several of them were not League members, but even so they thought so highly of the League and its work for authors that they turned in their pieces anyway. Two of them said they had always meant to join and they have since become members.

The authors in the Guild *Writer's Book* have reached high places in their careers. The best literary agents, literary lawyers, publishers and editors of magazines wait receptively for their next article or story or novel. Why shouldn't these authors think that they have outgrown the protection and advice which the Authors Guild gives? Their continued loyalty grows out of a double root.

One fork is this, as a Guild member put it. Whenever an agent or an author and a publisher agree upon a contract, they work with a third unseen presence at the table, the knowledge of work which the Guild has done upon the fine-print clauses in the contract, the awareness of practices advised and established. However these professional authors may have outgrown an immediate need for assistance, they recognize a debt to the Authors Guild for benefits which they share. We might add here that some top-flight writers are less clear sighted. They share the benefits, too, but they suffer a stubborn myopia when looking toward the source.

The second fork of this root from which the loyalty behind this volume grows is this: these writers have a better memory than others. They remember their own inexperience, their early lack of any knowledge about the business end of writing, their naïve and eager longing just to get into print, let the rights fall where they may. They remember the day when an agent had no interest in such small fry. They know that one important function of the Authors Guild is to help inexperienced writers to a good start, to take the place of the competent agent who has too long a list of important authors to bother with this newcomer, to prevent mistakes which might live longer than the first book. Because these authors in the Guild *Writer's Book* remember the days of their writing-youth, they know the value of this organization for writers, the Authors League of America. So much for the motives behind the contributions to our *Writer's Book.*

The stories about the collecting of the material would fill another volume; who was in Asia or Africa and couldn't be reached in time; who was too busy or too exhausted from a book and then changed his mind; who meant to hoard his stuff for a book of his own. Someday we might write that book, calling it *Sidelights on Authors,* or a *Study in the Differences between the Male and Female Writer.*

The Authors Guild presents its *Writer's Book* with pride and gratitude in the authors whose fine work fills its pages.

HELEN HULL, *Editor*

The idea for *The Writer's Book* originated at a meeting of the Authors Guild Council. Paul Gallico, then president, appointed Helen Hull as chairman of a committee to plan the contents of the volume and to gather the material. Elizabeth Janeway and Helen Hull drew up a possible table of contents. Necessity and further suggestions from Guild members modified the original plan somewhat, always, we hope, in the direction of a better book.

The secretaries of the Guild have given valuable assistance in such matters as locating addresses and sending out letters.

Helen Hull and Elizabeth Janeway have written the brief notes which introduce the articles.

The Guild wishes to thank the authors and the publishers who have made this Writer's Book a fine collection.

Contents

CONTENTS

THE WRITER'S BOOK

1

In Search of Readers

PEARL S. BUCK

Pearl S. Buck was born in Hillsboro, West Virginia, but she lived most of her early years in China. Her parents, whose lives she has recorded in two biographies, were missionaries. After boarding school in Shanghai she came to America by way of Europe and England and finished her education at Randolph-Macon College, Virginia, before returning to China. She won prizes, first, as a child when writing for a juvenile weekly in Shanghai. *The Good Earth* was her second novel and won the William Dean Howells Medal as well as the Pulitzer Prize. Still known primarily as a novelist, she had won recognition as a nonfiction writer as well before she received the Nobel Prize in 1938. She has written juveniles and *The Big Wave* received the award of the Child Study Association for 1948. Her most recent works include *Hidden Flower* (1952); *The Man Who Changed China: the Story of Sun Yat-sen* (1953); *Johnny Jack and His Beginnings* (1954); *My Several Worlds* (1954); and *The Imperial Woman* (1955).

Epic simplicity, universality, are the hallmarks of Pearl Buck's work. The feeling of deep connection with her readers of which she speaks here is surely a subjective aspect of this universality. Such simplicity cannot be taught. But it can be denied and lost. *Communication,* says Mrs. Buck to the young writer, is quite as important—no, more important than self-expression. And this is a healthy and a needed message.

E. J.

In Search of Readers

THE ramifications of a novelist's life are many and often confusing. To write a novel is no longer merely to write a book. The novel is only the beginning. The means whereby the content of a book can be conveyed to the public are manifold.

Yet not all novels do reach the readers for whom presumably they were written. A certain number of novels, perhaps, were written, or their authors say they were written, for the satisfaction of self-expression. Perhaps all novels are partly written for this reason. Yet it is doubtful whether even the necessity for self-expression is wholly satisfied if readers are lacking. Self-expression must pass into communication for its fulfillment, and communication, for a writer, means readers.

There are, of course, two kinds of writers, among others. One is the kind who wants the select reader, the gourmet in style. This writer cries down the mass magazine and the reprint house. A few who taste and ponder, who read and reread, are more prized by him than the crowd who gulp and wait to gulp again. The second kind of writer—and I must confess that I belong to this classification—has a sneaking and unalterable fondness for the crowd. The average person, fool that he often is, interests and amuses me more than the rare and extraordinary individual. The ways of common people are enchanting and funny and profound. They relax the mind and hearten the spirit. I can appreciate the person in a million. I enjoy his friendship and ponder endlessly on his complexities, whether male or female. But when I sit down to write a book I find myself writing about the behavior not of a Proust but of a garage keeper or a grocer, a peasant or a bandit, and since these crowd to the point of my pen so easily, it must be that it is they who haunt my subconscious mind.

So far this is the prelude to answering the question that has been put to me: How, I am asked, does one write a good novel that is also a good magazine serial?

It is a question which I have never thought to ask myself. One writes the best novel of which one is capable and if it sells also as a serial, then this is a piece of good fortune. Of one thing I am sure—that for me, at least, to write a serial first and then make a good novel out of it would be impossible. Novelists, generally speaking, are not serial-minded. There are many excellent serial writers, and theirs is a work not to be scorned, even by the literary minded. But, still generally speaking, they are not usually novelists. They, in turn, having written a good serial, must consider it luck when they also manage to have written a good novel. Most of them do not so manage, just as most novelists cannot write a good serial. The techniques of novel and serial are so different that rarely indeed, and in my opinion never, can a good novelist write a good serial, that is, not if he sets about writing a good novel and a good serial combined. The two do not combine. The only way a good novel can be made into a good serial is for a trained serial editor to take the novel and do the cutting and adjusting necessary. To such changes the novelist must, if he wishes to appear in a magazine, simply be blind. If he values his manuscript more than his reader, or the extra money he can earn incidentally, such changes will be torture to him, and he must keep a firm grip on himself and ignore what appears in the magazine. After all, his book is secure and with patience one day it will be in his hand, whole and as he wrote it. The magazine reader, he is told, and I suppose truthfully, is never the same as the novel reader.

But there are other novelists, of whom again I am one, who while they wish that all readers would read their books whole and entire, yet are so enchanted by the reader in all aspects that they welcome even partial readers. These writers seek constantly to find communication with all kinds of people, those who fear a book and therefore find comfort only in the ephemeral nature of publications which they can use to start the fire with or to wrap around winter clothes to keep out moths or only to fill the garbage collector's wagon. There are persons who honestly do not see the use of books in the home, either for information—have they not radio and even television?—or for decoration—is there not the wallpaper? Such persons buy magazines for many reasons, for crossword puzzles, for recipes, for fashions, for jokes, for pellets of curious information, for selected facts, for ideologies, and for serials and stories. Yet, says the writer who finds readers enchanting, is it not better to accept these than to let them go without communication?

I should say, then, that the writer who finds people enchanting may often find himself in magazines. There is a tendency among the sober-minded nowadays to declare that art and story are far apart, and that where there is real art in writing there cannot be story and where there is story there cannot be art. Maybe—maybe! And yet Henry James, who has risen from the dead recently, at least halfway, managed to get in a deal of story along with a plethora of art, and Charles Dickens, though he was a storyteller above all else and thereby lost much in art, yet had such an art to his storytelling that few persons can escape him altogether even today, though he lies so long dead. And George Eliot, that somber softhearted giantess, told her stories as she saw them, grave and gay in a sort of ponderous mixture, and there was art in that. I sometimes wonder if art today is not used as one of those modern machines, called the defense escape. That is, writers who have no gift for the telling of stories must needs have art or else what have they at all? But to the born storyteller God still gives the art of life and nature, as a matter of course. And where do stories come from in the mind and heart of the writer who finds people enchanting, except they come from the people who enchant him? And what are readers except people and what are people except potential readers?

It may be seen dimly what I am getting at, I think. I have discovered that people like to read about themselves, and not about the writer. Proust was complex enough to contain within himself an unusual number of persons, yet even so the number was limited. It took much art to keep such a few interesting, and the reader of magazines, perhaps, is used to richer fare. The life of the average person is fairly crowded with a number of people on any given day. The inwards of any writer, however complex, soon begin to pall. Variety in people is amusing and informing at the same time. A good novel, therefore, has more chance as a serial, granted the writer wants a serial, if it is full of people and not just full of the author, or even just full of what is called art. The more common the people are, the more lifelike they are, since most of us are wholly common and even the rest of us are partly common. I have met some kings and queens in my day and they also contained elements of commonness. I have yet to see the entirely uncommon person, male or female. No, what makes a novel an improbable serial—given the proper editorial hand, which any magazine seems to have—is not enough people, and worst of all, nothing but the self of the writer. The good novelist must not be an introvert, if he is thinking at all of magazine publication. The only difference that seems practical between an introvert and extrovert is that the introvert thinks himself the most interesting person in the world, and the extrovert finds himself boring and so gladly turns to anybody else he can find.

The novelist, therefore, who is an extrovert by nature or cultivation, stands a fair chance, if he writes his very best, of having his books published also as serials. When I say by implication that an introvert can develop extrovert tendencies, useful to his writing, I say what I believe. Introversion, at least if extreme, is a sign of mental and spiritual immaturity. Some writers, of course, like other persons, never become mature. If they can struggle to maturity, however, they, like others, will find themselves increasingly tiresome, and begin to look elsewhere for their material. On the whole, most novelists become extroverts at least for this reason if for no other. In private life they may continue introvert but professionally they do tend to become extrovert. This is to their advantage, if they are contemplating the magazine market.

More than this I cannot hazard on the subject of magazine serial writing, in combination with the writing of novels. I am not a serial writer. A few early attempts in that direction were lamentable failures, accompanied with anguish and chagrin on my part. I do not know to this day what makes a good serial. I leave that in the hands of the editors who do occasionally buy one of my novels for serial use. I continue to write novels, and being pleased with readers, I am grateful if I can find them elsewhere than among book lovers.

2

What Is a Good Novel, and What Is It Good For?

IRA WOLFERT

After graduating from the Columbia University School of Journalism, Ira Wolfert began his career as a sports writer for the *New York–American.* As a war correspondent, he served in the South Pacific, in the Normandy invasion and with the First and Third armies in France, Belgium and Germany, and for his telegraphic reporting on world affairs, was presented with the Pulitzer Award in 1943. In addition, he is the author of *Battle for the Solomons* (1943); *Tucker's People* (1943); *Torpedo Eight* (1943); *One Man Air Force* with Capt. Don Gentile (1944); *American Guerrilla in the Philippines* (1945); *An Act of Love* (first published in 1948; completely retold version, 1954); and *Married Men* (1953). He has also written numerous short stories and articles.

Ira Wolfert's double-barreled title may have a shock-effect upon fiction writers and readers, suggesting that he has found an answer, absolute and universal, to two questions which we have thought must always have relative answers. A novel is good when the reader finds it so. Critics disagree, arguing about technique, material, style, and attitude in terms of their own theories and predilections. Readers disagree on the basis of their own social and moral prejudices, preferences, and habits of reading.

Novelists themselves haven't offered definitions. Some writers have been articulate about their working processes, leaving us records in notebooks and journals. They have hoped their works would be good, without analysis of that quality. Their toil has implied that they expected their product to be good for something. Other novelists refuse comment. They won't open the oven door lest the cake fall. They hope to keep their secrets of creation, whether from modesty, fear of intellectual interference with an emotional process, or a highly individualized unwillingness to share experience. They know that the technique which the beginning writer longs to have exposed to him is not a matter of superimposed forms, but a slow struggle to achieve a secret purpose.

Ira Wolfert has looked at his own purpose and, in his account of it, lifted the good novel into the clear air of all fine aesthetic experience. His phrasing of the possible effect of a novel (when good) is full of excitement for any serious writer. For he lifts it above the plane of rules and theories into the high altitude of experience communicated to the reader.

H. H.

What Is a Good Novel, and What Is It Good For?

ALTHOUGH many have succeeded, no one has ever tried to write a bad novel. But, what is a good novel? And what is it good for? By and large, there are no definitive answers to these questions. Each reader must supply his own, and then it is definitive only for him.

But I think there are certain general principles that guide readers in making their definition and guide writers, either consciously or unconsciously, in their striving. People read novels for all sorts of purposes—for "escape," for entertainment, to find out what happens next, to get approval for their own sins, to find out how others have handled certain intimate situations they have been involved in, and to learn an etiquette of deportment for intimate situations they expect to be involved in. There are many other reasons. However, they go only to explain why so many bad novels are read as well as good ones.

A good novel may serve some or all of these purposes, but it also must do something more. It must, first of all, be an experience for the reader, an invasion of the privacy of his mind creating varying amounts of commotion there. That is, it must take its place in the world as a forceful product of creative energy.

This creative energy must also have a very special shape. It must be in the form of the novel—and now we are in trouble. What is a novel? Writers have made it pretty much what they pleased, but good novels do have one common denominator in their structure: they are prose translations of ideas into the language of human life being lived.

The good novel need not have human characters—or Charles Dickens would be held in very small esteem indeed, and certain important animal stories could not be regarded as novels at all. It need have hardly any narrative. Nor need it contain either/or—that is, either characters or narrative. Most of them manage to, but certainly the narrative of *Wuthering Heights,* taken by itself, would raise a lather on those who swallow soap operas without breathing back a bubble. Nor can its characters be regarded as people. They are instead human emotions made to live buffeting in hollow shells carved awkwardly to resemble people. Yet *Wuthering Heights* is a very good novel. It translates ideas into the language of life being lived.

Certain writers about writing have demanded of novels before calling them good that they be "larger than life." It is a confusing phrase, meaningless on the face of it. But let us take it for granted that they have not said what they meant. Nothing can be larger than life, nor can any novel be even as large. It cannot even be as large as the life into whose language it translates its ideas. For a work of art must be, as Goethe put it, "boundless within." Its pages must be haunted by a sense of despairing failure. For if there is no overtone of shortcoming, of truth lying beyond what it declares truth to be, then it is not alive.

But I have never been able to take lightly the demand that a novel be "larger than life." While the phrase is meaningless, it seems to yearn in the direction of a meaning. If the meaning it gropes toward is that a novel, to be good, must leave its reader with a knowledge that his own self is "larger" than he understood it to be when he began its pages, then I agree. It seems a reasonable demand to make of a man who has knocked down a wall of your brain and thrust himself in and made a commotion there without getting booted out.

So now, in a process of elaboration for purposes of clarification, we can enlarge the general principle that a novel must be a translation of ideas into the language of human life being lived, and add to it the following: the translation must be made with such accuracy as to increase the reader's knowledge of his own self.

This is the answer I make to the questions: what is a good novel, and what is it good for? I use the word "knowledge" in the dictionary sense of conscious awareness, and the word "self" in the special sense of the scientist who has grappled with the problem of making precise what the layman means when he blithely says "I"—as in "I love," or as in "What's in it for me?" The I-me referred to has three parts: the memories and experiences in its consciousness, and that "ground-stuff" (as Erwin Schroedinger calls it) which has made it conscious of its memories and experiences.

So a novel, to be good and good for something and to be larger than the life of its reader, must make its reader consciously aware that he has memories he did not know he had, or that he has had experiences he has not previously been aware of, or must enlarge his concept of his own "ground-stuff." In brief, the ideas it translates accurately into the language of life being lived must be both honest and revealing.

The good novels have done this to varying degree. The primary interest of the novelist—as of all workers who have put creative energy into constructive use—is the "ground-stuff" of man. This is the goad, I think—perhaps the only one—that stings forth creative energy in man and makes it set itself afresh in each generation a task that has been called impossible by four thousand recorded generations and has been shirked by none of them. This "impossible" task is to lift up into the realm of factual information an intuition about life with which all men are born, a sense of connection with purpose.

Some novelists have attacked the task directly, some indirectly. Some concentrate on experiences, and write of contemporary life. Some concentrate on memories, and write historical novels, epics and myths. Some have burrowed directly into the "ground-stuff" and have written novels of philosophy and revelation. But whatever the approach, whatever the direction of travel, the goal is the same—the "ground-stuff" within one in which lies the meaning of the intuition, perhaps, to use an old-fashioned word, God.

There have been many theories why all the roads creative endeavor has ever taken have led to the one place. Leucippus sought the unity in multiplicity. Modern science gives him the answer: multiplicity is merely different aspects of the same unity. Lovers give him the answer. When two lovers look into each other's eyes, they see a unity. They lose their selves in each other's self, and thereby increase their wisdom to the point where they can hear life sing. The various bibles of the world have given the answer: Love Thy Neighbor; We are all children of the same God; Athman = Brahman, the personal self equals the eternal self. However it is phrased, it means at least this much: that the "ground-stuff" of man has in it something in common not only with all his contemporaries, but with all his ancestors and, it may reasonably be predicted, with all his descendants.

Else, would novels survive? Would the story of an ancient prince who slew his parents for a kingdom have anything to say otherwise to people for whom not only the murderer is dead but the kingdom itself is dead? Dostoevski unhinged a brain for me to look into. The brain was dead before I was born. It was owned by a man whose name I cannot pronounce. He lived in a part of the world I have never visited, and in a society which has now ceased to exist. He struggled with problems which are not mine. I look into his brain and say, "God, what a lunatic!" But would my tone have quite so much fervor if, in looking into that brain, I did not see myself?

Each age has favored its own technique for securing knowledge of the "ground-stuff," and in our own age the technique of the scientist has dominated. The scientist believes that if enough relationships are illuminated, then that to which all else is related will be. If enough truths are discovered, the truth will be. He has parted company with the Upanishad who seeks to discover truth by staring motionless at his own navel, and insists on trying to look from without rather than from within. He will not trust his own senses. They are within. They are subjective. They are sentries manipulated for its own purposes by the dragon guarding the secret within the "ground-stuff." The scientist has to use his eyes, but he reinforces them and checks up on them with the mechanical tools of arithmetic—numbers, not words, never words.

Words are subjective. Objectivity is the touchstone. A man to look within himself must first crawl outside his own skin.

When I say that the scientist has dominated our age, I mean that he has dominated writers, too. The novelist followed the scientist and in modern times has produced novels that adhere very closely to the technique of the laboratory. Even a kind of arithmetic has been invented to replace words in recording reactions: "He saw it was going to be good between them now"; "He said nothing"; "It was all right." These are not words that create meanings. They are ciphers into which meanings may or may not be read. They are the words of a galvanometer needle coming fugitively to rest at varying places on a dial. They do not try to tell you what to think. They only try to massage you into thinking.

Some very good writing has been done in numbers rather than words and a great many people—myself included—have read these works avidly and gratefully. But it is not necessary to write in numbers to write good novels in the modern manner. Good naturalistic novels have been written, and good realistic ones. There are good slice-of-life novels, and good novels of reportage, good regional novels, and good novels of social comment. But they, if they are modern, have one thing in common. Henry James, for example, and James Farrell have one thing in common. They record the experiences of the "ground-stuff" objectively. Writing about themselves, which is what all fiction writing is always about, they try to keep themselves out of it. They don't succeed, as the scientist doesn't, but like the scientist they try.

I have chosen to juxtapose Henry James and James Farrell only to startle you into recognizing a point. I was unable to think of two styles that seemed on the surface to differ more radically. Henry James would have a character "loiter" on a street corner, where James Farrell would have him "futz around." But, isn't this true? That style is inseparable from content, that in the example cited the difference lies exclusively in the experience the novelist has recorded? The manner of recording is the same. Both James, Henry, and Farrell, James, recorded an experience with as much precision as objectivity can provide. Where they parted company was in the experience they recorded. A man "loitering" on a street corner is doing something quite different from a man "futzing around" on the same street corner.

The different experiences recorded make for different classifications of novels; the manner of recording makes all the classifications one. They are novels inhibited by science. Now science is a very severe priesthood. It worships its Book (of arithmetic) as fanatically as the ancestral monks of three and five hundred years ago worshiped their Book (of revelation). Science rejects dogmatically, it will not admit the natural existence of or concern itself with experiences that cannot be described in numbers. A great many thoughtful people (not all of them charlatans) have recorded evidences of extrasensory perception. But science will not have it until a galvanometer needle pointing to a number on a dial hands down The Law. Psychoanalysis has gained a dubious resting place in the outer court of the church only because the galvanometer needle quakes to its tread. It does not yet point to a number, but it is not entirely indifferent; it does tremble.

In joining the priesthood, novelists have been quite as severe as scientists. Where the good novel of the past would have felt naked to appear in public without the prose equivalents of poetry, painting and/or music, the good novel of our day uses them either sparingly or not at all. In the hands of a writer of prose, it was decided, music, painting and poetry are treacherous instruments more likely to lead away from objectivity than toward it. Explaining anything to the reader, of course, died instantly; he must be shown only the number on the dial. The *avant garde* marching toward the second half of the twentieth century raised a banner with a strange device: the novel naked, rampant on a field of ripped and rended fig leaves. Their prescription was—bare sentences. *Das Wasteland Über Alles.* The novel's characters must be made nervous by words more than four letters long. Their aspirations must be mute. Their sufferings and joys must be made to seem inexpressible by being unexpressed. They have no thoughts that cannot be stated explicitly by writing "He said nothing." They have no interest in thoughts. Best of all, they don't even have brains to think them with.

No one can have any real quarrel with the ideal of objectivity. But the inhibitions novelists have placed upon themselves in its wake have lent a certain grayness to our literature. Art has been called a process of withholding, but how does that pertain where the subject is man? The subject itself has been withheld from the artist. Yet the outburst, the outpouring, the novel that empties its author has all but disappeared. Deviled by the god of science, novelists are afraid to let themselves go. They will not follow where their passions take them. Where they used to get drunk on the juices of life, they now prefer a martini dry. Where they wrote with fists, they now trill their fingers along an abacus.

But not the good ones, not the big boys, and my own feeling is that the novel which records experiences objectively is here to stay quite awhile. There is nothing necessary about inhibitions. They are by-products of an individual response to life, not the framework of the modern novel. The modern novel is a form which has the room in it for a large-scale man to throw himself beyond the known into the unknown toward the unknowable.

Science and its galvanometer needle will continue to dominate. But something new is now slowly making its way past literary chatter into the attitude of a man toward himself—that almost-science created by Freud and his followers in the field for which he pioneered a technique of medical exploration. The unconscious has always bulked large in all art. The artist did not need Freud to tell him it existed. The novelist's debt to him and his followers is that now the experiences of the unconscious may be recorded objectively as inseparable from the experiences of the conscious—the two together being one.

What is to be gained by that? I can testify only from my own experience. I write novels that are objective, naturalistic, realistic works of reportage and social comment. They contain all the poetry, painting and music of which I am capable. It may seem that I am trying to ride off in all directions at once, but actually I ride in the one direction—the direction of recording experiences objectively. The experiences I record, however, include not only what was said and done, thought and felt—these set down as objectively as my abilities permit. But they also include a character's unthought thoughts and, the feelings he hardly knew he had—these, too, set down as objectively and precisely as is possible for me. And I search for the meanings of my character's words and deeds, what these words and deeds actually meant to the man who had committed them, even when he was not consciously aware of what he was doing.

I am not the only one striving in this field, but I speak of my work because that is what I know best. When an author goes into the unconscious of his characters, he encounters great dangers for his craft. All writers write out of their own personalities, I think, but now the author is more directly at grips with himself. He must confront himself head-on if he is to write what he knows is instead of what he fears is. All writers write what interests them and hope it will interest others. But now the writer is in danger of becoming absorbed in matters so private to him that no one else can share his emotion in them. He is in danger of becoming medical and, thus, trivial. For the analyst, the drama of a man in battle with his fate may be a fright the hero had as a child. For the novelist, this fact may or may not be relevant but if he stops there he is not creating a character. He is diagnosing him. And finally, there is the greatest danger of all—the tax placed upon the reader. Writing is communication and without readers a writer is a man without a woman, a general without an army. The reader asked to travel with an author into the unconscious is required to absorb into his own conscious mind a great deal that he, for comfort's sake, is willing to leave in his unconscious. He must make an effort, and since most readers like to sit still while reading and relax, as in a movie theater, and most find themselves becoming bored while thinking, find their attention wandering and unwilling to return, the danger of a writer becoming "meaningless" or "dull" or "pretentious" or "phony" or "intoxicated with his typewriter" is great.

But greater than the dangers are the prizes. The stature of man lies in his unconscious, his greatness and the facts about it. There is where his music is. No man is less than an epic creature in his unconscious. No man is less than a poet there, or less than universal. In each man lies the world. The great ideas have not been invented; they have been discovered. The philosophers, the artists, the men of religion and of science have invented nothing. They have only discovered what exists in themselves. And if it exists in one, it exists in all.

You have only to look to see that this is true. You, as a novelist, have only to trace down into the deep from which they sprung the words, deeds, thoughts and feelings of your characters and then you will see what is so—that man has been created equal, although not equal to expressing himself in the face of the enemies of expression. You may ride part of the way into that deep on the back of the psychoanalysts, but the rest of the inscrutable way you must make alone if you seek to discover in yourself a good novel that will be good for something.

3

T. M. on the Problem of the Artist

THOMAS MANN

Born in Germany in 1875, Thomas Mann, Nobel Prize winner for literature in 1929, achieved great success at the age of twenty-five with the publication of *Buddenbrooks*, a success which was continued through the publication of *The Magic Mountain, Joseph and His Brothers, Joseph in Egypt*, and other works. He left Germany when the Nazis came into power and later openly denounced them. He lectured at Princeton and lived for a time in California, but returned to Europe after the war and spent his last years in Zurich. His final work, *Confessions of Felix Krull, Confidence Man*, was published shortly after his death in 1955.

Thomas Mann has allowed us to select from his novelette *Death in Venice* certain passages which comment directly upon the problem of the artist in European civilization during the years which preceded and foretold the two world wars. We recognize this novelette as one of the most beautiful examples of this form of fiction. Through and behind the narrative of the disintegration and final destruction of the writer Aschenbach is the study of the artist with his years of discipline, his laborious hours of training himself in his art, his dignified acceptance of fame, and then the thrusting up from depths unknown to him of desires first to escape in travel, then to escape in passion, and finally to escape into the last desperate transformation of death. Thomas Mann, in these selected passages, speaks with more insight and power than any comment.

H. H.

T. M. on the Problem of the Artist

From *Death in Venice*

ASCHENBACH had sought the open soon after tea. He was overwrought by a morning of hard, nerve-taxing work, work which had not ceased to exact his uttermost in the way of sustained concentration, conscientiousness, and tact; and after the noon meal found himself powerless to check the onward sweep of the productive mechanism within him, that *motus animi continuus* in which, according to Cicero, eloquence resides. He had sought but not found relaxation in sleep—though the wear and tear upon his system had come to make a daily nap more and more imperative—and now undertook a walk, in the hope that air and exercise might send him back refreshed to a good evening's work.

....

. . . he felt the most surprising consciousness of a widening of inward barriers, a kind of vaulting unrest, a youthfully ardent thirst for distant scenes—a feeling so lively and so new, or at least so long ago outgrown and forgot, that he stood there rooted to the spot, his eyes on the ground and his hands clasped behind him, exploring these sentiments of his, their bearing and scope.

True, what he felt was no more than a longing to travel; yet, coming upon him with such suddenness and passion as to resemble a seizure, almost a hallucination. Desire projected itself visually: his fancy, not quite yet lulled since morning, imaged the marvels and terrors of the manifold earth. He saw. He beheld a landscape, a tropical marshland. . . .

He had, at least ever since he commanded means to get about the world at will, regarded travel as a necessary evil, to be endured now and again willy-nilly for the sake of one's health. Too busy with the tasks imposed upon him by his own ego and the European soul, too laden with the care and duty to create, too preoccupied to be an amateur of the gay outer world, he had been content to know as much of the earth's surface as he could without stirring far outside his own sphere—had, indeed, never even been tempted to leave Europe. Now more than ever, since his life was on the wane, since he could no longer brush aside as fanciful his artist fear of not having done, of not being finished before the works ran down, he had confined himself to close range, had hardly stepped outside the charming city which he had made his home and the rude country house he had built in the mountains, whither he went to spend the rainy summers.

And so the new impulse which thus late and suddenly swept over him was speedily made to conform to the pattern of self-discipline he had followed from his youth up. He had meant to bring his work, for which he lived, to a certain point before leaving for the country, and the thought of a leisurely ramble across the globe, which should take him away from his desk for months, was too fantastic and upsetting to be seriously entertained. Yet the source of the unexpected contagion was known to him only too well. This yearning for new and distant scenes, this craving for freedom, release, forgetfulness—they were, he admitted to himself, an impulse towards flight, flight from the spot which was the daily theatre of a rigid, cold, and passionate service. That service he loved, had even almost come to love the enervating daily struggle between a proud, tenacious, well-tried will and this growing fatigue, which no one must suspect, nor the finished product betray by any faintest sign that his inspiration could ever flag or miss fire. On the other hand, it seemed the part of common sense not to span the bow too far, not to suppress summarily a need that so unequivocally asserted itself. He thought of his work, and the place where yesterday and again today he had been forced to lay it down, since it would not yield either to patient effort or a swift *coup de main*. Again and again he had tried to break or untie the knot—only to retire at last from the attack with a shiver of repugnance. Yet the difficulty was actually not a great one; what sapped his strength was distaste for the task, betrayed by a fastidiousness he could no longer satisfy. In his youth, indeed, the nature and inmost essence of the literary gift had been, to him, this very scrupulosity; for it he had bridled and tempered his sensibilities, knowing full well that feeling is prone to be content with easy gains and blithe half-perfection. So now, perhaps, feeling, thus tyrannized, avenged itself by leaving him, refusing from now on to carry and wing his art and taking away with it all the ecstasy he had known in form and expression. Not that he was doing bad work. So much, at least, the years had brought him, that at any moment he might feel tranquilly assured of mastery. But he got no joy of it—not though a nation paid him homage. To him it seemed his work had ceased to be marked by that fiery play of fancy which is the product of joy, and more, and more potently, than any intrinsic content, forms in turn the joy of the receiving world. He dreaded the summer in the country. . . . What he needed was a break, an interim existence. . . . Good, then, he would go a journey. Not far . . .

. . . .

The union of dry, conscientious officialdom and ardent, obscure impulse, produced an artist—and this particular artist. . . .

Aschenbach's whole soul, from the very beginning, was bent on fame—and thus, while not precisely precocious, yet thanks to the unmistakable trenchancy of his personal accent he was early ripe and ready for a career. Almost before he was out of high school he had a name. Ten years later he had learned to sit at his desk and sustain and live up to his growing reputation. . . . At forty, worn down by the strains and stresses of his actual task, he had to deal with a daily post heavy with tributes. . . .

Remote on one hand from the banal, on the other from the eccentric, his genius was calculated to win at once the adhesion of the general public and the admiration, both sympathetic and stimulating, of the connoisseur. From childhood up he was pushed on every side to achievement, and achievement of no ordinary kind; and so his young days never knew the sweet idleness and blithe *laissez aller* that belong to youth. A nice observer once said of him in company—it was at the time when he fell ill in Vienna in his thirty-fifth year: "You see, Aschenbach has always lived like this"—here the speaker closed the fingers of his left hand to a fist—"never like this"—and he let his open hand hang relaxed from the back of his chair. It was apt. And this attitude was the more morally valiant in that Aschenbach was not by nature robust—he was only called to the constant tension of his career, not actually born to it.

By medical advice he had been kept from school and educated at home. He had grown up solitary, without comradeship; yet had early been driven to see that he belonged to those whose talent is not so much out of the common as is the physical basis on which talent relies for its fulfillment. It is a seed that gives early of its fruit, whose powers seldom reach a ripe old age. But his favorite motto was "Hold fast" . . . Besides, he deeply desired to live to a good old age, for it was his conviction that only the artist to whom it has been granted to be fruitful on all stages of our human scene can be truly great, or universal, or worthy of honour.

Bearing the burden of his genius, then, upon such slender shoulders and resolved to go so far, he had the more need of discipline—and discipline, fortunately, was his native inheritance from the father's side. At forty, at fifty, he was still living as he had commenced to live in the years when others are prone to waste and revel, dream high thoughts and postpone fulfillment. . . . Outsiders might be pardoned for believing that his [books] were a manifestation of great power working under high pressure, that they came forth, as it were, all in one breath. It was the more triumph for his morale; for the truth was that they were heaped up to greatness in layer after layer, in long days of work, out of hundreds and hundreds of single inspirations; they owed their excellence, both of mass and detail, to one thing and one alone: that their creator could hold out for years under the strain of the same piece of work, with an endurance and a tenacity of purpose like that which had conquered his native province of Silesia, devoting to actual composition none but his best and freshest hours.

For an intellectual product of any value to exert an immediate influence which shall also be deep and lasting, it must rest on an inner harmony, yes, an affinity, between the personal destiny of its author and that of his contemporaries in general. Men do not know why they award fame to one work of art rather than another. Without being in the faintest connoisseurs, they think to justify the warmth of their commendations by discovering in it a hundred virtues, whereas the real ground of their applause is inexplicable—it is sympathy. Aschenbach had once given direct expression—though in an unobtrusive place—to the idea that almost everything conspicuously great is great in despite: has come into being in defiance of affliction and pain, poverty, destitution, bodily weakness, vice, passion, and a thousand other obstructions. And that was more than observation—it was the fruit of experience, it was precisely the formula of his life and fame, it was the key to his work . . . and reading [his pages, one] might doubt the existence of any other kind of heroism than the heroism born of weakness. And, after all, what kind could be truer to the spirit of the times?

....

Yes, personally speaking too, art heightens life. She gives deeper joy, she consumes more swiftly. She engraves adventures of the spirit and the mind in the faces of her votaries; let them lead outwardly a life of the most cloistered calm, she will in the end produce in them a fastidiousness, an over-refinement, a nervous fever and exhaustion, such as a career of extravagant passions and pleasures can hardly show.

....

Thought that can merge wholly into feeling, feeling that can merge wholly into thought—these are the artist's highest joy. And our solitary felt in himself at this moment power to command and wield a thought that thrilled with emotion, an emotion as precise and concentrated as thought: namely, that nature herself shivers with ecstacy when the mind bows down in homage before beauty. He felt a sudden desire to write.

....

This life in the bonds of art, had not he himself, in the days of his youth and in the very spirit of those bourgeois forefathers, pronounced mocking judgment upon it? And yet, at bottom, it had been so like their own! It had been a service, and he a soldier, like some of them; and art was war—a grilling, exhausting struggle that nowadays wore one out before one could grow old. It had been a life of self-conquest, a life against odds, dour, steadfast, abstinent; he had made it symbolical of the kind of overstrained heroism the time admired, and he was entitled to call it manly, even courageous.

....

For you know that we poets cannot walk the way of beauty without Eros as our companion and guide. We may be heroic after our fashion, disciplined warriors of our craft, yet are we all like women, for we exult in passion, and love is still our desire—our craving and our shame . . . since knowledge might destroy us, we will have none of it. . . . Knowledge is all-knowing, understanding, forgiving; it takes up no position, sets no store by form. It has compassion with the abyss—it *is* the abyss. So we reject it, firmly, and henceforward our concern shall be with beauty only. And by beauty we mean simplicity, largeness, and renewed severity of discipline; we mean a return to detachment and to form. But detachment . . . and preoccupation with form lead to intoxication and desire, they may lead the noblest among us to frightful emotional excesses, which his own stern cult of the beautiful would make him the first to condemn. So they too, lead us to the bottomless pit. Yes, they lead us thither, I say, us who are poets—who by our natures are prone not to excellence but to excess.

4

The Novel of Contemporary History

JOHN HERSEY

Born in Tientsin, China in 1914 of American parents, John Hersey attended Yale and Clare College, Cambridge, England. Private secretary to Sinclair Lewis in 1937, he has been an editor of *Time* and their correspondent in the Far East. Acquiring his knowledge from on-the-spot coverage of the battle fronts in the Pacific, he wrote *Men on Bataan* (1942) and *Into the Valley* (1943); the latter being an account of a group of Marines in the valley of the Matanikan River on Guadalcanal. He returned to the Orient in 1945 where he gathered together the experiences of six survivors of the atom bomb and wrote *Hiroshima* (1946). His first novel *A Bell for Adano* (1944), which is set in the Italian war theater, received the Pulitzer Prize and was a highly successful play and motion picture. His second novel, *The Wall*, was published in 1949, and his third, *The Marmot Drive*, in 1953.

With the statement that fiction can be stronger than truth, John Hersey hands back to the novelist some belief in the value of his work. Criticism has suggested that the novel might be an outmoded form, and bewildered readers have wondered whether statistics and summarizing general statements might give them more enlightenment about what was happening to the world. The novelist may well have admitted that he could not present nor interpret a whole world. He may have doubted whether his particular ability to set down a few characters, with their suffering and their delight, their growth or their destruction, could any longer result in communication, without which he had no urge to write.

Mr. Hersey knows that events, historical, social, or individual like love and death, happen not in statistics and generalities, but to human beings one by one. He knows that however huge the world may be, what happens still happens to men and women one by one, and is felt by each of them. The fiction writer deals with men and women one by one, and still, as always, draws his readers into a direct, imaginative sharing of more lives than he alone can live.

Mr. Hersey speaks primarily of the novel dealing with contemporary history and the novel of social protest, citing by way of proof a proud list of novels to which he might well add his own books. What he says is true of all good novels.

H. H.

The Novel of Contemporary History

TRUTH is said to be stranger than fiction; fiction can be stronger than truth.

Palpable "facts" are mortal. Like certain moths and flying ants, they lay their eggs and die overnight. The important "flashes" and "bulletins" are already forgotten by the time yesterday morning's paper is used to line the trash can to receive this morning's coffee grounds. The things we remember for longer periods are emotions and impressions and illusions and images and characters: the elements of fiction.

What do we know of wars from the history books we once read in school, nodding sleepily but impelled from page to page by the specter of a failing mark in our next term paper? Most of us know what little we do of the Napoleonic wars, not from histories, but from Tolstoy's *War and Peace*, of the American Civil War, not from the voluminous military commentaries on that so "military" war, but from Crane's *The Red Badge of Courage* and the stories of Ambrose Bierce and Margaret Mitchell's *Gone With the Wind*, of the Spanish Civil War, not from news dispatches at the time, but from Hemingway's *For Whom the Bell Tolls* and Malraux's *Man's Hope*. The First World War seemed true to us only when we read Dos Passos' *Three Soldiers* and Hemingway's *A Farewell to Arms* and Remarque's *All Quiet on the Western Front*; the Second World War has only begun to reveal its repugnant self to us as we have read Mailer's *The Naked and the Dead*, Michener's *Tales of the South Pacific*, Shaw's *The Young Lions*, Cozzens' *Guard of Honor*, and Wolfert's *An Act of Love*.

Writers of fiction in these times should be very glad and humble. It is an ironical fact that the great industries of mass communications, built at the cost of millions of dollars, and profitable, too, in the millions—newspapers, magazines, radio, television—these marvelously intricate industries have somehow failed to communicate clearly one thing: human truth. Novelists have often failed in this task, of course, but usually they have come a great deal closer than the huge businesses which profess that very task. All alone at their desks, thinking back and trying to recapture impressions and feelings, dealing with the baffling, shadowy components of human character, advantaged only in the wonderful, flexible form they use, these individuals have frequently been able to do what the powerful organs of "fact" could not do: make reality seem real.

Fiction is a clarifying agent. It makes truth plausible. Who had even a tenable theory about the Soviet purge trials until he had read Koestler's *Darkness at Noon*? Who understood the impact of Italian Fascism upon peasants, on the one hand, and upon thinking men, on the other, until he had read Silone's *Fontamara* and *Bread and Wine*? Who claims to be able to argue about the collectivization of the farms in the Ukraine who has not read Sholokhov's novels of the Don country? Whose mind imagined the nature and meaning of the fall of France in 1940 before he had seen the novels of Sartre and Camus? Who can know what the American twenties were like without having read the novels of Scott Fitzgerald and Dos Passos and Faulkner and O'Hara?

All right, these novels did not set forth the whole truth; human truth is not compressible within cardboard bindings. Furthermore, novels do not reach nearly as many people nearly as quickly as do the instruments of mass communications. Granted. Granted and deplored. What is argued here is only this much: among all the means of communication now available, imaginative literature comes closer than any to being able to give an *impression* of the truth. Nor does the admirable speed of mass communications vitiate this. It would not be fantastic to say that a careful reading of American novels of the thirties and forties would have given better guidance on the outcome of the 1948 Presidential election than an even more careful reading of that very year's and each very moment's newspapers did give.

This essay, then, is concerned with a specific genre: the novels which deal with contemporary events. Among such events, we may include any of the sort that might be written up in the newspapers—a broad category, we must remember, embracing war and politics (the front page), love (the society page), death (the obituary page), and other such time-honored commerce of the novel form. Some of the novels cited above, in the effort to prove that fiction is more adhesive and persuasive to the human mind than fact, were written long after the events they set forth. Yet there is a unity to that list of examples, of purpose and effect, if not of quality, which shows that this genre of the contemporary historical novel is indistinguishable from that of the historical novel in general. Indeed, the superior novel of contemporary events will in time come to be regarded as a historical novel.

Recently it has become too easy to dismiss the entire genre of novels concerned with recent events as being "journalistic" books and therefore somehow less than novels. There is a reason for this error, but not an excuse: within the genre there have been bad books. With regard to historical novels, there has been a similar tendency to oversimplify: the reputation of the whole genre has suffered because some of its books have worn bosoms on their jackets rather than vice versa. The imputation of guilt by association is unfortunate in any field. The type of the contemporary historical novel needs only time to be vindicated—time for the poor novels to be forgotten and for the good ones to be dispassionately read.

What should be the aims of a writer who undertakes a novel of contemporary history? What are valid standards for this genre?

Above all, this kind of novel should make anyone who reads it better able to meet life in his generation—whenever that generation may be. This is the highest aim of any piece of fiction; in only one respect is this aim especially pertinent to the novel of contemporary history: the presently living generations have been more confused and harassed than most others have been by the history in which they have participated. In this very fact lies fiction's main chance. Fiction is not afraid of complexity, as journalism is. Fiction can deal with confusion. A journalist is not allowed to be confused; he must *know.* But it is not necessarily a disadvantage for a novelist to be confused *as a citizen and a human being*—provided he has discipline *as a writer.* Indeed, the novelist's confusion may be a virtue, for it may allow him to come into harmony with his readers, who are very likely confused themselves.

The task of this kind of novel, however, is not to illuminate events: it is to illuminate the human beings who are caught up in the events. Character is the proper focus of novels of any genre. Again, here is a special strength that novelists always have at hand and that journalists rarely have: it is possible in fiction to make a reader identify himself with the human beings in the story—to make a reader feel that he himself took part in the great or despicable events of the story. The image of a single protagonist, in which the reader may see his own image—this is far more moving, more persuasive, and more memorable than the most raucous headlines and the most horrible statistics and the most authoritative editorials that could possibly be published in a newspaper. Journalism allows its readers to witness history; fiction gives its readers an opportunity to live it.

The novel of contemporary history must carry conviction. It must seem to be true. It must suffer a most difficult test. Those who participated in the events with which it is concerned, reading it, must be able to say, "That is exactly how it was!", and at the same time, those who did not take part in the happenings, and who perhaps have not been able even to imagine such happenings, must be able to say, "That is how it must have been!" Thus a definite scrupulousness and thoroughness are required of the writer, who must have done even more careful research than an orthodox historical novelist, since the latter has no actual witnesses to contend with; but also the writer must be selective and skillful in weaving, so that his mere accuracy or factuality does not flaunt itself and offend the human story he has to tell.

An especially difficult requirement for the contemporary historical novelist is that he must make his story timeless rather than timely. Attaching his narrative, as he is, to events which contemporary readers recognize as being near to their own experience, if not actually part of it, he will find it very hard not to address himself directly to them, with all their special and temporary feelings about the events in question—rather than addressing himself to human beings of any time, present or future, who have no feelings about the events because they are remote from them. His concern must be to see whether he can discover the constants in human character.

This writer must be unusually conscious of style and form, for it is because of lapses in these areas that the derogatory label, "journalistic," is most frequently and most justly attached to his kind of work. Even the writer who did not train as a journalist, the "pure" novelist, must, in undertaking a work of this kind, keep on guard against any manifestation of the journalistic style, which has made such devastating inroads, unnoticed and scarcely commented upon, into other genres of the novel, especially here in America. He must at all costs avoid the mannerisms and clichés of "journalese." He must avoid the newspaperman's way of burking crises, of taking verbal short cuts, or thinking in terms of "lead," "body," "recap," "angle," "quotes," "color," "punch-line," "by-line," "head-line." He must shun glibness, and the appearance of it. Oversimplification is his poison. Punditry, editorializing, sounding like a columnist—sins all! He must be careful how he eyes even the virtues of the best journalistic writing—directness, clarity, fleetness of the metrical foot; he must approach a vernacular style with the utmost caution. On top of all this he must, like any novelist, seek a style which is at once unobtrusive and yet personal.

The writer in this genre, on the hunt for a personal style and form, is obliged to ask himself why he writes. It is an axiom of criticism that characters in a novel must be credibly and clearly motivated, yet it is not often required of a writer that he understand his *own* motivation. Why does he write the kind of novel he writes? In the field of the contemporary historical novel, there are several valid motivations on the conscious level, it seems to me, which may in combination lead to the desired result—namely, a good novel. There are others which certainly doom the result in advance.

The valid motivations are:

A search for understanding. The writer who uses his writing in an honest effort to comprehend the forces of contemporary history, and their effects on individual human beings, will usually find responsive readers, for this effort can be said to have a certain universality in these times. The effort may lead the writer into some special, private theory of history, which in itself may be distorted or even untenable; but that does not matter, so long as the desire to understand, which led to the theory, was in the first instance real. Thus it was in part a rather petulant and narrow theory of history that led Tolstoy into and through the greatest novel of all times, *War and Peace*; readers may argue with his theory, or even be bored by its reiteration throughout the novel, but they cannot help admiring the force of Tolstoy's conviction, they cannot help sharing Tolstoy's manifest desire to understand the shaping of events by people and of people by events.

A desire for communication. This is, of course, a motivation for any writer, but in the area of contemporary events, there is one special reason why this is an important drive: it is in this area that communication between human minds tends to break down. Oceans, boundaries, iron curtains; local prejudices, nationalisms, class lines; special interests, hardened traditions, intransigeant beliefs—all these tend to block the flow of ideas and images between man and man. A writer who is able, by pointing up the unchanging, universal qualities in his characters, to penetrate the mental and emotional tariff walls between people and to re-establish that free trade without which man cannot live in peace with his fellows—this writer is certain to find readers everywhere.

Anger. The genre of this essay is related, not only to the orthodox historical novel, but also to the novel of social protest. A writer who comes to his work in anger may, if his passion is not simply hysterical, command an audience. The anger must be to some extent justified; it must be directed against a recognizable and formidable object. Humorless anger is dead anger, and of course a protest touched with irony and shadow will be more persuasive than one all black and white.

A will for world citizenship. The best novels can never be employees of politics; yet there is one politics from which every novel can and must take orders: the politics of universality, of humanity.

The invalid motivations, which are liable to destroy a novel before it is even written, are:

Catharsis. If a writer uses a novel as a vessel into which to pour his unconscious inner turmoil and confusion and drives, he is certain to repel readers. Of course a writer who is soundly motivated will put into his work much that is unconscious and much that he neither sees himself nor understands. This is a matter of degree, and the difference lies in the writer's discipline *as a writer*, or lack of it.

Money. Any novel of contemporary events which is written for the sole purpose of making money will almost certainly be a bad novel and not make money. Herein lies the chief difference (up to the present time) between the novel of contemporary history and the orthodox historical novel. It has proved possible, in the latter field, to write books as merchandise and to make the merchandise move off the shelves. But so far, in the field of the *contemporary* historical novel, form and formula have not found a meeting point.

All this has been set down to urge the following conclusion: Much nonsense has been written about "journalistic" novels. The novel of contemporary history is an established form. It has dignity, purpose, and separateness. Like any novel form, it can be, and often is, abused. But it is sometimes excellently used.

The author of this essay acknowledges in it a certain pontifical tone. It is easier to write about writing than it is to write the sort of writing that ought to be written about.

5

The Novel as Social Criticism

ANN PETRY

Ann Petry was born in Old Saybrook, Connecticut. She has had two novels published—*The Street* (1946) won the 1945 Houghton Mifflin Fellowship Award; *Country Place* was a selection of the British Book Club. Her first juvenile, *The Drugstore Cat,* appeared in 1949 and her second, *The Narrows,* in 1953. A short story of Mrs. Petry's is included in Martha Foley's *Best American Stories 1946;* and a novelette appeared in Edwin Seaver's *Crosssection 1947. Harriet Tubman,* a biography for young readers, was published in 1955.

Mrs. Petry speaks of fashions in literary criticism, meaning perhaps that criticism moves in waves, lifting to the crest at different times certain types of novels and rolling neglectfully over others. We might speculate as to whether criticism helps to establish a style in the novels written during a certain period, or whether a successful novel drags in its train a series of hopeful imitations, or—and this speculation is the sound one—whether the prevailing wind of any given period carries the pollen in its own direction.

Is the novel of social comment out of style now, along with the term "proletarian" which was a key word to favor in the thirties? Should a novelist be a reformer, an informer, or merely a performer of his art? Mrs. Petry expands the concept of the novel as social criticism until it includes practically all novels which present their characters as living human beings. She answers with warmth and sincerity the questions implicit in the subject of her article.

Mrs. Petry's first novel *The Street* is evidence of the truth in her quotation from Remarque. Lutie with her hopes, her struggles and her failure tells the reader something he should know about Harlem streets, something he can not easily dismiss. The vitality in Mrs. Petry's characters has, as Remarque said, made the reader understand.

H. H.

The Novel as Social Criticism

AFTER I had written a novel of social criticism (it was my first book, written for the most part without realizing that it belonged in a special category) I slowly became aware that such novels were regarded as a special and quite deplorable creation of American writers of the twentieth century. It took me quite awhile to realize that there were fashions in literary criticism and that they shifted and changed much like the fashions in women's hats.

Right now the latest style, in literary circles, is to say that the sociological novel reached its peak and its greatest glory in *The Grapes of Wrath*, and having served its purpose it now lies stone-cold dead in the market place. Perhaps it does. But the corpse is quick with life. Week after week it sits up and moves close to the top of the best-seller list.

It is my personal opinion that novels of this type will continue to be written until such time as man loses his ability to read and returns to the cave. Once there he will tell stories to his mate and to his children; and the stories will contain a message, make a comment on cave society; and he will, finally, work out a method of recording the stories, and having come full circle the novel of social criticism will be reborn.

Its rebirth in a cave or an underground mine seems inevitable because it is not easy to destroy an old art form. The idea that a story should point a moral, convey a message, did not originate in the twentieth century; it goes far back in the history of man. Modern novels with their "messages" are cut from the same bolt of cloth as the world's folk tales and fairy stories, the parables of the Bible, the old morality plays, the Greek tragedies, the Shakespearean tragedies. Even the basic theme of these novels is very old. It is derived from the best known murder story in literature. The cast and the setting vary, of course, but the message in *Knock on any Door*, *Gentleman's Agreement*, *Kingsblood Royal*, *Native Son*, *The Naked and the Dead, Strange Fruit, A Passage to India,* is essentially the same: And the Lord said unto Cain, Where is Abel thy brother: And he said, I know not: Am I my brother's keeper?

In one way or another, the novelist who criticizes some undesirable phase of the status quo is saying that man *is* his brother's keeper and that unless a social evil (war or racial prejudice or anti-Semitism or political corruption) is destroyed man cannot survive but will become what Cain feared he would become—a wanderer and a vagabond on the face of the earth.

The critical disapproval that I mentioned just above is largely based on an idea that had its origin in the latter part of the eighteenth century, the idea that art should exist for art's sake—*l'art pour l'art*, Poe's poem for the poem's sake. The argument runs something like this: the novel is an art form; art (any and all art) is prostituted, bastardized, when it is used to serve some moral or political end for it then becomes propaganda. This attitude is now as fashionable as Dior dresses. Hence, many a critic who keeps up with the literary Joneses reserves his most powerful ammunition for what he calls problem novels, thesis novels, propaganda novels.

Being a product of the twentieth century (Hitler, atomic energy, Hiroshima, Buchenwald, Mussolini, USSR) I find it difficult to subscribe to the idea that art exists for art's sake. It seems to me that all truly great art is propaganda, whether it be the Sistine Chapel, or La Gioconda, *Madame Bovary*, or *War and Peace*. The novel, like all other forms of art, will always reflect the political, economic, and social structure of the period in which it was created. I think I could make out a fairly good case for the idea that the finest novels are basically novels of social criticism, some obviously and intentionally, others less obviously, unintentionally, from *Crime and Punishment* to *Ulysses*, to *Remembrance of Things Past*, to *USA*. The moment the novelist begins to show how society affected the lives of his characters, how they were formed and shaped by the sprawling inchoate world in which they lived, he is writing a novel of social criticism whether he calls it that or not. The greatest novelists have been so sharply aware of the political and social aspects of their time that this awareness inevitably showed up in their major works. I think that this is as true of Dickens, Tolstoy, and Dostoevski as it is of Balzac, Hemingway, Dreiser, Faulkner.

A professional patter has been developed to describe the awareness of social problems which has crept into creative writing. It is a confused patter. Naturalism and realism are terms that are used almost interchangeably. *Studs Lonigan* and *USA* are called naturalist novels; but *The Grapes of Wrath* is cited as an example of realism. So is *Tom Jones.* Time, that enemy of labels, makes this ridiculous. Dickens, George Sand, Mrs. Gaskell, George Eliot, Harriet Beecher Stowe, wrote books in which they advocated the rights of labor, condemned slums, slavery and anti-Semitism, roughly a hundred years ago. They are known as "the humanitarian novelists of the nineteenth century." Yet the novels produced in the thirties which made a similar comment on society are lumped together as proletarian literature and their origin attributed to the perfidious influence of Karl Marx. This particular label has been used so extensively in recent years that the ghost of Marx seems even livelier than that of Hamlet's father's ghost—or at least he, Marx, appears to have done his haunting over more of the world's surface.

I think it would make more sense if some of the fictional emphasis on social problems were attributed to the influence of the Old Testament idea that man is his brother's keeper. True it is an idea that has been corrupted in a thousand ways—sometimes it has been offered to the world as socialism, and then again as communism. It was used to justify the Inquisition of the Roman Church in Spain, the burning of witches in New England, the institution of slavery in the South.

It seems plausible that so potent an idea should keep cropping up in fiction for it is a part of the cultural heritage of the West. If it is not recognized as such it is almost impossible to arrive at a satisfactory explanation for, let alone classify, some of the novels that are derived from it. How should *Uncle Tom's Cabin*, *Germinal*, and *Mary Barton* be classified? As proletarian literature? If *Gentleman's Agreement* is a problem novel what is *Daniel Deronda*? Jack London may be a proletarian writer but his most famous book *The Call of the Wild* is an adventure story. George Sand has been called one of the founders of the "problem" novel but the bulk of her output dealt with those bourgeois emotions: love and passion.

I think one of the difficulties here is the refusal to recognize and admit the fact that not all of the concern about the shortcomings of society originated with Marx. Many a socially conscious novelist is merely a man or a woman with a conscience. Though part of the cultural heritage of all of us derives from Marx, whether we subscribe to the Marxist theory or not, a larger portion of it stems from the Bible. If novelists were asked for an explanation of their criticism of society they might well quote Richard Rumbold, who knew nothing about realism or naturalism and who had never heard of Karl Marx. When Rumbold mounted the scaffold in 1685 he said, according to Macaulay's *History of England*: "I never could believe that Providence had sent a few men into the world, ready booted and spurred to ride, and millions ready saddled and bridled to be ridden."

Similar beliefs have been stated in every century. Novelists would be strangely impervious to ideas if a variant of this particular belief did not find expression in some of their works.

No matter what these novels are called, the average reader seems to like them. Possibly the reading public, and here I include myself, is like the man who kept butting his head against a stone wall and when asked for an explanation said that he went in for this strange practice because it felt so good when he stopped. Perhaps there is a streak of masochism in all of us; or perhaps we all feel guilty because of the shortcomings of society and our sense of guilt is partially assuaged when we are accused, in the printed pages of a novel, of having done those things that we ought not to have done—and of having left undone those things we ought to have done.

The craftsmanship that goes into these novels is of a high order. It has to be. They differ from other novels only in the emphasis on the theme—but it is the theme which causes the most difficulty. All novelists attempt to record the slow struggle of man toward his long home, sometimes depicting only the beginning or the middle or the end of the journey, emphasizing the great emotional peaks of birth and marriage and death which occur along the route. If it is a good job, the reader nods and says, Yes, that is how it must have been. Because the characters are as real as one's next door neighbor, predictable and yet unpredictable, lingering in the memory.

The sociological novelist sets out to do the same thing. But he is apt to become so obsessed by his theme, so entangled in it and fascinated by it, that his heroes resemble the early Christian martyrs; and his villains are showboat villains, first-class scoundrels with no redeeming features or virtues. If he is more pamphleteer than novelist, and something of a romanticist in the bargain, he will offer a solution to the social problem he has posed. He may be in love with a new world order, and try to sell it to his readers; or, and this happens more frequently, he has a trade union, usually the CIO, come to the rescue in the final scene, horse-opera fashion, and the curtain rings down on a happy ending as rosy as that of a western movie done in technicolor.

Characterization can be the greatest glory of the sociological novel. I offer as examples: Oliver Twist, child of the London slums, asking for more; Ma Joad, holding the fam'ly together in that long westward journey, somehow in her person epitomizing an earlier generation of women who traveled westward in search of a promised land; Bigger Thomas, who was both criminal and victim, fleeing for his life over the rooftops of Chicago; Jeeter Lester clinging to his worn-out land in futile defiance of a mechanized world. They have an amazing vitality, much of which springs from the theme. People still discuss them, argue about them, as though they had had an actual existence.

Though characterization is the great strength of these novels, as it is of all novels, it can also be the great weakness. When society is given the role of fate, made the evil in the age-old battle between good and evil, the burden of responsibility for their actions is shifted away from the characters. This negates the Old Testament idea of evil as a thing of the spirit, with each individual carrying on his own personal battle against the evil within himself. In a book which is more political pamphlet or sermon than novel the characters do not battle with themselves to save their souls, so to speak. Their defeat or their victory is not their own—they are pawns in the hands of a deaf, blind, stupid, social system. Once the novelist begins to manipulate his characters to serve the interests of his theme they lose whatever vitality they had when their creator first thought about them.

And so the novelist who takes an evil in society for his theme is rather like an aerial trapeze artist desperately trying to maintain his balance in mid-air. He works without a net and he may be sent tumbling by the dialogue, the plot, the theme itself. Dialogue presents a terrible temptation. It offers the writer a convenient platform from which to set forth his pet theories and ideas. This is especially true of the books that deal with some phase of the relationship between whites and Negroes in the United States. Most of the talk in these books comes straight out of a never-never land existing in the author's mind. Anyone planning to write a book on this theme should reread *Native Son* and compare the small talk which touches on race relations with that found in almost any novel on the subject published since then. Or reread Act I Scene 1 of *Othello,* and note how the dialogue advances the action, characterizes the speaker and yet at no point smacks of the pulpit or of the soapbox. When Iago and Rodrigo inform Brabantio that Desdemona has eloped with Othello, the Moor, they speak the language of the prejudiced; but it is introduced with a smoothness that hasn't been duplicated elsewhere.

One of the most successful recent performances is that of Alan Paton in *Cry the Beloved Country.* The hero, the old Zulu minister, wrestles with the recognized evil within himself, and emerges victorious. Yet the miserable existence of the exploited native in Johannesburg, the city of evil, has been revealed and the terror and glory of Africa become as real as though one had lived there. It is written in a prose style so musical and so rhythmic that much of it is pure poetry. *Cry the Beloved Country* is proof, if such proof is necessary, that the novel of social criticism will have a life as long and as honorable as that of the novel itself as an art form. For this book is art of the highest order, but it could not possibly be called an example of art for art's sake. It tells the reader in no uncertain terms that society is responsible for the tragedy of the native African.

In recent years, many novels of social criticism have dealt with race relations in this country. It is a theme which offers the novelist a wide and fertile field; it is the very stuff of fiction, sometimes comic, more often tragic, always ironic, endlessly dramatic. The setting and the characters vary in these books but the basic story line is derived from *Uncle Tom's Cabin*; discrimination and/or segregation (substitute slavery for the one or the other) are evils which lead to death—actual death or potential death. The characters either conform to the local taboos and mores and live, miserably; or refuse to conform and die.

This pattern of violence is characteristic of the type for a very good reason. The arguments used to justify slavery still influence American attitudes toward the Negro. If I use the words intermarriage, mixed marriage, miscegenation, there are few Americans who would not react to those words emotionally. Part of that emotion can be traced directly to the days of slavery. And if emotion is aroused merely by the use of certain words, and the emotion is violent, apoplectic, then it seems fairly logical that novels which deal with race relations should reflect some of this violence.

As I said, my first novel was a novel of social criticism. Having written it, I discovered that I was supposed to know the answer to many of the questions that are asked about such novels. What good do they do is a favorite. I think they do a lot of good. Social reforms have often received their original impetus from novels which aroused the emotions of a large number of readers. *Earth and High Heaven, Focus,* and *Gentleman's Agreement* undoubtedly made many a person examine the logic of his own special brand of anti-Semitism. The novels that deal with race relations have influenced the passage of the civil rights bills which have become law in many states.

I was often asked another question: *Why* do people write these novels? Sometimes I have been tempted to paraphrase the Duchess in *Alice in Wonderland* by way of answer (I never did): "'Please would you tell me,' said Alice a little timidly . . . 'Why your cat grins like that?' 'It's a Cheshire cat,' said the Duchess, 'and that's why.'"

Behind this question there is the implication that a writer who finds fault with society must be a little wrong in the head. Or that he is moved by the missionary spirit or a holier-than-thou attitude and therefore is in need of psychiatric treatment. I think the best answer to that question, on record, is to be found in Robert Van Gelder's *Writers and Writing.* He quotes Erich Remarque (*All Quiet on the Western Front, Three Comrades, Arch of Triumph*) as saying that people cannot count with their imaginations, that if five million die in a concentration camp it really does not equal one death in emotional impact and meaning—the death of someone you have known and loved: "If I say one died—a man I have made you know and understand—he lived so, this is what he thought, this is what he hoped, this was his faith, these were his difficulties, these his triumphs and then he—in this manner, on this day, at an hour when it rained and the room was stuffy—was killed, after torture, then perhaps I have told you something that you should know about the Nazis. . . . Some people who did not understand before may be made to understand what the Nazis were like and what they did and what their kind will try to do again."

It is with reluctance that I speak of my own writing. I have never been satisfied with anything I have written and I doubt that I ever will be. Most of what I have learned about writing I learned the hard way, through trial and error and rejection slips. I set out to be a writer of short stories and somehow ended up as a novelist—possibly because there simply wasn't room enough within the framework of a short story to do the sort of thing I wanted to do. I have collected enough rejection slips for my short stories to paper four or five good sized rooms. During that rejection slip period I was always reading the autobiography of writers, and in Arthur Train's *My Day in Court* I found a piece of rather wonderful advice. He said that if he were a beginning writer one of the things that he would do would be to enter Mabel L. Robinson's course in the short story at Columbia University. Needless to say I promptly applied for admission to the class.

I spent a year in Miss Robinson's short story class. And during another year I was a member of the workshop that she conducts at Columbia. What I didn't learn through trial and error I learned from Miss Robinson. She taught me to criticize what I had written and to read other people's creative efforts with a critical eye. Perhaps of even greater importance she made me believe in myself.

As partial payment for a debt of gratitude I am passing along Arthur Train's advice. If the walls of your apartment or your house are papered with rejection slips I suggest that you apply for admission to one of Miss Robinson's classes.

6

Imagination and Experience

FRANCIS STEEGMULLER

Francis Steegmuller was born in New Haven, Connecticut, July 3, 1906, graduated from Columbia in 1927 and took an M.A. in English Literature there the next year. While at Columbia he wrote *O Rare Ben Jonson* (Knopf, 1927), *Java-Java* (Knopf, 1928), and *Sir Francis Bacon* (Doubleday Doran, 1930). He taught for two years at Dr. Alexander Meiklejohn's Experimental College at the University of Wisconsin in Madison, wrote *The Musicale* (Cape and Smith, 1930), a novel that annoyed Madisonians considerably, joined for a time the staff of *The New Yorker*, then turned to free-lance writing. With Marie Dresden Lane he wrote *American on Relief* (Harcourt, Brace, 1938), an objective picture of the relief setup, and then went to France to complete his research for *Flaubert and Madame Bovary, A Double Portrait* (Viking, 1939), a book about Flaubert and his times that Harry Hansen says "reads like a novel" though it is firmly rooted in scholarship. His most recent works include *States of Grace* (1947); *Maupassant: A Lion in the Path* (1949); *Two Lives of James Jackson Jarves* (1951); *Selected Letters of Gustave Flaubert* (1954); and *Grand Mademoiselle* (1955).

The writer may refuse to see and to accept the limitations and the scope of his imagination. He finds his own material commonplace and thinks to escape its dullness by flight into more romantic farther fields, taking passage on what he calls his imagination. He does not trust his own experience, he does not value it; he does not know that within that experience, provided he can penetrate deeply enough, he possesses on the one hand all that he can achieve of originality in creative work, and on the other all he can know of universality. The scientist does not tire of his present knowledge, abandon it, and take off at a great leap into some startling discovery. He proceeds by scrutiny of his knowledge, by rearrangement of bits of what he knows until one day, in a fresh combination of a few old items, he has a discovery.

The writer may limit himself precisely to what he has seen and felt, thus turning himself into a reporter, a naturalist. He is like the scientist who hangs on to Newton's law or who knows the earth is flat. The writer may possibly be unaware of his own processes, writing without looking at the source, weaving blindly among his impulses and dreams. If a genius sits at the door of his unconscious, if the writer is a gifted poet, he may turn out a fine book. Often, however, the writer who rejects his own experience, his background, himself in short, bogs down in imitative work. He has not learned that imagination is the faculty of rearranging the known, of transmuting it into a new and sometimes wonderful piece of creation. Imagination is not, as some writers think, a rocket to a distant star.

Readers, too, have odd notions about the relation between the book and the writer, between his imagination and his experience. They like to identify the fiction characters as actual living people whom the author might have known, fitting the likeness to the person by tags of red hair or the site of the house. They can't see the imagination at work for these motes of dust in their eyes.

For these reasons the following pages from Francis Steegmuller's book, *Flaubert and Madame Bovary*, may prove enlightening. They show in full clear light the way Flaubert worked, the original incident from which he planned his work, the whole process of transmuting his knowledge of place, people, customs, attitudes into his novel. His identification with his heroine, his visit to the agricultural show, his use of Louise, his creation of the pharmacist, his belief that "everything one invents is true" (a recognition of the universal in his particular characters), all throw light on the relation between Flaubert's imagination and his direct experience. The lines of comment on his struggle for the right style in phrase and rhythm are final evidence that for all the book may have started from a story of neighborhood gossip, the book in its finished form is a work of art, a product of creative imagination. Henry James in his *Notebooks* gives the sources of many of his novels and shorter pieces: he shows us part of the process of transmutation. André Gide in his *Journals* traces the development of *The Counterfeiters*. Occasionally scholars construct from careful research the sources of some great poem. For its complete illumination of this intimate and living relation in creative work between experience and imagination, Steegmuller's study of Flaubert repays the reader.

H. H.

Imagination and Experience

Selections from *Flaubert and Madame Bovary*

ONE day, however, in the midst of his monologue of lament and querying, he noticed that Bouilhet had assumed a far-away, inattentive look—very different from his own when Bouilhet's difficulties had been under discussion. He was saying nothing. He seemed to be weary of the whole subject of Flaubert's perplexities, for when he finally did speak, after a long pause, it was about an entirely unrelated matter. Unaccountably, he began to talk about the visits he had paid, in Gustave's absence, to Madame Flaubert at Croisset.

Generally, he said, he had found her alone, with only little Caroline and the servants; few of her Rouen friends ventured as far as Croisset to call, contenting themselves with seeing her during the winter, when she moved into the city and lived in a few rooms near the hospital; only Achille and his wife drove out to the house beside the river, and even they, Louis gathered, very seldom. One day, however, his visit had coincided with that of an old lady of very provincial, almost rustic manners—clearly not a Rouennaise—who treated Madame Flaubert with considerable deference and who was accorded, in turn, more warmth than Madame Flaubert was accustomed to bestow on non-relations. When Bouilhet was presented to her, and heard her name, Madame Delamare, he knew at once who she was. He had known her son, and when he said so the old lady immediately began to weep and to bewail his untimely end, the tragedies which had overtaken him, the woman who had caused his ruin. Madame Flaubert and Bouilhet did their best to repair the damage which Louis's well-intentioned remark had caused, but the old lady's grief had recalled to Bouilhet the whole story of Eugène Delamare and his misfortune, which had recently been the subject of much comment in Normandy. And now he reminded Flaubert of it. Why he should do so Flaubert could not imagine: he was quite familiar with the story himself. He had known Eugène Delamare, he knew Madame Delamare and had often seen her at Croisset. The only detail new to him was Delamare's death, which had occurred during his travels. But Louis went over the tale from beginning to end.

Delamare, a few years older than Flaubert and Bouilhet, had been an impecunious and mediocre medical student at the Rouen hospital under Dr. Flaubert. He had never passed all his examinations, and like many another young Frenchman of the time who could not afford to continue his medical studies to the end, had contented himself with becoming not a full-fledged doctor, but an *officier de santé*—an inferior category of licensed medical man then in existence. He had become the local health officer in a country town near Rouen, and after the death of his first wife, a widow older than himself, he had married a charming young girl of seventeen or eighteen, the daughter of a near-by farmer. She was pretty, had been educated in a Rouen convent, where she had read romantic novels, and was delighted to escape from her father's farm until she discovered that marriage with an adoring nonentity and life in a small country town were even more oppressive. She quickly came to despise her husband, longed for a more vivid life, began to spend too much money on clothes, disdained her neighbours, took lovers, sank even more deeply into debt, boredom, and nymphomania, and finally poisoned herself. During the nine years of their marriage, Delamare had been perfectly blind to his wife's extravagances and infidelities; he could not endure life without her and with the revelations of her behavior, and he too killed himself. Their child, a little girl, had been taken in by old Madame Delamare, who had always hated her unbalanced daughter-in-law. They lived in poverty in a village near Croisset, and from time to time the old lady paid a visit of respect to the widow of the great man under whom her son had studied, and accepted Madame Flaubert's gifts.

Such, in brief, was the story of Eugène Delamare's tragic marriage. Bouilhet, however, recounted it to Flaubert in detail. He reminded him of the black-and-yellow striped curtains in young Madame Delamare's parlor, which had first caused her to be thought pretentious and extravagant by her mother-in-law and her neighbours and had been gossiped about all over Normandy; of the way she had instructed her peasant servant to address her in the third person; of her prettiness, her *chic*, her haughtiness and nervousness, her at-homes on Friday afternoons which she herself was the only one to attend, the unpaid bill she had left at a lending library in Rouen. He recalled Delamare's heavy appearance and manner, his good-natured mediocrity, his satisfaction with his situation in life, the confidence, almost the affection, with which he was regarded by his country clients.

And then, after mentioning all the details of the Delamare case that he could remember, Bouilhet returned, as abruptly as he had left it, to the subject of Flaubert's literary perplexities. The story of Delamare's marriage, he announced without preamble, was the story for Flaubert to write. He had decided that while Flaubert was away. And when Flaubert jumped to his feet with the same cry he had uttered two years before on hearing the verdict on *Saint Antoine*, Louis asked him to sit down, and to listen, and continued.

He pointed out the advantages of the story. He had been quite wrong, he said, to suggest shifting the scene of a realistic novel to Flanders; Flaubert knew Normandy to the last detail, that knowledge he must exploit, and Normandy must be called Normandy, not Flanders. Some Normans would complain, but that was a minor matter. The background of the story of Delamare was utterly Norman. Life on Norman farms and in small Norman towns, a rural Norman medical practice, Flaubert could describe with brilliant effect. What was Eugène Delamare but the incarnation of all that was dullest in the bourgeois? What was his wife but a bourgeois victim of romanticism? And what categories of humanity were better suited to Flaubert's pen than those? The whole thing would give him an opportunity to paint provincial life as it deserved to be painted. And he repeated what he had said two years before: there was no need for Flaubert to concern himself, as Balzac had chiefly concerned himself, with bourgeois money matters. Young Madame Delamare had run into debt, but precisely because she had had no thought of money. A novel on nonmaterial bourgeois themes, written with style, would unquestionably be something new. And now that Balzac was dead, and there were no novelists of any power or originality writing in France, such a book might very easily be the thunderclap with which Flaubert had always sworn he would appear.

But the vulgarity of it! Flaubert protested. That, although he made many other objections as well, was his loudest cry when Louis finally allowed him to speak. Even if he could ever bring himself to admit that a drama which could be enacted in a Norman town was fit to take the place of *Saint Antoine*, that dramatization of the thought of the entire world, it would scarcely be such a story as the Delamares'. In the Flemish novel, at least, the heroine was to have been visited by religious mania, to have entered into mystical trances, suffered from hysterical afflictions; and all this, her character once determined, would have given Flaubert scope. Whereas with the Delamares everything was commonplace, even the vices were mediocre! How could he bear to spend several years describing such people as those? The prospect revolted him.

Even so, Bouilhet insisted, the idea was good—not only good in itself, but good for Flaubert. Delamare was mediocre, his mediocrity was the mediocrity of the bourgeois; about the mediocrity of the bourgeois Flaubert always had much to say; he had lampooned it in the *Garçon*, he had written from Damascus about a *Dictionnaire des Idées Reçues*; why should he not express himself in a novel, which would be more effective than either? And young Madame Delamare was a character with even greater possibilities. Flaubert could show what there was—not only in her, but in the very air of the times—to lead her to her fate; the essence of the tragedy was her disgust with the surroundings in which she found herself, and beyond which she had somehow learned, however futilely, to look; it was the infection of romanticism, and that too was one of Flaubert's favorite topics.

But even admitting the excellence of the themes, Flaubert demanded, how could he write the story? Eugène Delamare did not baffle him; the medical background and the mediocrity he could describe—but the lady! A woman unbalanced in no mystical way but in regard to the matters of daily life, a woman who was pretentious, nervous, discontented, burdened by a dullard of a husband, a George Sand heroine without the halo of nobility: how could he paint *her*?

To this question Bouilhet made no reply, letting it hang in the air as oddly as he had previously seemed to be avoiding all mention of Flaubert's problems. The subject was changed as though by mutual consent; during the next few weeks, whenever they met, they conversed about other things—chiefly about the Orient; and Flaubert quietly set to work and finished the synopsis of *Don Juan*.

Despite long talks with Bouilhet, however—long discussions as to the best setting for the story, the best names for the characters, the best types of minor characters, the best sequence of events—the novel took shape but slowly in Flaubert's mind, and too fragmentarily to make possible the drawing up of an outline or synopsis. Several things did become clear. First, it was obvious that the book would be concerned far more largely with Madame Delamare than with her husband, who formed, rather, a part of the general background which she found so intolerable. Second, the opportunity of painting a scathing picture of the bourgeois, and of describing various aspects of the romanticism which had always so fascinated him, already offered itself as certain consolation for the loss of the color, magnificence, and antiquity in which he loved to bury himself. And third, the task might be less intolerable if he remembered to think of the book as an exercise. If it taught him the lessons of exactness, simplicity, and force which Bouilhet felt it would, and which he knew he needed, then later he could return to the themes which he loved, and his writing on them would be all the stronger. To concern himself with the bourgeois in a novel that would take at least two years to write would be an ordeal, but he would suffer it. Since discipline was needed, he would discipline himself.

But even though he realized these things, and realized that this novel was worth far more, as an idea, than either of the other more exotic subjects which he had considered, it was still an unattractive and depressing prospect, and he welcomed the arrival of an excuse which allowed him to forget about it for at least a short time: he welcomed the arrival of Maxime Du Camp, who came down to Croisset for a visit.

He had been back only a few months, and already *Madame Bovary* was under way. So recently returned from Eastern scenes, he was plunged far more intimately than ever before into the depths of Norman life, the life which hitherto he had always avoided by seeking refuge in some exoticism of time or space. It was, of course, Louis Bouilhet who had achieved Flaubert's rapid return to work. Had it not been for him, *Madame Bovary* would doubtless never have been begun. But could even Louis have persuaded him actually to undertake and pursue a subject so lacking in glamour, had it not been for the Oriental journey? The two years in the East had been a purge, so to speak, of Flaubert's romantic longings: of his lusts after exoticism in all its forms, of his need for brilliant color, heat, violence, grandeur, and filth. Now, with those boiling desires drawn off—at least for the moment—he had for the first time in his life the courage to concern himself with the details of daily existence in a small French town, which he saw with new eyes. Never before could he have endured the company of the Bovarys!

Sundays, as usual, Bouilhet appeared. He liked to play games with Caroline or cards with Madame Flaubert and Uncle Parain; sometimes it was difficult for Flaubert to draw him into the study until the evening. But Sunday night, invariably, Flaubert read him what he had written during the week—sometimes only a page, or two, or three. Questions of style, of content, of treatment were thrashed out: it was some time before Bouilhet was satisfied with the sentence rhythms which Flaubert was to employ. Long and oratorical sentences were of course taboo, and while the simplicity of the style of the Breton book remained a model up to a certain point, the poet now thought that *Madame Bovary* should be written in prose that was more distinguished, more originally beautiful. Together they read over sentences dozens, even hundreds of times; and then, when each sentence seemed right, they read over the paragraphs into which they were combined. Gradually, out of single sentences that were simple and direct, Flaubert learned how to construct paragraphs and pages that were also simple and solid, but shimmering and rich as well; inversions, shifts of emphasis, variety in sentence length resulted in a style that was more compelling and stronger than the monotony of the romantics. In the end, Bouilhet was delighted by the impact of the result, and so was Flaubert; but it soon became clear that this new style was not something which once conquered could thereafter be employed with ease and swift carelessness. Every sentence, every paragraph, it seemed, would have to be forged painfully, read aloud, and worked over again and again, like lines of verse; the book could advance only at a snail's pace; it would take years! It was a staggering prospect!

Sometimes, in fact, particularly at the beginning, the prospect was almost unbearable: the unexalted subject, the stubborn style, the fewness of the pages so far written filled Flaubert with desperation, and in the letters to Louise with which he varied his solitude as he had done in the past he cried out his difficulties. "I am advancing so painfully, spoiling so much paper, scratching out so many lines! My sentences are slow to come, for it is a very devil of a style that I have adopted. A curse on all simple subjects! If you knew how I tortured myself you would have pity on me, and if you knew the utter flatness of the monotony in which I live you would be astonished that I notice even the difference between winter and summer, day and night."

One day Flaubert spent at an agricultural show in a near-by town: the scene in which he was to describe it would not be written until the winter, but the show was given in summer, and notes must be made now. Another afternoon he spent staring at the Norman countryside through pieces of colored glass, to be able to describe the effect. Evenings, after dinner, he sat with his mother and Caroline on the wrought-iron balcony of the summerhouse beside the river; night gradually fell; on the towing-path across the Seine they could distinguish from time to time the silhouette of a horse pulling a noiselessly slipping boat; the moon was reflected in golden spangles in the still blackness of the river; eel-fishers' boats drew quietly away from shore. They sat there peacefully until Flaubert rose, saying: "Time to get back to Bovary," and then all returned to the house.

. . . The ability vividly to express a host of different points of view, always in accents of passionate sincerity, is perhaps the opposite of a handicap to a young man whose set task is the gradual bringing to life of the elaborate and solid plan of a novel with a large cast of characters. Flaubert considered *"ne pas conclure"*—"draw no conclusions"—to be the only motto for a sensible man, and the amusing thing is that even when he was talking about his work he could not help differing with himself.

"You should write more coldly," he informed Louise one Sunday morning. "We must be on our guard against that kind of intellectual overheating called inspiration, which often consists more largely of nervous emotion than of muscular strength. At this very moment, for example, I am keyed up to a high pitch—my brow is burning, sentences keep rushing into my head; for the past two hours I have been wanting to write to you and haven't been able to wrench myself away from work for an instant. Instead of one idea I have six, and where the most simple type of exposition is called for I find myself writing similes and metaphors. I could keep going until tomorrow noon without fatigue. But I know these masked balls of the imagination! You return home with death in your heart, done up, having seen only falsity and uttered nothing but nonsense. Everything should be done coldly, with poise."

Later, however, when he was finally in the midst of the adultery he had so longed to reach, and which he knew would "make the whole effect of the book," the story was different. "This has been one of the rare days of my life passed completely in illusion from beginning to end. At six o'clock this evening, as I was writing the word 'hysterics,' I was so swept away, was bellowing so loudly and feeling so deeply what my little Bovary was going through, that I was afraid of having hysterics myself. I got up from my table and opened the window, to calm myself. My head was spinning. Now, at two in the morning, I have great pains in my knees, in my back and my head. I feel like a man who has been making too much love—a kind of rapturous lassitude. Will what I wrote be good? I have no idea—but one thing is sure, that my book has been going at a lively rate for the past week. May it continue so, for I am weary of my usual snail's pace. I fear the awakening, however, the disillusion that will come from the recopied pages. No matter; it is a delicious thing to write, whether well or badly—to be no longer yourself but to move in an entire universe of your own creating. Today, man and woman, lover and beloved, I rode in a forest on an autumn afternoon under the yellow leaves, and I was also the horse, the leaves, the wind, the words my people spoke, even the red sun that made them half-shut their love-drowned eyes . . ."

It was scarcely an echo of moments of coldness or poise when he declared that he was "nauseated by the vulgarity of his subject." At times his disgust for the people he was describing was so great that he wrote brutal scenes, full of contempt, which it was impossible to keep but which relieved his feelings. And he was least cold of all, perhaps, when to his delight the veracity of some part of his creation was demonstrated. "I had a great success today. You know that yesterday Rouen was 'honoured' by a visit from the Minister of War. Well, I discovered in this morning's *Journal de Rouen* a phrase in the Mayor's speech of welcome which I had written the day before, textually, in my *Bovary* (in a speech by a prefect at an agricultural show). Not only were the idea and the words the same, but even the rhythm of the style. It's things like this that give me pleasure. When literature achieves the accuracy of an exact science, that's something!"

Indeed, it was only when he was composing his novel—and not even when he was talking about it, and certainly not when he was talking about other things—that the power of Flaubert's writing, with its constantly shifting points of view, was enhanced rather than vitiated, one indication among others that he was a born novelist. He thought about politics and society, these days, more than he had before beginning *Madame Bovary*, and he had ever more ideas about art; but it was undoubtedly his realization that it was *in his book* that he was consistent and always in touch with reality that caused him to make, with regard to *Madame Bovary*, a claim he was never to make with regard to any of his utterances on society or politics or art: "Everything one invents is true, you may be perfectly sure of that. Poetry is as precise as geometry. Induction is as accurate as deduction. And besides, after reaching a certain point one no longer makes any mistake about the things of the soul. My poor Bovary, without a doubt, is suffering and weeping at this very instant in twenty villages of France."

Emma Bovary had begun, perhaps, as young Madame Delamare, and there was no question but that she had subsequently taken on a resemblance to Louise Colet. The adultery scenes, in particular, contain whole phrases and passages of feeling that had been born in Paris or Mantes. But by now the largest part of her character was being modeled on that of someone whom Flaubert knew far better than either of those. "*I* am Madame Bovary"—"*Madame Bovary, c'est moi!*" —the retort he would soon be making to anyone who asked him the identity of his model, could have been made now. "One no longer makes mistakes about the things of the soul": that was why *Madame Bovary* was coming true.

The book was now half done.

Before Bouilhet's departure for Paris Flaubert had created Homais, the pharmacist who lived across the square from Madame Bovary and from whose "capharnaum" she was to steal the arsenic for her death. Homais was Flaubert's final crystallization of the Garçon, of the sententious and absurd bourgeois with a little learning and a head full of *idées reçues*, and he painted him as "at once comic and disgusting, essentially and personally fetid." The man became so completely alive that Flaubert was soon quoting him in his letters. "As my pharmacist would say . . ." he wrote, or: "In the probable words of Homais . . ." He delighted in writing Homais' report on the local agricultural show for a Rouen newspaper: "Why these festoons, these flowers, these garlands? Whither bound this crowd, like the waves of a raging sea, under the torrents of a tropical sun pouring its heat upon our fallows? Etc."

When he was not actually writing, he was studying and observing. He read books on popular beliefs, books of popular medicine. He attended the funeral of the wife of an old friend of his father's, a botanist, one of the few people in Rouen whom he respected. "The poor old man will be pitiable. Perhaps I shall find something there for *Bovary*. Such exploitation as this would seem odious if I were to talk about it, and yet is there anything wrong in it? I hope to make others weep with this man's tears, which I shall transmute by the chemistry of style."

He was finding, to his own intense interest, that he must not always be completely truthful and accurate in detail. To secure greater vividness and verisimilitude for the whole, some parts had to be distorted; strolls in the countryside had to take a longer time, journeys to Rouen a shorter, than they did in life—or else the general action would appear to be telescoped or tenuous. If the stroll or the journey was the vehicle of the action, he learned to lengthen it, filling it with conversation, incident, and significance; if, on the contrary, it was merely a transition between more important scenes, it was compressed, subordinated; hours and minutes were blandly lied about. The transitions were at times more difficult to write than the scenes which they linked: "Bouilhet was satisfied with my horseback ride, but before this passage I had one of transition which contains eight lines and took me three days. There is not a superfluous word in it, nevertheless I have to cut it down still further because it drags." The policy of reading everything aloud was adhered to: it was the only way to test sonority and tempo. And just as he struggled to make the style smooth and harmonious with no loss of vigor—he wanted "not a single flabby phrase"—so he realized that the action, too, must move smoothly, and with ever-increasing speed and complete inevitability, toward the closing tragedy. In life, the story of the Delamares might conceivably have had a different ending; but in *Madame Bovary*, even in the earliest chapters, Flaubert mentions details whose presence has no meaning apart from their relationship to the catastrophe. The end is inevitable, none other is conceivable, considering the details out of which Flaubert made up his narrative. He gave much effort to the precise description of objects and of tiny events, but before being carefully described they were just as carefully chosen.

The spring was a particularly beautiful one. "You are right, poor fellow," he wrote to Bouilhet, "to envy me the trees, the river bank, and the garden—everything is splendid here. Yesterday my lungs were tired from smelling lilacs, and tonight in the river the fish are cutting incredible capers, like bourgeois invited to tea at the Prefecture." He took many walks in Rouen, for it was Rouen which he was now describing: the scenes of Madame Bovary's second affair had in life been enacted in the Hôtel du Grand Cerf at Mantes, but Rouen was their setting in the novel. "I am singing the cafés, the taverns, the wine-shops at the foot of the rue des Charrettes. I am in the midst of my Rouen scenes, and have been making tours of inspection of the brothels, the green bushes before the cafés, the smell of absinth, cigars, and oysters." Homais considered Rouen a Babylon, and it enchanted

Flaubert to write in such terms of the city which he found so dreary. Rouen became almost one of the characters. "What a look Rouen has—is there anything more heavy and depressing? At sunset yesterday the walls were oozing such ennui that I was almost asphyxiated as I passed!" Taking his notebook, he spent a morning on a hill to the south of the town, observing the view over its spires and chimneys and the winding river that Madame Bovary had from her carriage as it reached the summit of the hill after the journey from the country beyond; in the afternoon he sketched out the description, and it was eventually rewritten five times. To give to these chapters the unmistakable stamp of Rouen, he found a place in his text for an object which existed nowhere else—the *cheminot,* a kind of Rouennais breakfast bun in the form of a turban, for which he endowed Homais with a particular fondness.

As before, he found himself littering his pages with metaphors—this easy method of giving color to a drab subject remained a temptation until the end. And it was all too easy to fall into analyses of character, a device of Balzac's which Flaubert considered a blemish in any work of fiction and a confession of weakness in any author—characters should reveal themselves in their actions. When he could, he read his beloved classics, and he railed as usual against the age in which he lived. "I have lately been astonished to find in Buffon's *Préceptes du Style* our own theories on the said art," he wrote to Louis. "How far one is from such ideas nowadays! In what an aesthetic void exists this glorious nineteenth century!" And as two of the least aesthetic objects of the unaesthetic century he pointed to Queen Victoria and Prince Albert, who were that summer the guests of France at the Exposition Universelle in Paris.

The autumn was as beautiful as the spring. "The leaves are falling. The garden paths, as you swish along them, are full of Lamartinian sounds which I like extremely. My dog Dakno lies beside the fire the whole day, and from time to time I hear the tugs on the river." Even with Bouilhet away, he had almost never enjoyed Croisset so much as this autumn before the completion of Madame Bovary. In September, on the date which marked the fourth anniversary of the beginning of the book, he hoped that "in a month Bovary will have her arsenic in her belly," but it took a little longer than that. He ran into difficulties in calculating his heroine's debts, and had to proceed slowly, consulting frequently with Rouen notaries. The exact effects of arsenic poisoning had to be studied. "I am sinking under the burden!" he cried to Bouilhet; but he had to keep working steadily all the lonely winter. "When I was describing the poisoning of Emma Bovary," he recorded later, "I had such a taste of arsenic in my mouth and was poisoned so effectively myself, that I had two attacks of indigestion, one after the other—two very real attacks, for I vomited my entire dinner." For his description of the wake around Madame Bovary's bier he drew on his memories of his watches beside the bodies of his sister and of Alfred, and his portrait of Dr. Larivière, the famous physician who was called to Madame Bovary's bedside too late, is a portrait of his father, who in life had been the head of the hospital in which Eugène Delamare had studied.

. . . There was a letter from an unknown gentleman, inquiring as to the original of the character of Emma Bovary, and to him Flaubert replied as follows:

"No, Monsieur; no model posed for me. Madame Bovary is a pure invention. All the characters in the book are completely imaginary. Yonville-l'Abbaye itself is a town which does not exist; the Rieulle is a nonexistent stream, etc. That has not kept people here in Normandy, however, from choosing to discover that my novel is full of allusions. But if I had made them, my portraits would be less lifelike; for in that case I should have kept my eyes on individuals, whereas my desire was to portray types."

There was a letter from another gentleman, in Reims, who thanked Flaubert for having written the novel because it had avenged him for the infidelities of his wife. All the pharmacists of the Seine-Inférieure recognized themselves in Homais, and some of them discussed the advisability of calling on Flaubert and slapping his face. And several years later Flaubert discovered that in Africa there was a Frenchwoman named Madame Bovaries, who resembled Madame Bovary not only in being the wife of a doctor, but in other particulars as well. Flaubert was often asked who had been his model for Madame Bovary, but he invariably replied that he had invented her. "*Madame Bovary,*" he always declared, "*c'est moi!*"

7

The Craft of Crime

RICHARD LOCKRIDGE

A former newspaper reporter and drama critic on the *New York Sun*, Richard Lockridge is the author of numerous mystery novels written independently and with his wife, Frances Lockridge. Together they have created the Mr. and Mrs. North series. He served as a lieutenant in the U. S. Navy during the war doing public relations work. A member of the Authors Guild Council, he has been a leader in its book contract negotiations.

Mr. Lockridge, in his clear and succinct discussion of how to write a good modern mystery novel, offers several suggestions which add up to this conclusion: to write a good mystery novel you must write a good novel. In the first place the characters must have not merely tags of identification, but reality enough so that the reader shares their experiences, however harrowing, and has enough concern about their fate to follow the story eagerly to its end. Then the scenes must have vividness enough to draw the reader within their drama. Whatever the material or plot of a novel, these two qualities are fundamental, an illusion of reality about the characters, and a chance for imaginative, vicarious experience in the scenes.

The mystery novel begins with murder, and in today's model ends with what Mr. Lockridge calls a gimmick, the single or perhaps double revealing clue. Within that pattern it requires for its success the same labors and intentions from the writer which lead to good fiction in any form. This conclusion may stir more novelists into trying mystery novels, and it should show mystery writers how to write better mysteries.

H. H.

The Craft of Crime

THE lending library shelves from which I choose rather too many of the books I read are segregated in the book shop and collectively bear a label—MYSTERIES. The designation covers a multitude of sins, some more flagrant than others, and the books assigned to the section make strange shelf-fellows. Kenneth Fearing's *The Big Clock* has been stabled there, and Robert M. Coates' *Wisteria Cottage*, although neither of these excellent books was reviewed as a mystery. Agatha Christie's, Rex Stout's, Erle Stanley Gardner's and Leslie Ford's works appear in this section from time to time; so do those of Manning Coles and Eric Ambler. Early Graham Greenes are present and along with them are collections of ghost stories and, of late, specimens of the science fantasy genre, now resurgent. Once I found William Faulkner's *Intruder in the Dust* displayed there, but that turned out to have been in error or, perhaps, in subconscious criticism.

In the broadest sense, and that of the greatest significance to a writer, these books are alike in being fiction. (There are true crime books among them, but they are merely fictionalized, which is another matter.) In a narrower sense, most of them are alike in being fiction which has to do with the crime of murder; with violent death brought about, and brought about feloniously, by human agency. They differ in various fashions, quite aside from the differences a reviewer may detect in the skill of their authors. Some of them are "novels," by the simplest criterion which comes to mind—they are reviewed by the men who commonly review novels and other serious matters. Some of them are spy thrillers. Some of them are of that species now called "suspense novels," with the implication that a story in which the identity of the murderer is not concealed is inherently better than a story in which it is. This represents an effort on the part of publishers to get books moved up a critical notch, which is a fine idea when it works, as now and then it does. Mr. Greene's early books are, in his own aptly chosen word, "entertainments." The rest are properly—and unashamedly—mysteries or detective stories. (It was once the custom to make a distinction here, as it was once the custom to distinguish between Angora and Persian cats. The distinction was gradually abandoned in both instances for the same reason: nobody could tell which was which.)

But all of them, the lending library says, are "mysteries" and the designation is as good as any for working purposes and for the purposes of the worker in the field. And all of them are, for better or worse, products of the fiction writer's craft. No single thing is so important for a mystery writer, experienced or tyro, to remember; none, one sometimes reluctantly concludes, is so often forgotten. These are stories, not puzzles. They are, within their limits—which are not so circumscribed as is commonly supposed—novels, not parlor tricks. They are good or bad, successful or unsuccessful, not in relation to the trickiness of their plots, to their "gimmicks," to the obscurity of their poisons or the ingenuity of their murderers. They are good or bad, and by and large they sell or do not sell, because the characters who people them are alive or are puppets; because the reader is interested in what happens to the characters or does not care at all; because the people of the story speak and act as do people who do not live in stories, and feel as they do, so that the reader feels with them. The problems of those who write mysteries are thus, basically, the problems of all who write fiction, whether for the pulps or for posterity. The mystery novel writer who does not always remember this has mistaken his trade.

He has, of course, a good many other things to remember: things which grow immediately out of the kind of fiction he is writing. He is writing plot fiction and, unless he happens to be Mary Roberts Rinehart, plot fiction of a more or less fixed length. The length is, roughly, between 65,000 and 75,000 words; 80,000 is usually acceptable; much under 65,000 brings one close to that no-editor's land between the novel-length and what has, I guess, to be called the novelette. In this space—long when one is filling it; not long (one always hopes) to the reader—the mystery writer must introduce his characters, differentiate them one from another and bring them alive. He must, at the same time, involve them in interesting and exciting happenings which center about at least one murder and include a threatened miscarriage of justice which will discommode (perhaps by hanging) his hero or heroine. He will probably wish to incorporate romance, a little or a lot—a lot, of course, if he hopes for serialization in the slicks, but then all of it, as goes without saying, essentially virginal. He had best have a physical "chase" during which villainy seems very likely to knock virtue in the head, and almost must have a final scene of confrontation in which the murderer, writhing and kicking at the end of the line, is drawn into the net. In addition to these standard ingredients, the writer who hopes to be distinguishable from any of the hundreds—perhaps thousands—in practice must get in a reasonable number of identifying peculiarities, such as humor, toughness, personal idiosyncrasies of style or, if it happens to be conveniently possible, general superiority of conception and performance such as one finds, for example, in E. C. Bentley's *Trent's Last Case* and in the earlier books of Dorothy Sayers.

It is obvious that the necessity to incorporate all this and character too in a manuscript of fairly fixed length raises a central problem of technique, and one which is by no means always solved even by the most experienced. Since the plot is, by definition, basic, and action, in the modern form of the mystery, essential, the temptation is always present to economize on characters. Many succumb to this temptation; the complaint of reviewers that the characters in many mysteries lie flat on the page is not entirely unjustified and the answer that it is technically somewhat difficult to make them do otherwise is without validity.

It is not, of course, suggested that mystery characters be developed with Dostoevskian thoroughness, which would be inappropriate even if it were not, for quite a few of us, impossible. One may write of crime and punishment, fortunately, without being able to write *Crime and Punishment*. The mystery writer has many characters to present and must get on with it or back his book goes to that circulating library whence, ninety-nine times out of a hundred, it came. He will almost inevitably use tricks—his characters may fancy cats or orchids; they may speak in an idiom unknown this side S. S. Van Dine; they may drink only milk when all about them are gulping rye or they may, in what has always seemed to me rather an oversimplification of the problem, take off their shoes whenever they sit down. But these are identifications, nothing more, and are to be used as aids to, not substitutes for, characterization. In the same way, names carefully chosen for dissimilarity one to another are helpful, as anyone may notice who reads mysteries replete with "Johnsons" and "Nortons," "Burts" and "Kirks" or, for that matter, "Valeries" and "Dianas." But one sentence of honest characterization is worth all these devices. I cannot suggest to anyone how such sentences are to be achieved; I can only note their great desirability.

In my own practice, which is fortunately with a collaborator, we more often begin with characters than with plots. Quite frequently the lady who is, in no merely complimentary sense, my inspiration in these matters starts it all with a list of people she would like to find in a book. A church organist, one of these was, and another a volunteer social worker who, to the regret of both of us, died in the second chapter, just as she was beginning to come alive. Then we begin to shake these characters into the pattern of a plot; *A* will do for the murderer; *B* seems a suitable first victim, and so on.

This way seems to us as good as any other and, in such matters, as indeed in most others, one is forced back to the frame of personal experience. There are other ways known to us: one may begin with motive; sometimes with locale; now and then, but rarely, with a plot twist. Probably it does not matter much where one begins, so long as one begins somewhere—and some time. The beginning is almost always, again so far as we are concerned, made by an effort of will: a "come-next-Monday-we-start-a-new-one" decision. A mystery writer who waits patiently for a mood to encompass him, for an idea to strike, may find starvation, or other employment, striking first. The professional in this field cannot—as can, say, the professional in the field which J. P. Marquand adorns—write one book every three or four years. Three or four a year would be more like it; Mr. Gardner does, I suppose, rather more.

Even for those less prolific than Mr. Gardner, plot consumption is rapid and ingenuity suffers strain. But fortunately it is unnecessary to begin with a unique plot, or even a strikingly novel one. Motive is even less likely to be original, however anxiously one may twist its tail. Probably with exceptions, of which I can at the moment remember none, it is the treatment which is important, as in any other form of fiction. The structure may be, and usually is, tried and true; there is still no objection, per se, to the ancient with millions dying of poison in the ancestral mansion, surrounded by eager heirs. If there were, dozens of mystery writers would be out of business.

The basic motive, and the one generally easiest to handle, is that of gain. In life, nine out of ten who are done to death possess something their murderers want, almost always money. There is no apparent reason why this percentage should not obtain in fictional murder, and by and large it does. The widest area of exception is, obviously, the spy novel, where no motive is required to explain the wickedness of the villain. He is wicked because he is on the other side, and this goes without saying. The spy novel has another advantage: there is no risk that the reader may, even momentarily, find his sympathies misplaced, while in a proper mystery he may sometimes be perverse enough to prefer your guilty to your innocents. But spy novels are easiest to write, and to sell, in time of war, which may be an excessive price for an author's convenience.

Once you have, in whatever order you choose, invented basic plot and characters, one more prewriting step remains. This, of course, is the matter of unraveling what you have raveled up. How, in short, does your detective find out who did it? He may no longer, as he could in Sherlock's time, pick up significant clues and pocket them, with neither by your leave nor explanation to the reader. He may not—at least not too obviously—rely on intuition, although most of the operatives in the "hard-boiled" group seem to utilize little else. And if he relies on the method of slow accumulation, working with a stop watch in one hand and notebook endlessly in the other (Early English School) the reader will grow bored even before the author does. The modern answer, by and large, is the gimmick—the single, or perhaps double, revealing clue, which the reader might also notice were he bright enough. These are hard to come by; unlike motives, they should have a measure of originality. At this stage of the preliminary work there is, I am sorry to say, nothing to do but think.

With all this done, there remains only the writing—only that one sustained action which will decide whether the book will be published, whether if published it will sell, whether it will be distributed by one of the mystery book clubs, reprinted by the dollar book publishers, and the forty-nine cent ones and by those whose printings cost a quarter in the drug store racks; whether it will be serialized or condensed in a magazine, be made into a play or a motion picture, serve as the basis of a radio series. If the characters lift themselves, for however brief a time, from the page; if the scenes are vivid and stir the reader's imagination so that momentarily he lives them too; if the action similarly catches the reader up, so that he reads faster and faster to learn what happens next—well, if these things happen in the book, you have *genus*, fiction; *sub-genus*, mystery. You may even have something you can sell for money.

But how this is done nobody, I think, can tell anybody else.

8

The Mystery Novel

REX STOUT

Primarily a mystery novelist, Rex Stout is best known to readers as the creator of Nero Wolfe. President of the Writers War Board, 1941-1946, and president of the Authors Guild, 1943-1945, he is Chairman of the Writers Board for World Government.

Rex Stout's article concerns one particular form of mystery novel, the detective story of the classic pattern. His concentration on this one form gives his discussion of its structure a precision and a usefulness for which detective story writers will be grateful. He lays down a few clear principles and, reading them, we understand better why Nero Wolfe has become a familiar, popular, and at times highly exciting character. He is, as Mr. Stout states, the hero of the detective stories through which he moves, slow of bulk and swift of mind. The reader wishes to learn how Nero Wolfe unravels the puzzle. He knows that the story is, as Mr. Stout says, designed concealment, and that Nero Wolfe will ferret out the hidden facts. Willingly and with increasing interest the reader follows the detective. Readers remember not the plots nor the criminals of the Nero Wolfe stories, perhaps not often the actual method of discovering the proper clue; they remember the detective.

The structure is simple, the principles are few. All you have to do is to create a Sherlock Holmes, a Father Brown, or a Nero Wolfe!

H. H.

The Mystery Novel

SO MANY different kinds of stories are being published as "mystery novels" that I should at once declare myself not qualified to speak as an expert on writing tales which (a), admit the reader as eyewitness to a murder in the first chapter, seeing the culprit plain; or (b), merrily celebrate Homicide Week, starting out with a couple of dozen cops, amateur sleuths and assorted civilians, and ending with less than a dozen survivors; or (c), snap the heroine in a portentous tremble in the first paragraph, and in 271 pages work her up to a frantic palsy; or (d) or (e) or (f).

The only kind of mystery I know anything about, as a writer, is the detective story of the classic pattern. In it, ipso facto, the detective himself (or herself) is and must be the hero. That is the central concept which must govern throughout, from the first groping for a plot up to the last page of revelation and triumph.

It is permissible to get the reader interested, if you can, in the difficulties and dexterities of the other characters, but those concerns must always be tangential. If you place an attractive young woman on the spot as a murder suspect, it is to be hoped that the reader will be anxious to see her cleared, but it is essential that he shall be even more anxious to learn how the hero brings it off. This necessity obviously controls the whole operation. Say, for example, that you hit upon a novel and ingenious murder method, or alibi, or concealment of motive. That's fine; but unless you can devise detection of it by the hero equally novel and ingenious, you may have a good story but you won't have a good detective story. Surely this is elementary. But in the scores of unsolicited "ideas for a story" that have been offered to me by amateur philanthropists, there has never been one that did not ignore it. That may not matter much, since none of the stories ever got written, but it does matter that it is also frequently ignored in stories that do get written.

That, I think, is the only unexceptionable rule for writing good detective stories. Lists of pontifical dicta have been drawn up by various experts, but they seem to me to be nonsense. There's nothing against having a corpse found in a locked room for the hundredth time, or pinning the crime on the butler, or trotting out a flock of false clues, if by excellence of writing or invention of a new twist or brilliance of performance by the detective you can make a good fresh tale of it. The most frequently repeated rule, generally assented to, is the most nonsensical. It says, "You must play fair with the reader," meaning that in the course of the narrative the reader must see and hear everything that the detective sees and hears. I don't know why people like S. S. Van Dine and R. Austin Freeman and Dorothy Sayers have insisted on it, since every good writer of detective stories, including them, has violated it over and over again. A dozen times and more Watson says something like this: "I did not see Sherlock Holmes again until late in the evening, when he returned to Baker Street hungry and exhausted." And the reader does not learn what Holmes did that afternoon until after the culprit has been exposed and taken into custody, and Holmes has lit his pipe and started to enlighten Watson. It is the same with Dupin, Lacoq, Father Brown, Poirot, Wimsey, Perry Mason —practically all of them.

No; even that rule is not valid. Indeed, it would be quite possible, and should be a lot of fun, to write a detective story in which, up to the moment of revelation, the reader is kept in ignorance of the identity not only of the murderer but also of the detective. There would be, of course, a nominal detective-hero, either official or amateur, whose activities and exploits would be the main thread, and at revelation-time up would pop one of the other characters (the last one on earth you would suspect) who would explain how the detective had concentrated on the wrong clue, cracked the wrong alibi, and nabbed the wrong party. That would make it a double revelation, exposing not only the real villain but the real hero. Someone should try it. It could be a first-rate detective story, and certainly it would make a monkey of the above-mentioned sacred rule.

Perhaps I should add the parenthesis that if the rule that you must play fair with the reader is restricted merely to this, that you mustn't lie to him, then of course it holds for detective stories as it does for all stories.

The Mystery Novel

If I presumed to write a 300-page book telling people how to write detective stories (which God forbid), at least 290 pages of it would be devoted to the unique technical problem of the genre. I have already suggested it in stating the one rule which I think is inviolable: the hero (or heroine) must be the detective.

That sounds simple but heaven help us. Let's say you have the required qualifications for a storyteller; you can create people in your mind that you get excited about, you can devise and develop a plot situation, you have a sense of structure and form, and you can write readable narrative and dialogue. Thus equipped, you can write good stories, but it doesn't follow that you can write good detective stories. For them you need something more. You need, not the kind of mind that likes to solve puzzles, but the kind that likes to construct puzzles, which is quite different. You also need considerable ingenuity if they are to be not only puzzles but good ones.

That kind of mind is essential. If, having the other qualifications but not that one, you try doing a detective story, you will probably make a mess of it. For it works this way. Your main characters, three men and three women, are in your mind, created and named and known. You are familiar with the criss-cross of their emotions and relationships and with the major developments as the plot proceeds, on to the high climax, the murder of *A* by *B*. It's quite a story. But not being a nitwit, you realize that while it is quite a story it is not a detective story, since in a detective story the murder of *A* by *B* must be not the climax but the beginning. That's a complication and a nuisance, and you proceed to take care of it by rearranging the plot, making some of the best incidents postmurder instead of premurder, and you're getting along fine when all of a sudden—who the devil is this?

Oh my lord, it's my detective! Now I have him to contend with!

But at least you still have your story. *B*, *C*, *D*, *E* and *F* (*A* being dead) are still with you and still in a fix. All you have to do is move the spotlight . . . but that changes everything. That marvelous showdown scene between *D* and *F*, and the one with *B*, *C* and *E*—they have to be discarded, since it would be too damn banal to have the detective eavesdrop on them, and if he doesn't know of them what good are they? So it goes until at length you become aware that you have no story left; the detective has stolen it. This is the crisis. You have three alternatives:

1. Kick the detective out and write the story straight, without him.
2. Keep the detective in, as an unavoidable and pestiferous intruder.
3. Let him have it. Transfer your major interest from the alphabet to the real hero.

If you choose the first, good luck. If you choose the second, you'll need more than good luck. If you choose the third, it all depends.

For your trouble has only started. A maddening surprise is laying for you. Granted that you successfully transfer your excitement from the characters you lovingly created to the intruder, and that you replot the whole thing into puzzle form and enjoy it, which you can't do unless you have the kind of mind above mentioned, then is when the fun starts. Having cleared these hurdles, having accepted, and not forlornly, the fact that the story is no longer about what the three men and three women have said and done but is about the hero's process of discovering what they have said and done, you start to write it; whereupon the surprise bangs you in the nose. You realize to your dismay that you can't write it. Instead of writing it you have to conceal it.

As replotted, in Chapter IV the hero is to suspect that *C* is a phony because he spelled honor without a u, which no Oxford man would do. In Chapter VII he is to eliminate *E* from suspicion because she eats canned pineapple with a spoon instead of a fork. And so on. Since the story is now about the hero's process of discovery, and since those are vital and exciting items in that process, of course they are to be highlighted? Oh no. On the contrary, though the facts themselves are to be related, their significance, which is what makes them interesting, is to be hidden at any cost. Telling a story is designed exposition; telling a detective story is designed concealment. Unless you fully understand the nature of this unique technical challenge, better not try it.

If you do try it you should not let yourself be annoyed at the restriction of the medium you have chosen, any more than a poet working on a sonnet should be annoyed at the restriction of the traditional rhyme pattern. It is the only way to get the effect you are after, and surely it is worth it. In *The Maltese Falcon* every word and sentence is in preparation for the impact of those nine words on page 257: "But never mind that. Why did you shoot him?" That was what Hammett was after all the time. The point always to be remembered is this, that what makes it exciting is not the discovery that Brigid killed Thursby, but that Sam Spade knew it—and how he found out. If you do remember it, and plot and write accordingly, you may not come up with a Sam Spade, but it will be a real detective story, and you can count on your share of my two dollars and fifty cents.

9

Conflict and Plot

ARTHUR KOESTLER

Born in Budapest, Hungary, in 1905, Arthur Koestler has served as a correspondent in Europe and Asia. He volunteered in the French army in 1940 and then in the British Army in 1941. He is the author of *Spanish Testament* (1938); *Gladiators* (1939); *Darkness at Noon* (1941); *Scum of the Earth* (1941); *Arrival and Departure* (1943); *The Yogi and the Commissar* (1945); *Twilight Bar* (1945); *Thieves in the Night* (1946); *The Tragic and the Comic* (1948); *Insight and Outlook* (1949); *Promise and Fulfilment* (1949); *Age of Longing* (1951) and an autobiography, *Arrow in the Blue* (v. 1, 1952; v. 2, 1954).

This chapter on "Conflict and Plot" from Arthur Koestler's recent book, *Insight and Outlook*, offers to the writer two major concepts which may serve to increase his power as he writes and to extend his horizon as he looks over his material. In the first part of the chapter Koestler states that the reader must identify himself not only with the hero but also with the villain if he is to share fully the dramatic experience in the story. Often the writer is entirely on the side of the angels, scorning the evil characters. The reader then enters the conflict only partially; he does not feel the deep opposition of human values. "By suffering with Desdemona and identifying ourselves with Othello's despair, we are compelled to hate Iago; but we can only hate Iago if . . . he too is a projected aspect of us." The dramatist or novelist who understands this concept may perform the miracle for which he always works, that of drawing the audience or the reader into emotional participation in his product.

Then the later pages of the chapter should help the writer who worries lest all plots have been used and no new one is left for him. All have been used, in the sense of the conflict which makes for drama. But these conflicts are eternal in man's relation to every aspect of his life, and yet in each period they differ in their dress of time, of custom, of current codes of morality. Koestler classifies these conflicts, and his list of the archetypes stimulates the writer into a fresh consideration of his own environment, with the evidence he has gathered in his own experience of the repeating rhythm of these archetypal conflicts, and the "new ways of combining several conflicts into composite patterns."

H. H.

Conflict and Plot

A Chapter from *Insight and Outlook*

IN THE hierarchy of bisociative processes that constitute art, the most powerful effects are derived from intersections of conflicting fields.

The conflict may be set inside one character (Antony the soldier versus Antony the lover), or between two or more characters, or between a character and a nonhuman agent or principle such as chance, fate, God. Conflict between characters may again be subdivided into clashes between different temperaments or ideas or scales of value, or between competing interests of the same kind, for example, sexual rivalry. The conflict may be explicitly stated or merely implied in the plot. But the common principle in all these variations is that each of the conflicting characters or ideas must be right within its own terms of reference, that the audience should be compelled to accept both conflicting fields as valid, and that the conflict should thus be carried into the reader's or spectator's mind as a clash between two simultaneous and incompatible identifications.

Conflict thus always reveals a paradox in the human condition. The paradox may be a superficial one, as in the case of divided sympathies for two competitors, with the resulting desire to help both, that is, to harm both. If traced to its roots, this paradox will resolve itself in the more fundamental conflict between the sympathetic and competitive aspects of human nature, in the polarity between the self-asserting and self-transcending urges. The dilemma has been referred to a level from which a deeper insight into the human condition is possible; the particular conflict has been earthed in the acceptance of its fundamental insolubility.

The function of conflict is essentially the same in drama, epos, or novel. And the process of experiencing conflict is essentially the same for artist and audience. Let the author be Shakespeare and his experience the process which occurred in his mind on reading Plutarch's life of Caesar. By a series of acts of imagination, the author identifies himself with each of the characters in turn—Caesar, Brutus, Antony—projecting some aspect of himself into each of them and speaking through their mouths; or, we may just as well say, introjecting them into himself and lending them his voice.

This, then, is the experience which the author wants his audience to share. He provides as stimuli actors on a stage or words in print. In both cases his experience will be shared only if the audience responds to the stimuli; otherwise the words will remain a dead letter and the stage a trite mummery. To elicit this response, Brutus and Caesar have to be alternately presented in situations where they capture the sympathy of the audience and compel them to adopt the thought-patterns now of Caesar, now of Brutus; to build up inside their own minds fields of behavior corresponding to both Brutus and to Caesar. By creating this double sympathy and double identification, the author leads his audience to a powerful climax where the conflict is experienced as a bisociative clash of two fields in the spectator's own mind. Thus a conflict of values is externalized by the artist in creating character, and internalized again by the audience in absorbing it.

The precondition for conflict giving rise to aesthetic experience is that both antagonists must exist in their own right. The villain must express some common villainousness in ourselves; he must enable us to experience what it feels like to be frankly a villain. By suffering with Desdemona and identifying ourselves with Othello's despair, we are compelled to hate Iago; but we can only hate Iago if he has come to life for us and in us; and he has only come to life in us and commands a certain amount of our sympathy because he too is a projected aspect of us, is the embodiment of our frustrated ambitions and jealousies, the bite of the underdog; for everybody is somebody's underdog. Without this silent complicity of ours, Iago would be merely a stage prop, and we could hate him no more than a piece of cardboard. Thus, while satisfying the integrative tendency through identification with one character, art at the same time neutralizes aggression by compelling us to understand, and even sympathize with, his antagonist. It automatically mirrors both sides of the medal, while in our practical pursuits we only see one at a time.

Literature admits of no black-and-white technique; the more evenly our sympathies are distributed between the antagonists, the more latent aspects of our own personality become actualized, the more significant the work becomes. Caliban and Prospero, Faust and Mephisto, Don Quixote and Sancho Panza, Christ and the Great Inquisitor—each of these couples fights an everlasting duel, in which we act as seconds for both. In each pair two universes clash, two self-contained frames of reference, two hierarchies of values intersect. All great works in literature contain variations and combinations of such archetypal conflicts rooted in the human condition, which first occur in mythology and are restated in the specific terms of each period. Poetry, according to Gerhart Hauptmann, is "the distant echo of the primitive word behind the veil of words." In the same sense, the action of a drama or novel is always the distant echo of some primitive action behind the veil of the period's costumes and conventions. There are no new themes in literature, just as there are no new human instincts; but there are in each period new sublimations, new settings and rules for fighting out the old battles yet again; and new ways of combining several conflicts into composite patterns, that is, plots.

These archetypal conflicts are derived from the basic paradoxes of man's biological and social make-up. They are of a limited number, and they all recur in countless symbolic variations in mythology, folklore, and literature. I shall confine myself to a few typical patterns.

CONFLICT BETWEEN MAN'S DESIRE FOR (a) OMNISCIENCE OR (b) OMNIPOTENCE—AND THE NATURAL OR DIVINE LIMITATIONS IMPOSED ON HIM (MAN VERSUS UNIVERSE)

Examples: the forbidden fruit (a); Jacob's struggle with the angel (b); the Tower of Babel (a+b); Ecclesiastes (a); Prometheus (b);

Faustus (a+b); Buvard and Pécuchet (a); and a whole host of broken Promethean heroes in recent fiction by authors as wide apart as Dostoevski and H. G. Wells. We note that in the later developments of the theme the law of progressive implicitness makes itself felt in the more discreetly allusive, almost shamefaced way in which the Promethean impulse is presented. We also note that, with the growing recognition of man's limitations and cosmic insignificance, a process of resigned skepticism sets in which makes the Promethean hero appear either as a madman (Wells's Dr. Moreau, Stavrogin in *The Possessed*, and their innumerable imitations), or as a fool (Buvard and Pécuchet).

CONFLICT BETWEEN MAN'S INSTINCTS AND THE SOCIAL LIMITATIONS IMPOSED ON HIM (MAN VERSUS SOCIETY)

This archetypal pattern branches into several categories and subcategories such as:

1. *Sexual conflicts:* (a) sexual drive versus incest taboo (see for a full list Reik's *Das Incest-Motiv in Dichtung und Sage*); (b) sexual drive versus monogamy and convention (at least half of the total bulk of world literature, from Vulcan-Mars to Madame Bovary, Anna Karenina, and variations of the triangular and polyangular situation); (c) woman's sexual drive versus her drive for emancipation (Amazon myths, women in male disguise, bluestockings from Lysistrata to Ibsen and Ann Veronica); (d) sexual drive versus other social obstacles (*Romeo and Juliet, Paul et Virginie,* etcetera); (e) sexual drive versus spiritual aspirations (or the conquest of the flesh, from Buddha to Aldous Huxley).

2. The *self-assertive power-drive* of the individual *versus social obligation* toward (a) the tribe, (b) the nation, (c) the social class, and (d) society in general. Examples range from *Coriolanus* through *Le Rouge et le Noir* to the stereotyped Soviet novel.

3. The *self-transcending tendencies* of the individual *versus social pressure,* or *Sensitive Hero and Callous World:* (a) with emphasis on *aesthetic* self-transcendence: the artist and society, the ivory-tower motif, most school memoirs and autobiographic novels (*L'Éducation Sentimentale, Of Human Bondage, Jean Christophe*); (b) with emphasis on *ethical* integration. Here the hero's system of values differs

from the conventional values of his time, and he appears in consequence as either naïve or mad or an inspired fool (Perceval, *The Lay of the Great Fool*, Don Quixote, Eulenspiegel, Dostoevski's *The Idiot*, Shaw's *Adventures of a Black Girl in Search of God*, Camus' *L'Étranger*, and other variations on the gentle-savage-goes-to-town theme).

CONFLICT BETWEEN TWO INCOMPATIBLE LOYALTIES

In other words, conflict between two types of social integration, for example, *love versus patriotism* (Judith and Holofernes, Antony and Cleopatra, Katuschka and the Five-Year Plan, and the stereotyped secret agent's dilemma). This motif is the archetype of ethical conflict between different *aims* of the integrative tendency. . . .

CONFLICT BETWEEN ENDS AND MEANS

A variation of the previous, the conflict being between metaphysical and secular values, for example, the sanctity of individual life versus the interest of the group. Examples range from Abraham's haggling with the Lord to spare Sodom for the sake of five righteous men, through Dostoevski's *Great Inquisitor* to Aldous Huxley's *Grey Eminence.*

THE IMPACT OF TIME

This is a subcategory of the first conflict on this list: the desire for immortality versus death. It is expressed, among others, in the motif of the struggle of generations—from David and Saul to *Fathers and Sons.* A variant of this are serial novels and family sagas—*The Rougon-Maquarts, The Forsyte Saga, The Thibaults, The Old Wives' Tale,* where the theme is not focused in one conflict but appears in the form of a continuous friction of the characters against time, and their attrition by it. In other words, the conflict is between factors in human nature which are outside time (instinct, tradition) and those which are a function of time (biological decay and social change).

FATE VERSUS VOLITION

This is again a subdivision of the first motif mentioned, but one of special importance in the progress of literature. It is an archetype of great plasticity which undergoes periodic changes according to the prevailing conception of fate. In the book of Job, destiny is embodied in a jealous god who insists on the absolute, groveling submission of the human will. In *Oedipus Rex* destiny appears in the shape of wily and malevolent powers who trick Oedipus into fulfilling his predestined fate while conceding the appearance of his acting by free will; their traps appear as hazards (Oedipus meeting his father on the crossroads, and so forth). Such fateful hazards remain for a long time the main levers of destiny's interference with man. The turning point came with the Renaissance; the change is apparent in the new developments in Elizabethan drama. Romeo and Juliet still both die as a result of unfortunate misunderstandings ("Oh! I am Fortune's fool"—"One writ with me in sour misfortune's book"). But, roughly from Henry IV onward, all major characters in Shakespeare are the victims not of outer, but of their inner destiny; not of blind fate, but of their blind passions. Cassius: "The fault, dear Brutus, is not in our stars, but in ourselves"; Hamlet: "Call me what instrument you will, though you can fret me, yet you cannot play upon me"; Iago: " 'Tis in ourselves that we are thus or thus. Our bodies are our gardens, to the which our wills are gardeners. . . . If the balance of our lives had not one scale of reason to poise another of sensuality, the blood and baseness of our natures would conduct us to most preposterous conclusions: but we have reason to cool our raging motions, our carnal stings, our unbitted lusts."

The conflict between volition and fatality thus becomes internalized and transformed into the dichotomies of reason and passion, of spirit and flesh, of mind and body, and is finally immersed in the antinomy of free will versus determinism by heredity and environment (Ibsen, Strindberg, Zola, naturalism). Atoms, chromosomes and natural laws take over the role once played by the gods and fates; "destiny from above" has become "destiny from below"; but the essence of the predicament remains the same.

10

Writing for the Women's Magazines

FAITH BALDWIN

Born in New Rochelle, New York, in 1893, Faith Baldwin moved with her family to Brooklyn when she was seven. Educated at schools there and at a school in Briarcliff Manor, New York, she was in Germany prior to the entry of the United States into the First World War, and returned to do community service work at Camp Upton. Married in 1920 to Hugh H. Cuthrell, she has four children. In addition to juveniles and verse, she has written some sixty stories and novels.

Thirty years cannot wither nor custom stale Faith Baldwin. Her first book appeared in 1921 and her reign as queen of the women's magazines began at about the same time. Challengers come and go, but she is still queen today, and shows every sign of reigning for at least thirty years more over an enormous and contented population of readers.

This is no mean achievement—and let no one imagine that Faith Baldwin has done it by discovering the "formula" for "formula fiction" and cashing in on it. Her only formula is interest. She is eternally interested in what interests other women, and able to tell them about it amusingly, pleasantly, but above all, sincerely. Long may she reign!

E. J.

Writing for the Women's Magazines

IT BECOMES increasingly difficult to particularize about magazines, as the line of demarcation between the so-called women's and the general magazines is not nearly as sharp as it used to be; except that in the former we look for the nonfiction departments which have to do with home making, fashions and the like. But editors of the general magazines have always appealed to women, while magazines such as *Collier's* or the *Saturday Evening Post*, which are assumed to be slanted to the masculine taste, are also aware that women know how—and what—to read.

Practically all magazines use mystery stories, which have ardent followers both male and female; and several use westerns. In my house there are three very feminine readers who fall with screams of joy upon these and then pant to see them in the movies. How many men read the women's magazines I do not know but I suspect more than will acknowledge it. I did have a friend, however, who, when a story of mine appeared in a women's magazine, used to send his secretary out to buy it, and then hide it in a desk drawer, torn between loyalty to the writer and fear of a horrid ribbing at the hands of friends.

However, I feel it is fairly safe to remark that more women than men read magazines, all magazines. Perhaps their tastes are somewhat wider, more catholic? I used to amuse myself when traveling, by regarding the magazines read by my train companions. . . . I don't believe I ever saw a man reading a women's magazine, though plenty of women were reading the fiction weeklies and all read the general magazines.

It is true that the women's magazines per se are slanted to the taste of the woman reader. You will find some adventure yarns and humorous stories, but fewer than in general publications. Most magazines will occasionally buy a rousing historical story or period piece. You don't find as many "dialect" stories, or folkways tales in the women's magazines as in the others; nor as many nature stories. Domestic animal stories crop up in all magazines but one notes that the tame, rather than the wild, animal is more often found in women's publications; usually as a sort of four-footed Cupid and/or tear jerker. All magazine editors prefer American to foreign settings but most will use foreign settings if necessary to plot, particularly timely, or wonderfully exotic. The story which has a religious theme is being found more often nowadays in most magazines. It used to be predominant half a century ago. Perhaps to have faith has again become fashionable? One hopes so.

A run through of a year's files will find the preponderance of women's magazine stories dealing with not-too-long-married problems, (this includes budgets, in-laws, extra-marital-goings-on, and children) and romantic young love, whether in penthouse or trailer. Most editors wince if your characters have money. Although the richest girl or boy in the world theme is often received with acclaim. I differ with the idea that the forty-five dollar a week worker isn't interested in the doings of the rich. These make for glamour and escape. True, she likes to read about other forty-five-dollar-a-weekers, but sometimes it's fun to drink champagne instead of a less bubbly brew. Also, it astonishes her to read that even upper brackets have problems . . . if not the one problem which is of utmost concern when you don't get the raise. Anyway stories about the hideously rich, the yachted and custom-made heroines, the polo-playing hero and the lad who rises from rags to you-know-what will soon become period pieces.

It has been said that most magazines, particularly women's, cut their literary cloth to clothe the figures of the up-to-thirty-five-year-old group. It seems incredible to me that people past this age have forgotten how to read and that they wouldn't like sometimes to read about people not the age of their sons and daughters, married or unmarried. One's contemporaries are really quite rewarding. I know from experience that it is hard to convince editors (whatever *their* age) that people of—or past—forty are not senile, and might even have problems, emotions and—*mirabile-dictu*—romances, licit and illicit. Once in a while a writer does get away with this dangerous premise. Perhaps even young people like to read about their elders if only in order to feel superior? I don't know. One of the most successful short stories I ever wrote and which recently drew the attention of a housewife in

Turkey, dealt with a plain woman, married, past forty and with several children. However, she was dead as a mackerel before the story opened and represented only by her vigilant ghost, which was much more beautiful than she had been in life. And she was also unseen and unheard, which is unusual in a heroine, dead or alive, fiction or fact.

In this connection, I may remark that stories dealing with ghosts are not often received with open check books by editors, although we all know the exceptions to this rule. Other rules which are sometimes broken are, no stories in the first person; none in letter form. I've written and sold these also, but not often. Anyway I don't *know* the rules. They are made today and remade tomorrow. Editors' ideas change; so do editors. It is most disconcerting.

In general, I feel the most readily salable story from the women's magazine standpoint, and barring works of genius which don't often turn up—is that dealing with romantic young love or the not-too-long-married. Rereading that world-shaking statement, I see that it also applies to general magazines. Oh well, one must adopt a New England attitude, saying not yea, nor nay, but perhaps, maybe, and sometimes. Generalization is absurd.

There was a time when women's publications abhorred any straying from the fictional straight and narrow; then, they permitted it, if properly published. Nowadays the taboos have been relaxed and each magazine has its own list of thou-shalt-nots, applicable to situations, attitudes, and language. It is certain that a writer can be considerably more realistic in his approach to life than twenty, even ten, years ago.

But the happy ending is still preferred, although it may be indicated rather than stated . . .

I am an average reader, reading with my emotions, and identifying myself with the characters, to some extent. I think, "That once happened to me," or, "That might happen to me. What did I do, what would I do?" I do not read to find out what the competition is doing and saying; I read as the reader, who is not a writer, reads, for amusement, escape, pleasure, and even nourishing food for thought. I have read some terrible tripe, from my reader standpoint, in all the magazines, and some very fine stories in every category. You can't always win, and no magazine comes through with 100 percent fine fiction each month.

I have been, I often am disappointed in and distressed by editorial reactions to my own work, especially if I believed it was good and they knew it wasn't. Theirs is, after all, the last word; and while an editor is prone—even obliged—to tell writers what he believes they should write, and how they should write it, I am certain that no writer can turn the tables. Consider the situation calmly. The writer has something to sell; the editor something to buy. I doubt that it is ever a sellers' market in this field. The buyer is in the better position; and writers are a dime a dozen . . . It's an articulate era. And, as I have told writing classes over and over again, there has never been a time when editors didn't want to "discover" new talent and unveil, as it were, new names, for a variety of reasons, some extremely practical.

I assume that the editor arrives at his choice, as does the editorial reader, by a number of paths. He does not draw a story from a hat. He considers, no doubt, his personal taste, although some editors have actually been known to decide against theirs—and of course the tastes of his readers. This yardstick is arrived at in several ways, including letters from readers, polls—although I have never understood how these work—and circulation figures, and all seem to be tied up with advertising. It's all pretty mysterious to anyone who just sits down and beats her or his brains out trying to create characters, if not for the ages, at least for a calendar month.

The war has altered more things than come to the attention of the Congress. Apparently during the war people read more . . . they hadn't the gasoline to go racketing off on trips and if they were women with sons or lovers, or husbands, in the fighting, they sat at home and waited for the mail or went out to work and returned to fall into bed but not to sleep. Everyone read. Father, who couldn't go to war, read too; and grandfather. The magazines were in enormous demand; not only in homes but in camps and overseas. Advertisers had nothing on the shelves to sell but they advertised for something called good will. The magazine and book business flourished or so I have been told.

Now they tell me it has slumped. Maybe it's the opportunity to travel now; maybe it's television; maybe it's just something called leveling off. I wouldn't know.

I cannot believe that the time will come when no one will want to read. . . . Perhaps I'm wrong; I usually am. And the statistics recently printed which prove that England, for instance, reads far more than the United States, are a little staggering. I can speak only for myself when I say that the day will never dawn for me when I cannot derive pleasure from a magazine or from a book. It's all very well to look at a picture in the parlor—our ancestors had a lot of fun with the gadget called a stereopticon—but I do not believe that the imagination is stirred. And that seems important to me.

Back in the thirties when readership also fell off, when people didn't have the money for magazines or books, the magazines suffered, but came through. In those days writers who had, by then, achieved circulation drawing power were occupying a good position. The editors bought them and displayed their names on the covers. This was also a good time for the new writers with something to offer. It stood to reason that every story in every magazine could not be by a "name" writer; there was such a thing as a budget (and still is). Hence the writer who had no name at all, except that given him by his parents, came into his own. He didn't cost much, but he read very well. These writers, who began in the depression days, are name writers now, or many of them are. But it was the writer in the middle who went on relief; the man or woman who had been writing long enough and was sufficiently good to command an excellent price but whose name on the cover of a magazine had not yet the power to draw circulation like a magnet the steel filing.

I daresay this may happen again, perhaps is happening. Again, I don't know.

Yesterday, a perfectly strange young woman telephoned me. She was trying to write—as who is not? She had written, during the war, a number of fanciful, half-fiction letters to a relative abroad. It occurred to him and to those with whom he shared the letters, that she could make a living writing fiction. So she had tried, and reaped a crop of rejections.

Meantime she was supporting herself with various odd jobs and she called me to ask if she were too old to go to college and work her way through. I said No, because I do not believe that anyone who wants to go to college enough to work for it is too old, or ever will be. And she was twenty-four.

One of the things she asked me, and everyone asks me this—were the things she sent to the magazines read by the "proper people"? Practically every beginning writer harbors the delusion that his manuscript isn't read. You can't make people believe that every manuscript *is* read. Only a few, comparatively speaking, reach the fiction editor, and the editor-in-chief. But each is read by someone who knows his business and who can tell after three pages, or less, if it is worth while to go on reading. Not that the first or even second manuscript reader's choice is always selected. I have known manuscripts to have as many as eleven different people read them, and report upon them with favor only to be rejected at the top of this particular kind of pyramid.

There is no such thing as pull. The "name" writers are rejected as well as the no-name. The name may get a quicker reading, and usually does, but is as vulnerable as Miss Unknown to rejection and disappointment.

But people don't believe it.

As for formula, if I had a magic formula I would most certainly impart it, at great price, to the beginning writer and never do a day's work for the rest of my life except that work which I would really like to do and which would most certainly be rejected. I don't believe anyone has a formula. The excellent classes in diverse types of writing can teach the basic rules, but formula there is none. For as I have said, tastes change and editors alter and today's great story is rarely tomorrow's.

Editors have taught me a great deal, and I am grateful to them, from the national magazine editor who, some twenty-two years ago, bought my first serial—and saw to it that I rewrote it not once but six times. Editors know their jobs. I may think, and you may think, that they sometimes make grave errors. And they do. But they are not infallible, being human. Sometimes they may behave as if they were, but none is so unintelligent as to believe it.

I served the usual apprenticeship: books which were published but didn't sell; newspaper serial writing which taught me a modicum of suspense, of characterization (if sketchy) and continuity and which also taught me that I couldn't rope in a character and then unrope him because I became bored with the critter. I am grateful for all I learned by trial and error. I am grateful for my experience with ghost writing, collaboration and my adventures with the so-called pulps. Few writers begin in a national or slick magazine, but there again the exception proves the rule for some, of course, do.

During the war I believe it was necessary for a writer to infuse his stories with violent drama, action, and conflict. Because the factual newspaper headlines dealt with such drama, action and conflict that fiction necessarily paled beside it. What people lived couldn't be reproduced even in a carbon copy, the fictionized facsimile. There were editors, mainly of women's magazines, who for some time ignored, as far as possible, the war in fiction. But most of them had to come to it. There were readers who screamed that they wouldn't read stories dealing with any phase of the war, and those who said that ignoring the times we lived in didn't make sense. And it was hard to see how you could ignore the times. In a contemporary young love story you had to have a hero; ergo, he was either fighting, or 4-F or a VIP, or doing a job in Washington. Your heroine had to do something too, she had to, if married, look after herself and her family, or if unmarried, take to some form of war endeavor. You couldn't ignore the concomitants of a country at war: the food and housing problems, for instance. Your heroine couldn't jump into her jalopy or her convertible, as her circumstances decreed, and whip off to parts unknown. She hadn't the gas.

All the changes were rung: the problem of the stay-at-home, the temptations, the struggles, or the meeting of the very young heroine with the uniformed hero and the war marriage; and, afterward, the story of what happened to *that.*

Gradually, editors learned what they wanted. Now they are learning again. Most editors look ahead. They don't ask themselves what do people want to read today; they ask what will they want to read in, say, three months as it takes that long for a magazine to appear on the stands.

You have to keep looking ahead. The writer who knows what people will want to read in three months, six months, or a year will probably never have a rejection.

The shadow of fear and uncertainty lies over most of us; for us the future seems far from being as clear and open as we believed it would be. Editors know this, and I daresay many of them are feeling their way. They have no desire to increase or underline what fears their readers may secretly harbor; yet they must publish material which is always timely.

Some things are not dated; these are love and birth and death, all emotional problems and their solutions. A writer is lucky. He can set down a problem and solve it, to, he hopes, the satisfaction of an editor or reader. Sometimes he finds himself astonished to find that he cannot, in like manner, solve his own; nor write the happy ending.

I believe that not only for women's but for all magazines sincerity counts; integrity of the emotional content of a story; and good, recognizable characterization which brings with it the valuable reader identification.

For the taboos and angles—horrid word—of each magazine I see no better way to establish these than to read the magazines. In the final analysis, I suppose the best story in any magazine is the one the reader remembers and recommends to others. And as each reader may not remember nor recommend the same story, each writer has the opportunity to gain the only award which, for editor as well as writer, counts—the approbation of the person who buys and reads the magazine in which it is published.

11

Calamophobia, or Hints Toward a Writer's Discipline

JACQUES BARZUN

Born in Paris in 1907, Jacques Barzun came to the United States in 1919 and received his A.B. and Ph.D. from Columbia University, where he has been a full professor since 1945. He has written: *The French Race: Theories of its Origin* (1932); *Race: A Study in Modern Superstition* (1937); *Of Human Freedom* (1939); *Darwin, Marx, Wagner* (1941). He is coauthor of: *The New Invitation to Learning* (1942); *Romanticism and the Modern Ego* and *Teacher in America;* and he has edited *Pleasures of Music; Selected Letters of Lord Byron;* and *New Letters of Berlioz* (which he also translated).

The first sentence in Jacques Barzun's article, "No writer has ever lived who did not at some time or other get stuck," will bring a long and shuddering sigh of recognition from writers, no matter what they write or wish to write and no matter what stage of accomplishment and recognition they have achieved. They all know the dillydallying which wastes a precious morning, and the more devastating block which holds them back from production for weeks or months—and sometimes longer.

The first comfort Mr. Barzun offers is that this inability to get to work may afflict any writer. The second comfort lies in the interpretation of the block as doubt or fear rather than as some disturbance so far beneath the surface of consciousness that the writer can do nothing about it but suffer.

Then Mr. Barzun offers a series of simple, workable hints of the way in which any writer can push himself over this barrier of sterile doubt and fear (and sometimes the inertia of indolence, too) and get himself down to work. Perhaps all writers work out some form of self-discipline which helps them most of the time; then in a dry season they lose faith not only in themselves but in the routine they had evolved. At such a time they would do well to read again these "Hints Toward a Writer's Discipline."

H. H.

Calamophobia, or Hints Toward a Writer's Discipline

No WRITER has ever lived who did not at some time or other get stuck. Even the great producers such as Scott and Dickens suffered from the professional malady of being "for no good reason" (as we all say) unable to write. And for every writer in working trim there may be a dozen persons of great ability who are somehow self-silenced. At long intervals they turn out remarkable fragments—half essays or embryo stories; but they cannot seem to pull themselves together and finish anything, much less begin at will.

Now writing is not an art in which one can succeed by the production of interesting ruins, and since the total or partial paralysis of the writer's will is a fearsome and mysterious blight, most writers come to recognize the need of a discipline, of a set of ritual practices which will put the momentum of habit behind their refractory ego and push them over the obstacle. Scott confessed that he used his divided self in order to rule: hating the thought of commitment, he hardly ever wrote anything except to flee the necessity of writing something else. And Dickens tells of long mornings when he forced himself to stay at the desk making false starts, lest by giving up he should give up forever. For all his books already in print, he might just as well have been the common schoolboy who is told to write of his visit to Aunt Julia and who honestly finds nothing to say except that he arrived on Friday and left on Sunday.

It may be partly because we were all coerced in this fashion that writing on demand comes so hard later. If so, the old experience contains its own corrective, provided we are willing to look into it, that is to say to look into ourselves. If we ask what is the literary impulse par excellence we are, I think, bound to say that it is a desire to pull together one's conscious self and project it into some tangible constructed thing made up of words and ideas. The written thing may serve ulterior ends, as in exposition or polemic, but its first intention is to transfer a part of our intellectual and emotional insides into an independent and self-sustaining outside. It follows that if we have any doubts about the strength, truth, or beauty of our insides, the doubt acts as an automatic censor which quietly forbids the act of exhibition. Johnny cannot write about the visit to his aunt not merely because he did not initiate the literary idea, but because he feels like a fool relating the trivial things that happen every weekend: "They don't want to hear about that." Generalizing from his dominant conviction, we may say that the antiliterary emotion par excellence is fear. It acts precisely as when one attempts to speak a foreign language; one feels too damn silly for words—and one shuts up.

Obviously, if one were starving or in danger of assault words would come fast enough, the inner censorship lifted and all sense of affectation gone. This, then, is the desirable situation to create for oneself every morning at nine, or every evening at five. The hopelessly stuck would find it expensive but worth it to hire a gunman to pound on the door and threaten death as a spur to composition. Ideas would come thick and fast and yet be sorted out with wonderful clarity in that final message to one's literary executors.

The sober application of this principle suggests that the writer needs an equivalent of this urgency, this pressure. It cannot help being artificial, like any pulmotoring but, although it need have nothing to do with danger, it must generate some form of excitement. Most of those who have written extensively under varying conditions would say that the true healthful pressure and excitement comes from a belief that the things one wants to say form a coherent whole and are in some way needed; that is, the urge is a mixture of the aesthetic and the utilitarian impulses. This seems to be borne out by the observation frequently made that if one can only get something down on paper—anything—one feels no further hindrance to working. The final product may not contain a single sentence of the original, but in the successive drafts one has only a sense of pleasure at molding a resistant lump of clay—cutting away here and adding there in the double light of utility and harmony. It is at the outset, before the matter exists, that the great void paradoxically objectifies one's fear, one's conviction that "they don't want to hear about it."

To know how to begin, then, is the great art—no very profound maxim—but since in any extended piece of work one must begin many times, this is the art which it is essential to master. There is only one way: to study one's needs and quirks, and circumvent one's tricks for escape. The guidebooks will tell you that you should be full of your subject—a very good notion but too abstract. Fullness requires moral and mechanical aids and stout controls. For nothing is more common than to feel a stream of excellent ideas racing past and never a hook to lure them out into the open. This is especially true if one has previously tried to capture them and failed. We may say that our ideas feel like a whole world which is too big and whirling too fast to be pulled out in one piece. True, and this is why first aid at this point consists in not trying to have it born whole. Convince yourself that you are working in clay not marble, on paper not eternal bronze: let that first sentence be as stupid as it wishes. No one will rush out and print it as it stands. Just put it down; then another.[1] Your whole first paragraph or first page may have to be guillotined in any case after your piece is finished: it is a kind of "forebirth." But as modern mathematics has discovered, there can be no second paragraph (which contains your true beginning) until you have a first.

The alternative to beginning stupidly, with a kind of "Er-ah," is to pick out during the earliest mental preparation for the work some idea which will make a good beginning, whether for intrinsic or topical reasons, and let it pull the rest along. Thus I began this essay on the cheering note that those mighty engines, Scott and Dickens, also stalled, and I had this in mind long before I knew what would come next. The danger of this procedure is that a picturesque idea

[1] Another "painful" writer, André Gide, makes the same remark in another way: "Too often I wait for the sentence to finish taking shape in my mind before setting it down. It is better to seize it by the end that first offers itself, head or foot, though not knowing the rest, then pull: the rest will follow along." (*Journal*, June 4, 1930.)

can lead one too far back of the true starting line, and the cleverness or the charm of the idea make one unwilling to sacrifice it. Burke was rightly accused of beginning every speech by inviting the Speaker of the House to dance a minuet with him. Ruthless decapitation is the remedy; but note in passing that the error confirms our analysis of the writer's insidious desire to put a cozy padded vest between his tender self and that vague, hostile, roaming animal known as the audience.

Having begun, the writer of even moderate gifts will feel a certain warmth creeping into his veins and rising, as it should, to his head. (In writing, always keep your feet warm, unless you are a full-blooded Indian accustomed to thinking great thoughts while walking barefoot in icy streams.) This genial current, which might prove genius, must be maintained and a double circulation, physical and mental, established in which blood, ink, and thoughts perform their appointed roles. It is now more than ever important not to let the vigilant censor within freeze everything on a technicality. I refer to that sudden stoppage due to the lack of the right word. Some writers, it is true, are able once started to shape their sentences whole in their heads before putting them down—Gibbon was one of those. But most, I believe, do not. Hence it is fatal for them to feel the entire system of ideas, feelings, and tenuous associations which is now in motion come to a dead stop because some adjective which means "boring" and begins with *n* eludes them. Forget it. Leave a blank. The probability is that there is no such word; if there is, it will come up of itself during revision or be rendered unnecessary by it. This sets the rule, by the way, for revision itself: keep going at a reasonable pace to the end, skipping the impossible; then start afresh until you have solved the true problems and removed the insoluble. Remember Barrie's schoolboy who chewed a pencil to splinters and failed the examination because he sought a word halfway between mickle and muckle.

The same law of momentum applies to the search for transitions, to perfecting the rhythm and shape of sentences, even occasionally to the ordering of paragraphs. Don't haggle and fuss but reassure yourself with the knowledge that when you come back to settle these uncertainties and fill these blanks you will still have your mind with you. Especially for young writers who have experienced difficulty and discouragement, the proper aim is that of the learner on the bicycle—keep going, which means a certain speed. Cutting slow capers will come later.

II

More serious than being stopped by a word is the breakdown in ideas. This has to be judged and treated with an even sharper eye for evasion and fraud on the part of the writing self. For the possibilities are several: one is that you have written enough for one day and reached a natural stopping place. It is wise therefore to have not simply a set time for writing—it need not be daily and yet be regular—but also a set "stint" for the day, based on a real, not vainglorious estimate of your powers. Then, when you come to a natural stop somewhere near the set amount, you can knock off with a clear conscience.

Another cause of stoppage is that the work has reached a point of real difficulty—an intellectual decision has to be made, a turning taken, and your mind is balking at it from fatigue or other causes. Or again, it may be that by reason of faulty arrangement there is no obvious bridge from where you are to where you want to go. If the former is true, you must fight it out sooner or later, on the same principles that enabled you to make a beginning. If the latter, devices may help: go back to the beginning, or to some convenient break in the development and read ahead, making but few corrections—just enough to warrant the expense of time and eyesight, but not enough to bog you down. As you approach the halting place, you may suddenly see where you lost the true way and how to by-pass the evil spot altogether; or conversely you may find that your fresh running start carries you straight on and over the hump.

Why not an outline? Well, for my taste, outlines are useless, fettering, imbecile. Sometimes, when you get into a state of anarchy, or find yourself writing in circles, it may help to jot down a sketchy outline of the topics (or in a story, of the phases) so far covered. You outline, in short, something that already exists in written form, and this may help to show where you started backstitching. *Per contra*, a memorandum listing haphazardly what belongs to a particular project is most useful. In fact, if you would be a "full" man as you undertake a new piece of work, you should have before you a little stack of slips bearing the ideas that have occurred to you since the subject first came to life in your mind. Otherwise the effort and the sense of treasures just out of reach will be a drain and diversion of writing power. It is jottings of this sort that fill the "Notebooks" at the tail end of "The Works." When I say slips or notebooks, I mean any congenial form of memorandum, for I doubt whether a self-respecting man with a lively flow of ideas can constrain himself to a uniform style and shape of note-taking until the sacred fires have begun to cool—say around the age of fifty-one.

In all such matters, I believe in humoring to the greatest extent the timid and stubborn censor which stops work on flimsy pretenses. Grant, by all means, its falsely innocent preferences as to paper, ink, furnishings and quash its grievances forever. We know that Mark Twain liked to write lying in or on a bed; we know that Schiller needed the smell of rotting apples in his desk. Some like cubicles, others vasty halls. "Writers' requisites," if a Fifth Avenue shop kept them, would astound and demoralize the laity. Historically, they have included silk dressing gowns, cats, horses, pipes, mistresses, particular knickknacks, exotic headgear, currycombs, whips, beverages and drugs, porcelain stoves, and hair shirts. According to Mr. Bernard De Voto's latest novel, writing paper of a peculiar blue tint has remarkable properties, about which the author makes an excellent point very subtly: he shows his writer-hero as neurotically exigent on this "trivial" matter, but after we have mocked and put him down as a crank, his work turns out to be a masterpiece. Quite simply, by yielding on such apparently irrational details, the writer is really outwitting his private foe—the excuse maker within each of us who says: "I can't work today because I haven't any blue paper." Nor is this weakness limited to artists, whether genius or duffer. Before me is a letter just received from a distinguished scientific friend who says: "I have got down to honest work on my article, drawing up elaborate typed notes in what may be a desperate attempt to avoid the actual writing."

That is the true spirit: suspect all out-of-the-way or elaborate preparations. You don't have to sharpen your pencils and sort out paper clips before you begin—unless it be your *regular* warming up. Give yourself no quarter when the temptation strikes, but grab a pen and put down some words—your name even—and a title: something to see, to revise, to carve, to do over in the opposite way. And here comes the double advantage of developing a fixation on blue tinted paper. When you have fought and won two or three bloody battles with the insane urge to clean the whole house before making a start, the sight of your favorite implements will speak irresistibly of victory, of accomplishment, of writing done. True, you are at the mercy of the paper mills, as Samuel Butler was the slave of a certain thick book which he used to prop up his writing board at the exact slope of his desire,[2] but such attachments are changeable once they have become a way of tackling work. Even fundamental routines may be recast. I used to wonder how Jane Austen could possibly write in the midst of family conversation, when to me Crusoe's solitude was scarcely adequate. But I learned under necessity to compose (first drafts at least) while keeping a chattering and enterprising child out of mischief in my workroom. The one thing needful is to have an anchorage in some fixed habits and to deal with writer's cowardice precisely as one would with other kinds—facing pain or going over the top. For it is never the specifically literary faculty which balks; it is the affection for one's dear self seeking to protect it against the fearful dangers of laughter, criticism, indifference, and reprints in digest form.

Since habits are rooted in the physical part of us, some writers find it serviceable to begin by doing some act requiring no special thought but which insensibly leads to composition. This doing may be as simple as answering correspondence or (with Butler) "posting one's books"—i.e. transcribing notes. But most writers prefer not to spoil the day's freshness by a reminder that relatives exist, nor distract themselves with the scattered subject matter of their notes. The ideal situation perhaps is to awaken with the grand design in mind (it was the last thing thought of before falling asleep) to shave while a matching throng of ideas lathers up within, and to go straight to the blank sheet without exchanging words with any one.

Here a natural analogy with other arts suggests a few scales and runs on the typewriter, and it may well be that the writer's lack of anything so pleasantly muscular is a real cause of his frequent impotence; even the painter can busy his hands, craftsmanlike. The momentous ques-

[2] It was Frost's *Lives of Eminent Christians*, as he tells us in "Quis Desiderio?"

tion behind this comparison is of course the familiar one—pen or typewriter? It is no hedging answer to say, take your choice. But your choice (as I keep repeating) must be thoroughly considered. Is it possible, for instance, that like me you find it discouraging not to see whole paragraphs at a time and not to be able to cross out whole sentences at a time? If so, stick to the pen and use the typewriter to do your first revision as you transcribe. The plastic aspect of written matter is important, and the best revision is undoubtedly made from a clean copy embodying previous revisions. One reason why so much nineteenth-century work is good is that printers' revises were cheap and the writer carved direct on cold print.[3]

Many writers' liking to compose direct on the typewriter has to do with this clean look of near-print. Hence persons whose fingers are clumsy and whose typed odes are full of fractions and dollar signs should give up the instrument. According to biographers, what they usually take up instead is a short stubby pencil. I do not know why it must be squat, and I have only an abstract prejudice against it, so I mention it here to be fair in spite of myself. Let us by all means have poems, even if written with skewers in goose fat: the point is Suit Thyself but pay for it, i.e. work.

III

Numberless other facts, tricks, and generalities could be added to this already overlong set of hints. Writers young or old who take an interest in the bare processes of their art (as painters more frequently do) would be well advised to read at large in the considerable literature of exhortation and confession about writing. Nine-tenths of it is pedantic or platitudinous, but the other tenth is often amusing and likely to contain particles of illuminating truth, especially if written by a practicing writer. But again, the reader's object being ultimately to make personal applications, he should be particularly on the watch for statements—there must be more than one in the present essay—which make him exclaim: "What an idea! why, it's just the opposite."

The writer must indeed turn everything into grist for *his* mill and no other, as a result of which he acquires both self-knowledge and

[3] Proust's novel was, I believe, the last work to enjoy this advantage.

self-command. His last consideration is therefore his first: what is he afraid of? Only, after he has disciplined himself, he puts the question differently and asks: whom am I writing for? The century of the common man makes this no easy question to answer, for the common man is a social and political ideal, admirable in the spheres thus denoted. As a buyer and reader of books he does not exist; one finds humanity instead, which is diverse. One will write for different kinds of people at different times but at any one time there must be some imagined interlocutor, some animated ear trumpet, into which we pour our words. This may be posterity or the children aged eight to ten but either must be represented in our minds as by a lawyer in court. In judging our own work, we "suit" this mythical person, and our original verdict "they don't want to hear about that," takes on another meaning—critical yet productive—a kind of ideal collaboration.

This endless conversation in which the writer's censor turns into a helping representative of a given public, is of course most pleasantly realized when the writer has in truth "a reader"—a relative or friend whose judgment he can use.[4] Notice I did not say "whose judgment he will take." For the last step in the writer's liberation through discipline is the discovering of judicial distance—distance from himself, from his work, from his critic, and even from that fickle tiger, his audience.

The practical rules that follow are obvious. Do not read what you have written—much less what you are writing—to whoever will listen; indeed never read unpublished work (except perhaps poems) but give it to be read at leisure. Never show a first draft—except to an old and tried reader who knows from the crude signs what your work may become. Above all, do not talk yourself out of good ideas by trying to expound them to haphazard gatherings. In general, never choose your critic from your immediate family circle: they have usually no knowledge of the processes of writing, however literary they may be as consumers; and in their best-natured act of criticism one may hear the unconscious grinding of axes sounding like a medieval tournament.

No, your special reader (or two or three at most) must be chosen

[4] One thinks at once of Flaubert and Louis Bouilhet, and in our day of Gide and Roger Martin du Gard.

from those who care for writing as much as for you—no writer wants his work to shine in a *charitable* light. And even from your critic-by-appointment you must take only what goes with the grain of your thought and intent. This calls for delicate decisions, since it is always easy to cut off dead tissue and always hard to cut into the living cells that are not true flesh but tumor. The basic principle here as always is to protect the work and not the self.

There is one thing more. A man who writes, as Hardy said, stands up to be shot at, but Hardy was wrong to resent the shooting. So-called established writers who after years of work still wince at criticism are certainly not established in their own souls. Nor does one have to be callous or stubborn about reproof in order to feel solid and to accept one's errors and limitations with a composure which one can then extend to the errors and injustices of critics. Doing so habitually makes one more and more able to *see the work,* which is the prerequisite to producing it, pruning it, and preserving it against the ravages of time.

12

The Novelist

W. H. AUDEN

W. H. Auden was born in England in 1907. His first major work was *Poems* published in 1930. Following that came: *Orators* (1932); *Dance of Death,* a play (1933); *Letters from Iceland* (with Louis MacNeice) (1937); *Spain* (1937); *On This Island* (1937); *Selected Poems* (1938); *Education, Today—and Tomorrow* (with T. Worsley) (1939); *Some Poems* (1940); *Another Time* (1940); *Double Man* (1941); *For the Time Being* (1944); *Age of Anxiety* (1947); and *Nones* (1951). He is also the co-author, with Christopher Isherwood, of: *Dog Beneath the Skin* (1935); *Ascent of F.7* (1936); *Journey to a War* (1939); *On the Frontier* (1939). He has edited a number of poetry collections.

This sonnet by Auden is a keynote to fiction writing. In its terse ironic phrases it summarizes the life and labor of the novelist. Readers of books may look at it with surprise, but writers will recognize their days of throwing themselves out of gear, their Proteuslike struggles to project themselves into countless human situations.

H. H.

The Novelist

Encased in talent like a uniform,
The rank of every poet is well known;
They can amaze us like a thunderstorm,
Or die so young, or live for years alone.

They can dash forward like hussars; but he
Must struggle out of his boyish gift and learn
How to be plain and awkward, how to be
One after whom none think it worth to turn.

For, to achieve his lightest wish, he must
Become the whole of boredom, subject to
Vulgar complaints like love, among the Just

Be just, among the Filthy, filthy too,
And in his own weak person, if he can
Must suffer dully all the wrongs of Man.

13

The Publisher Speaks

THOMAS R. COWARD

Former special assistant in the Department of State, manager of the New York office of the Yale University Press, and editor of the Bobbs-Merrill Company (1922-27), Thomas Coward has been president of Coward-McCann, Inc., Publishers, since 1927. A contributor to literary magazines, he is director of G. P. Putnam's Sons, The Sporting Gallery and Book Shop.

In this Writing Book by Authors most of the talk concerns itself with writing, how, what, and why the authors write. Yet each article, either in direct statement or in hopeful implication, shows that the author reaches toward the goal of publication. His story or his book or his article is a communication to other human beings, and he is not satisfied until he finds his audience. You may break up this need into various parts, such as a desire to make a living, which is legitimate, or a desire to win recognition, which is common to all above the rank of vegetable. But beyond and above such desires is the strong compulsion of any creative worker to know whether he has succeeded in reaching outside his own narrow limits to his fellow men.

Here the author can no longer rely upon his own industry. He must turn his work over to some business already established for the purpose of handling this transformation of the private written word into the public printed word. He hunts for an editor or a publisher to accept his work and, finding one, thinks he is lucky. Sometimes he is.

What is the other side of this coin? What is the attitude of these arbiters of writers' destinies? Mr. Thomas R. Coward, president of Coward-McCann, tells how he looks at books and authors.

H. H.

The Publisher Speaks

SOMEWHERE that profoundly pompous Keyserling said in his Prussian wisdom that "marriage was a tragic tension." At least I think he said it, and nothing would induce me to undertake the boredom of wading through his pages to verify it. It will do as a text: The relationship in general between author and publisher may be loosely described as a marriage, and certainly, when there is not comic tension there is considerable tragic tension. If we may carry this idea further, the author is the wife, the source of life, the publisher the husband who must protect and provide for his wife and children. Now, of course, it is true (though some publishers, alas, occasionally forget it) that authors could in some way or other exist without publishers, but no publisher could exist without authors.

However, just as it is usually better for a woman and child to have a husband and father about, just so is it better, at least as things are set up now, for an author to have a publisher. There have been movements afoot to abolish marriage, and there have been movements to abolish publishers. Both, I suspect, are doomed to failure. Of course, a wife occasionally maddened over lack of attention (advertising), over insufficient support (meager advances), or seduced by flowers and honeyed words of "another man" (the artful letter, or cocktail-party whispered word of a rival publisher) does dispose of her husband in one way or another ("changes publishers"). But most authors usually stick it out, and generally for the eventual good of both parties.

A good deal of this "tragic tension" is due, as in real marriage, to a natural egotism on the part of each partner, and to a lack of agreement as to the duties and responsibilities toward each other. The publisher is often inconsistent. He likes to think of himself as in a "profession." He tries to forget that only a short time ago he would have been considered "in trade" and, indeed, is now as often as not. If the publisher would be content to think of himself primarily as a businessman, in the long run the partnership would run more smoothly. For no matter how much of a flair a publisher has for good books, for spotting talent in advance, for original advertising and promotion, unless his business instinct is sound, a smash-up is inevitable.

But the publisher cannot be solely a businessman, and there's the catch. Few authors, who for the most part are a highly sensitive, mercurial, melancholy lot, will choose a publisher solely because he is a good businessman. Indeed, the greater number of authors are afraid of businessmen or else despise them. Therefore, the publisher, while keeping a steely slate blue eye on the balance sheet, must at the same time turn a warm blue eye alight with understanding and affection upon his authors, particularly if they are men. Women usually take for granted that a certain business give and take is a necessary part of any business partnership. But not all women, and very few men.

To be sure, when some of these reach the best-seller lists, with the concomitant book club, motion picture, and serial money, they are apt to suffer a sea change and almost overnight develop a highly trained sense of business which would make them welcome additions to the money marts of the world. Then the positions are reversed, and the publisher finds himself begging for sympathy, understanding, and terms which will not bankrupt him, while the former warm eye of creation, now turned a steely slate, gazes sharply upon him.

Let us see what a publisher needs to be successful. First, as I have said, he must have business acumen, he must have a feeling for books, be ahead of his immediate cultural and political times, but not too far ahead, he must have natural enthusiasm and vitality, and he should like human beings. These are primary requisites, but he must also possess tact, an unlimited capacity for flattery, an ability to be creatively critical, and he must be able to write straightforward English. If he can read two or three other languages, so much the better. He should be able to rough it with Hemingway, go to the opera with Louis Bromfield, follow the hounds, ski at Sun Valley, be equally at his ease at Bleeks and the Knickerbocker Club; the headwaiters should know him at "21," at the Stork, at the Plaza Oak Room, at the Pump Room, at Romanoffs.

He must have the dignity of a Lord Chief Justice, the homely wit and cheer of a Will Rogers, and the common sense and affection of an old family doctor. He must be banker, lawyer, husband and wife, mistress, friend, press agent, and psychiatrist. He must be able to produce theater tickets on the aisle for a smash hit within twelve hours' notice, with a note to the star to greet his party backstage. He must stand as godfather, though he has not been to church, except for a funeral or marriage, in twenty years. He must know something of philosophy, of painting, sculpture, the graphic arts, music both classical and popular, the ballet, the theater, Saville Row, and the Foubourg, St. Honoré, and food and drink. And speaking of the last, how authors can drink!

Now to be serious for a moment. All publishers would rather publish a distinguished book than a run-of-the-mill product, even though the financial rewards may be less. Almost all publishers expect to, and do, give time and generous thought to the creative and personal problems of their authors. Indeed, these problems are often inseparable. A publisher unless subsidized cannot publish on as high a level as he would like to. There just aren't enough good books to go around, and a certain minimum of volume each year is essential to a publisher's existence. This is unfortunate in one way, and yet in another is a safeguard for the writing profession. If the number of publishers should shrink, there would be great danger of monopoly, and a great danger of a few large publishers standing on what has proved safe. The very fact that there are not enough proved books to go around drives the publishers to experiment, which means that an author with something new to say, or something old to say in a new manner, or both, has a good chance of publication, and of a more than routine welcome and critical help from the house he joins.

The publisher can be, and has been in countless cases, both financially and critically helpful to his authors. Beneath the natural strain of business and a multitude of duties, most publishers have a deep respect for books and for those who write them. The late Maxwell Perkins of Scribners had dozens of authors who took his advice on everything under the sun. Indeed, Perkins' understanding of and hold on his authors was such that, as the literary world knows, Thomas Wolfe left him, crying he was bewitched. Kipling, who came to dislike almost everything American, had a long and intimate friendship with F. N. Doubleday, and the late Nelson Doubleday until his death received royalty from "Uncle Rud" from the sale of the *Just So Stories.*

Let the author remember that his work is only one of many that the publisher must launch, and that Jones whose books sells five thousand copies expects, and should have, as much personal attention and thought as Smith, who is in the best-seller brackets. And let the publisher never forget that he is dealing with human beings whose last manuscript is for the moment the most important thing in the world, that has often cost tremendous effort and courage. It *can* be a good partnership if both sides will suffer each other patiently at times—or, at least, count to ten.

14

The Chances Against the Beginning Writer

JAMES A. MICHENER

James A. Michener, after Swarthmore and two years in Europe on a fellowship, began his career as a teacher, first in social science at the Quaker George School, and then at Harvard as visiting professor in history. In 1941 he went to Macmillan Company where he was, until 1949, managing editor of the high-school textbook division. During the war he served in the Navy.

Tales of the South Pacific, published in 1948, was the Pulitzer Prize novel for the year. His other works include *Fires of Spring* (1949); *Return to Paradise* (1951); *Voice of Asia* (1951); *Bridges at Toko-ri* (1953); *Floating World* (1954) and *Sayonara* (1954).

Perhaps no field of labor toward the ends of career and livelihood attracts so many naïve and hopeful aspirants as does the field of writing. A young man who wishes to become a plumber knows that he must learn to use certain tools, wrenches and blow torches, that he must learn certain skills, such as threading an inch pipe and fitting a joint, and that he must begin as plumber's assistant. But the aspiring writer often sees no gap between his desire and its fulfillment. His tools seem familiar, he is oblivious to the necessary skills. Hence the half a million novelists and the million and a half short-story writers of whom Mr. Michener speaks.

For these writers Mr. Michener's mathematical certainties will be startling and no doubt appalling. The chances against them are heavy. Perhaps nature spawns writers as she does frogs' eggs and the free-floating barnacle on the slim chance of survival of a few to carry on the species. Yet even the accidental writer knows that his work has neither completion nor satisfaction until it finds readers. If the chances are so slim, and the would-be writer loses his hopeful and naïve ignorance of the facts of publishing, will he abandon the attempt?

If his writing is, as Mr. Michener suggests, a daydream of a pleasant way to annex fame and fortune, he may decide the odds are too great. But if his desire to write grows out of an inner urgency, no mathematics will discourage him. He will believe Mr. Michener's final heartening statement that America is hungry for talent. With that mixture of humility and pride which hangs around creative work he will go on writing, hoping that the force which drives him is the product and the proof of his talent.

H. H.

The Chances Against the Beginning Writer

IF ONE considers the chances against a beginning writer, one is astonished that parents and teachers continue to goad young people with the pious statement, "You are a born writer." There are few harder ways to make a living; there are few fields of endeavor which can consume so much of one's energy in return for so little spiritual reward.

Throughout these remarks I shall keep referring to the two kinds of rewards a serious writer, or any other workman, has a right to expect: (1) He should have a reasonable chance to earn a modest living. (2) He should experience the intellectual and spiritual thrill of having his work considered on its merits. The purpose of the balance of my remarks is to show how great are the odds against a beginner's attaining either of these expectations.

The four artistic careers which excel serious writing in difficulty are, in order of hardship, poetry, sculpture, serious music, and painting. Bells should be rung and the entire village should meet for prayer when a young man or woman dedicates himself to one of those fields, and it is proper that a nation should prize above most things its genius in any of those endeavors. As a man who has knocked about the arts for some time, I can only say that in the presence of a poet I am struck with awe that I should behold so courageous a man. I never felt that way about generals or admirals, for our society is organized to protect the warrior.

Writing—and from here on I speak of novels, short stories, and articles, including essays and nonfiction; I cannot and do not wish to speak of radio, television, advertising, or movies—is a tough discipline. Any practiced writer knows that. I have written in several different fields and in my occupation I judge the writing of others, yet I have never been able to write anything that could stand in first draft. I have learned even to type letters on yellow sheets so that I can correct them into saying what I intended to say. There may be some fortunate people who can sit down and "dash it off." They are to be envied. Most others will sympathize with Kenneth Roberts, whose remarkable biography *I Wanted To Write* is recommended as the case history of the typical fellow who has to do it the hard way, when he says, "March 25, 1931: Struggled on in Chapter 12—a tough one. They're ALL tough."

But let's forget that writing is an artistic craft. (If you think otherwise, you'll rapidly learn when you try to "dash it off.") Let's assume that an imaginary young man has the basic skills of writing and that he knows how to apply himself. What are the chances against his winning the two rewards defined above?

They are staggering. Comparing various guesses, one can estimate that there are probably half a million people in the United States who are vaguely trying to write novels. The first novel of an unknown author competes against half a million people who also want their novels published.

If this young man submits his novel to a large company, his is one of 4,000 received that year. With luck, the company may be planning to publish 40 novels. The author therefore seems to have one chance in 100 of being published by that company. One large house reported that during one year it published about 5 percent of the manuscripts submitted (one in 20).

The following figures are often quoted as the normal experience of a successful publisher. He receives about 2,000 manuscripts a year and publishes 100 (one in 20); but all of the above figures are misleading because of 100 books published as many as 95 come from established professionals,[1] whose books are usually contracted for before they are written. This means that only 5 out of 1,905 unsolicited manuscripts are published (about one in 380). Since novels are more difficult to place than nonfiction, it is safe to reason that for every first novel published 450 are written!

But let's suppose our young author finds a publisher. What are the chances that his book will gain critical attention? (I consider this first because most serious artists are willing to struggle along on meager income if they know their work is good.)

Again the chances against critical attention are great. About 1,200 novels are published each year. A daily-review column can handle at most 313 books a year. If the reviewer were to report upon novels alone, he could do only one in four, and of the 313 he chose at least 200 would be by practiced novelists whose names had news value.

Actually, a daily reviewer may do no more than 120 novels a year, or one in ten of the total offered in any twelve months. Then knock out the columns given over to summaries of the season, special lists at Christmas, and other intrusions, and the unknown's chances of notice grow increasingly slim.

The Saturday Review of Literature may review as many as 380 novels a year. A Sunday book section may cover between 15 to 20 each week, but of these five to seven are murder mysteries. Thus the Sunday sections may review up to 675 serious novels a year. *Time* rarely reports on more than three a week, and *The New Yorker* may adequately notice an average of five a month.

A first novel that received good notices in *The New York Times* and *Herald Tribune* daily and Sunday columns; in the SRL, *The New Yorker*, *Time*, and *Newsweek*; and in the Sunday book sections of the *Philadelphia Inquirer*, the *Chicago Tribune*, and the *San Francisco Chronicle* would be almost certain to be a true best seller. But the

[1] A number of publishers might take exception to this statement, since these publishers (Harper & Brothers, among them) do attempt to have first novels represented on their annual lists and to achieve a balance between well-known authors and those who are beginners in the field.—THE PUBLISHERS

chance of any first novel's being even noticed by all eleven of these media is very slight.

Rather more likely is the depressing experience of one gifted young writer who recently published a quite respectable novel. His book was reviewed by neither of the daily columns. It was mentioned by none of the magazines, not even the SRL, and it was noticed by only three of the major Sunday sections. He had written a book that would bring modest credit to any writer, but the mathematical chances were against him.

Financially the story is even more depressing. The average first novel loses money for everybody, especially the writer. A recent survey of war novels written by unknown writers revealed that more than half lost money, that more than half sold less than 3,000 copies. Assuming a standard royalty, and a price of $3.00 for the novel, the average author made about $900 from his long hours of work, much, much less than he could have made as a plumber. Taking all the writers who could reasonably be called professional writers, the average income is less than $1,500 a year. I know, personally, less than ten writers who actually earn their living by writing. (I know many who have modest-salaried jobs and whose writing income helps add up to a pleasing yearly return.) And I know personally not one novelist who makes his living by novels alone. There must be quite a few who do—a leading editor estimated that about eighty did, counting the detectives and the horror boys—but I happen to know none. (Again, I know many who get a modest return on their novels every two or three years but who make their living by doing short stories or by selling to the movies.) The most relaxed writers I know are three who live on their wives' income.

Therefore it should be imperative for glib advisers of budding novelists to remind them that it is hard to find a publisher, that when a novel is published it is hard to get it reviewed, that when a book is reviewed it is difficult to sell enough copies to make money, and that when one does actually make some money it is usually not enough to live on. Those are the facts.

The writing of short stories pays much better but is far less rewarding spiritually. A man can spend ten years doing one reasonably good short story after another, and at the end of ten years he will have accomplished little that he can be deeply proud of. There are exceptions. Perhaps Wilbur Daniel Steele derived as much spiritual satisfaction from his superb tales as did Richard Wright from *Native Son*, but the average short-story writer composes in sand that is regularly washed by the waves of forgetfulness and indifference.

On the other hand, he does eat. A 100,000 word novel that earned $900, would, if broken up into twenty 5,000-word salable short stories earn about $20,000. But let's not make short-story writing sound too simple. It is much easier to write one novel than five first-rate short stories. Besides there are at least 1,500,000 people who are trying to practice this elusive art. They work on the untenable supposition that a person with no talent ought at least to be able to write 5,000 words if incapable of writing a novel. Richard Gehman, a successful writer, has uncovered the following depressing facts. A leading magazine, which publishes five stories a week, receives 6,000 each week to choose from! A magazine specializing in cultural leadership publishes two stories in each issue, selected from 5,000 submitted.

The short-story field is further restricted because so many amateurs have one or two good stories to tell. Here let me digress for three paragraphs on the important problem of amateur versus professional. Difficult though painting is, the professional artist does not have to compete for space in established galleries with enthusiastic amateurs. Most people are willing to admit that a painter must have certain basic skills and training. Serious painting—as contrasted to recreational—is left pretty largely to the professionals. But everyone is convinced he can write, and those who would shudder at the prospect of submitting an amateurish daub to the Metropolitan Museum have no compunction about thrusting their verbal daubs at the editors of the *Atlantic Monthly* or the *Saturday Evening Post*.

And they should have no compunction about doing so. Everyone who can speak can write, and everyone who can write at all ought to be able to write one novel and two short stories. Such writers are the amateurs, and they enrich our culture. But by definition the professional writer is the one who can write more than one novel, more than a lucky pair of short stories. Yet the professional is handicapped in either learning or practicing his art by the lucky amateur who has his two good stories to sell.

But in the long run it is the professional writer—and here I mean the dedicated writer, the writer who in Jean Paul Sartre's cogent phrase is committed—whom a nation must depend upon for its body of literature. It is reassuring to observe how many of our finest novels are written by the old hands; it is interesting to see how much even the magazines must depend for their best stories upon the practiced minds.

To return to the main argument, I would say that writing short stories is about the best paid, least rewarding, and most harrowing way of making a living through serious writing. It is the best paid because the big advertisers pay the big magazines to find good stories to lure the public back to the advertising pages. It is the least rewarding because few writers can build an artistic life on short-story writing; and it is the most harrowing because the short-story writer lives at the mercy of magazine editors, whose habits are more mercurial than Shelley's wild west wind. The story that is sold today might have been rejected yesterday for some irrelevant reason, and—here is where the harrowing part comes in—the story that would have been accepted yesterday is rejected today because: (1) "We've had two stories about daffy undertakers this year," (2) "The big boss liked it right up to the ending. Then he said no," (3) "We've had a shake-up here at *Everyday*, and the orders are we've got to use up our back inventory."

The chances are greatly against the young writer in this jungle of the short-story field. The competition is bitterly keen. Even though the market is extensive and remunerative, for every story needed by a magazine, there must be about 2,000 immediately available! So the average short-story writer probably makes about $400 a year. That is, fifteen people who are really trying to sell stories will probably sell seven, and the best writer of the fifteen will probably account for three of the seven, meaning that at least ten of the aspirants will sell no stories in a year!

Are the chances any better in the nonfiction field? No. For the beginner they are worse. Most nonfiction books are written by experts—and even when the amateur appears to have crashed into print it most often happens that a professional ghost was pushing the reluctant pen. Most nonfiction books make their authors little money. The principal reward is the momentary enhancement of the author's reputation among his business associates. Books like *The Egg and I, How to Win*

Friends and Influence People, and *Peace of Mind* are exceptions, and the beginning writer should not expect to duplicate those phenomena.

Nonfiction in the magazine field is quite properly the preserve of the established article writer. A high percentage of feature articles are assigned in advance to men and women already known to the editors. The beginning writer will find this a most difficult field to invade. One of the best approaches is through newspaper experience. Another is to haunt editors with three or four superbly done pieces—which no one will want—and the implied promise that you can do as well on any topic an editor might assign you. Editors like to know writers who can be depended upon.

Novels, short stories, nonfiction. I cannot state too clearly how difficult it is for a young writer to achieve success in these fields. Vague longings, the praise of one's family, and an apartment in New York have practically nothing to do with success in writing. A study of what can be accomplished in words, an above-average mental capacity, vivid feeling, intelligent analysis of one's own potentialities, and very hard work are the best paths to a career in writing. Nine young people out of ten are too lazy or too little gifted ever to complete the arduous training period. Never in a thousand years will nine out of ten who, in their twenties, vaguely "want to write" ever do so. The chances are all against them.

And yet, if I must denounce the idle, day-dreaming attachment to writing that is so prevalent, I must also report the magnificent opportunities that await the young writer with a true talent and the energy to perfect it.

In New York there are some publishing companies that may have to quit business because they cannot find enough good writers. It often happens that three days before a magazine is "put to bed" the editors frantically phone the principal agents begging them "for one good story." A large publishing house may spend up to $100,000 a year simply looking for new writers.

Let me make this very clear. If tomorrow word were mysteriously to circulate around New York that in Waco, Texas, an unknown Scott Fitzgerald had a suitcase full of stories which he was about to release, by nightfall every publisher would be making that young Texan enticing offers. He could have advances for five years. He could have a vacation in Alaska. The telegrams would pour in, and three or four of the smartest publishers would fly their leading editors down to try to sign the boy up on the spot.

In the meantime, the magazine offices would be going crazy. The fifteen largest periodicals would offer a new Hemingway, a new Willa Cather, or a new Philip Wylie almost any inducement; for this fact is paramount—America is terribly hungry for writing talent. Publishers are not fools; they know that they exist solely upon the talent of writers. When they go to bed at night, they dream that in the morning they will stumble upon a masterpiece by some unknown writer. That is why no manuscript is ever turned aside unread, either by a book publisher or by a magazine editor.

I sometimes feel I am in a crazy world when I watch editors beating their brains out, trying to find good novels or stories, while a million or more writers beat their brains out trying to sell what they have written. What it adds up to is cruelly obvious: There will never be enough good writers, and there will always be far too many who are wasting their time trying to be fifth-rate writers. Only by the brutal processes of trial and error can the gifted writers be weeded out from among the untalented; and if you who read this are young, and if you know that you have the talent to write, remember what Somerset Maugham said: "It is wonderful to be young and to know that you have the talent." What he did not bother to add was, "Because then the world will want you."

15

Techniques of the Modern Short Story

RICHARD SUMMERS

Born in Oshkosh, Wisconsin in 1906, Richard Summers graduated from the University of Arizona in 1925, received his M.A. at George Washington, and has done graduate work at Columbia University. He has taught English at the University of Arizona since 1928 where he is an associate professor and was once chairman of freshman English. Married, with three children, he is the author of two novels, *Dark Madonna* and *Vigilante* (a motion picture of which is planned), and has also written text books; *Craft of the Short Story, College Composition, Minimum Essentials.* He has written several popular adventure novels for young people and sold pulp westerns to Fiction House in 1931. In late years he has been author of a number of stories for the quality markets.

Mr. Summers ends his article with a comment so important to writers that it should not only close but also open his discussion of commercial and quality short stories. Here it is, a quotation from Hugh McNair Kahler, an experienced editor. "Nobody can write for an audience to which he does not himself belong, and the best work . . . has always been done by people who were concerned only with pleasing themselves. Given a reasonable degree of competence in the mechanics of the craft, there is an audience, large or small, for anything that any of us writes to please himself, since none of us is unique."

The writer must trust his own material, he must believe in his own convictions, he must write with full emotional sincerity. When he has developed some craftsmanship he should look around to find this audience to which by nature he belongs. If he begins by conscious imitation, he will cut off his talent at its source.

Mr. Summers gives a clear and lively analysis of the markets open to the contemporary short story. His discussion of the idealistic code, the fear-quelling rules which furnish the emotional appeal of commercial fiction certainly hints at wishful thinking in American readers, movie audiences and radio listeners. But even daydreams change their shape from one age to another, and the new generation of writers may have less patience with old platitudes.

H. H.

Techniques of the Modern Short Story

(As They Concern the Creative Writer)

As I often tell my students, there is nothing whatever I can say about the short story to which they cannot cite numerous exceptions. A short story must be unified; they can name a dozen sprawling, disunified and successful short stories to prove me wrong. A short story must have a single theme—Edgar Allan Poe's "element of artistic piquancy"; yet some stories contain no apparent theme, while others have several. A short story should not backtrack for fear of losing the feeling of immediacy, of happening at the moment. Countless stories have been written entirely in retrospect, successful stories.

How then can one be brash enough to discuss the techniques of the modern short story? I am brash enough only with my fingers crossed and a willingness to acknowledge in the beginning that you can prove me a liar, and that when I venture a resounding truth, it is only a relative truth after all.

Is the attitude of the writer toward his story and toward writing in general a part of technique? Most certainly it is. *Probably the writer's own emotions (synthetic or genuine) and his attitude toward the writing craft in total are the most important single element in the creative process* because largely they set the tone of the story. A hundred printed rejection slips, unless the young artist understands the reason for them, may destroy him more quickly than poverty, a nagging wife, war or pestilence. Chances are he sends out his stories hit-or-miss to the *Saturday Evening Post, Collier's, Ladies Home Journal,* and other leading national "slick paper" magazines, with bounding heart and baited breath slipping them into the mailing chute. He might as well unbait his breath and quiesce his heart. The story has about one-tenth the chance of being taken as has the first nickel in the slot machine of hitting the jackpot. Perhaps the story is "quality" or what is more likely, a half-baked mixture of "quality" and "commercial." Perhaps it is unpleasant or too realistic in tone. Perhaps it deals with a forbidden theme such as homosexualism or crashes into one of the many other taboos of the commercial market. Perhaps the preliminary reader doesn't like the opening sentence or opening paragraph and reads no further.

Almost all creative writing of every sort is done for a market. Whether it is a commercial market or not has nothing to do with the statement. If you acknowledge this truth, then whatever sort of writer you are, whatever the kind of writing you are doing, it is only basic common sense both to examine the needs of the market and to analyze the kind of product you are trying to sell.

Commercialism governs the commercial market for fiction just as it governs the commercial market for all other products, and the forces of supply and demand operate just as delicately. As a salesman you would not try to sell a woman a vacuum cleaner when she has expressed interest in a washing machine. You would be a poor salesman indeed if you endeavored to persuade her that what she needed was a vacuum cleaner, not a washing machine. You would, however, try to sell her a better washing machine than your competitor offered. Only by submitting a better story of the type suitable to a particular magazine or magazines can you compete with the writers already appearing in their table of contents.

You will find most of your competition at any large newsstand. There you discover pulp paper magazines of every sort—western stories, detective stories, "sweetheart" stories. You discover in the slick paper field quite a group of "confession" magazines, women's magazines, and the great "family" magazines (*True Story Magazine, Woman's Home Companion, Collier's* as examples). Even though the stories contained in these commercial magazines are different in content and aimed at different audiences and vary greatly in the excellence of their writing, they have certain qualities in common that bait a large body of the public to read them, and therefore they are stories that have been salable. These qualities will be discussed at length later on.

You will also find a very few magazines publishing stories quite different in content and technique from the foregoing: *Story Magazine, Harper's, Atlantic Monthly, The New Yorker, Mademoiselle.* And you would not even find at the typical newsstand any of the "little" magazines such as the *Partisan Review*, the *Sewanee Review*, the *Kenyon Review*, the *New Mexico Quarterly*, the *Southwest Review* and many others. Did you want to pursue this difference in fiction still further into the novel field, you would find the same differences and distinctions. You would discover that most best-selling novels, though not all, have the characteristics of some of the first group, while other novels have characteristics of the second group and usually smaller sales.

With a broad swipe let us divide the whole field of modern fiction and particularly the short story into the commercial and craft writing of the first group and the "quality" and experimental or art writing of the second group. (Of course there will be some overlapping, for there can be no absolute dividing line.) Commercial stories bring much higher prices in a much larger market than do "quality" stories—most of the "little" magazines pay nothing at all, but publication in them can give a good deal of satisfaction and may obtain critical attention. The large majority of "best short stories of the year" published in the various anthologies are usually chosen from the second group, the quality group.

And this returns us to the attitude of the creative writer toward writing. Some writers are, through temperament, family environment, education, the nature of their reading interest, better suited to commercial writing; others to quality or artistic writing. The young writer must make some sort of decision early in his writing career, a decision, by the way, that is often not a free choice. Normally he will be better able to write the kind of stories that he likes to read. If stories of young love (the most popular type of commercial story) give you a critical bellyache, it is not sensible to try to write them. If detective stories are odious to you, how ridiculous to believe you can compose them successfully. Rid yourself of the notion that you can dash off a dozen or so pulp-paper stories that you hate and sell them to support yourself while you are composing a serious "literary" novel. Your hatred will be evident between every line. The tone of the story will be wrong even though it might be technically perfect.

Let us examine the distinctions and differences between the commercial or craft story and the quality story. With close critical scrutiny anyone can observe some of the more obvious:

(1) The commercial story is well plotted, leads to a definite climax, and usually contains the traditional hero-versus-villain conflict. The quality story has little or no plot; it has forward movement and may reach a climax on a much lower plane of excitement. Usually the quality story abandons the hero-villain relationship entirely in favor of the social problem (which sometimes involves hero and villain as they represent social types), or in some cases the quality story conflict is within the mind of the leading character.

(2) The commercial or craft writer resorts to a variety of tricks of the trade. Carefully he foreshadows the exciting events to come, thus creating suspense. His opening sentence in a short story is almost invariably a catch line which he uses to bridge over introductory material that sets time, place, course of action, identification of main characters, and so on: "When John Jordan . . . died, everybody wondered sympathetically what was going to become of little Allie." "Neither Sophie nor I had any dates all that summer." "I had not seen Dr. Squirnes since before the war, and last winter, when I met him again, I was astounded at the change in him." These three opening passages were taken without selectivity from the current issues of *Ladies Home Journal* and *Redbook*. I repeat that they were the first three stories I examined. This opening catch line—foreshadowing—is so standard in the commercial story that lacking it a story may not pass the preliminary reader, who may conceivably read beyond the first line. Of course there are many other tricks and devices employed to retain reader interest and excitement, tricks which I have not space here to

analyze in detail. Foreshadowing is a device used not only in the opening line but also several times throughout the story. Surprise is used frequently, surprise in character revelation, in the unfolding of the action, and often mild surprise in the denouement (although the O. Henry trick ending is practically out of vogue except in the short shorts).

The quality story makes very little use of these artificial devices, the author relying on content and theme to keep the reader going. For contrast here are the opening lines to three quality stories: "Elizabeth Willard, the mother of George Willard, was tall and gaunt and her face was marked with smallpox scars." "I belong to a kind of club or association consisting of men more or less eminent in the various arts or professions." "Truly, Deaconess, I don't want for a thing, thank you kindly."

(3) Characters are more generally types—stage types—in the commercial story. This statement should not be misunderstood. The businessman, the doctor, the housewife, the social gadabout, the washwoman, the English aristocrat, the gangster, the policeman, the stenographer, the nurse, the pioneer woman, the cowboy, ad infinitum, that crowd the pages of our popular fiction are so thoroughly characterized and individualized that they have all the semblances of real people. But underneath, if you skin off their superficial qualities and manners and dialogue, they are very similar to all the other secretaries, housewives, colored cooks, gangsters, detectives, professors—who have little relationship to their counterparts in real life.

The quality writer tends to be interested in the insides, the inner workings, of real people he has observed, or of people as representative of various segments of our social order. Essentially he is a psychologist interpreting actual behavior of people under tension or stress. Sometimes these interpretations seem morbid and extreme.

(4) The craft writer makes a good deal of use of setting and background, sometimes having little relevance to the main line of the story. Clothes, food, rooms, buildings, outdoor settings, cars, streets, offices, whatnot.

Some quality stories have no setting at all, or only a very vague setting. Or the setting may be used as a portion of character revelation.

(5) The commercial story contains a good deal of action of one sort

or another—a shifting of scenes as upon the stage. This action or movement may be fast or violent in nature or it may be quiescent, but it is there nonetheless. The quality writer tends to limit himself to a single action or scene or series of closely related actions that form a unit, resulting in what is labeled the "episodic" story. Or there may be no action at all, the entire story done in retrospect in almost expository form.

(6) The style of the commercial story is likely to be the traditional (slick-paper) style, with smooth-flowing sentences, great clarity, obvious transitions, a considerable number of well-selected adjectives. This style is a direct inheritance from the nineteenth century English and American novelists—more particularly in the short story form from writers like Bret Harte and Thomas Bailey Aldrich and more modernly from O. Henry. From the latter the young writer can learn a good deal about commercial appeal, but he should not imitate because many of O. Henry's tricks have been outmoded.

There is another style in current vogue, especially in the detective story, but appearing in other stories as well—a style borrowed directly from the cult of the simple, of which Ernest Hemingway is the leading exponent. This new style involves the objective viewpoint of action, short direct sentences, few adjectives, very rapid action, and it results in a kind of modern melodrama that is sometimes very effective. Some of the leading exponents are such writers as Raymond Chandler, James M. Cain, Dashiell Hammett, John Latimer.

Quality writing ranges all the way from the extremely experimental style to a feeling of complete lack of style. In general, three influences are to be noted in the modern quality story and in novels as well. The most salable is the *New Yorker* type, the episodic story of social criticism that borrows much from the earlier works of James Joyce and from Katherine Mansfield and is exemplified in the works of such writers as Ruth Suckow, Katherine Brush, John Cheever. Then there is the "stream-of-consciousness" cult, which originally borrowed its technique from Freudianism, the concept that the individual's character is best exemplified in his subconscious or half-conscious thought stream. James Joyce's later works and the works of Virginia Woolf have strongly influenced trends in modern quality writing in both the short story and novel form. Finally the cult of the simple, previously mentioned, as conceived by Gertrude Stein in rebellion against what has been termed the "new Mandarin" style has profoundly influenced such writers as Sherwood Anderson, Ernest Hemingway, William Faulkner, Erskine Caldwell. All these movements were direct outgrowths of the development of European realism and naturalism.

Of course style is an integral part of subject matter, not an entity in itself. Commercial writing has borrowed some of the technique of all three of the foregoing movements.

(7) The commercial writer, like the journalist, accepts the stipulations and taboos of his craft. And magazine taboos are many and exacting. For example, a story cannot contain any affront to a particular advertiser or product or to advertisers in general—for they support the magazine and yield the profits. Nor can there be any insult to any large segment of the population, any statement that might alienate a large body of readers. Sexual perversion of all types, almost all stories dealing with insanity, death treated morbidly—in fact anything of an unpleasant nature is usually taboo. The halt, the lame, the blind, those afflicted with any but a temporary malady do not make good material for hero or heroine. Recently one of my advanced students produced a salable commercial story in all respects except that one of the heroine's arms was permanently stiff, a matter upon which the plot turned. This seemed a minor enough permanent affliction to pass the taboo, yet thus far the story has been rejected by two national magazines on the basis alone of this affliction.

In recent years some of the commercial magazines have broadened their editorial policy a bit—admitting to consideration and publication such tabooed matters as divorce, mild profanity, modified treatment of sex, crime—all these acceptable only provided the hero or heroine is in the right. In fact, stories appear occasionally which have all the semblance of certain types of quality stories, except that when you shuck them to the kernels, they are the same product in a different wrapper.

Yet something has been omitted in all the preceding discussion, some less tangible difference between commercial and noncommercial short stories hinted at with the statement that the commercial story must please the reader. What is this fundamental essence, this gourmet powder that gives a certain piquancy to the same ingredients that the "quality" writer might use in a different way? What does make the short story palatable to the vast mass of the reading public?

It is not contained in all the technical aspects discussed above, but reverts rather to the original discussion of the attitude of the writer toward his creative efforts. Expressed simply, it is this: *The commercial or craft writer is primarily an entertainer.* That is his purpose in writing and he is paid according to the degree of entertainment. *The quality writer, the creative artist, is fundamentally a teacher.* His purpose is to teach about life as he has observed it, about the quirks and foibles of people he has known. Because he is teaching a more intelligent audience, he is sometimes abstruse; he works in symbols, in unusual language seeking unusual effects. As a good teacher he often seeks to convey his message by implication, by saying much through what he has left unsaid. The craft writer soothes, reassures, excites; he is the clown on the stage, the acrobat, the magician, the lascivious heroine, the agile hero. The quality writer is a lecturer on the lecturer's platform or the preacher in the pulpit, often talking in parables.

The lecturer cannot compete with the actor either in the size of his audience or, as a consequence, in the compensation he receives for his services. It is no accident that forty million people every week read the comic books, while a serious art exhibit that draws four thousand is an unqualified success. As Katherine Anne Porter has so aptly phrased it: "You cannot secure your bread and freedom of action too. You cannot be a hostile critic of society and expect society to feed you regularly."

The secret ingredient that sells commercial magazines, that fills motion picture houses, that prevents the twenty million radio audience from clicking off their radios is the emotion and sentiment contained in the entertainment. Lacking this ingredient, no commercial writing can be successful. One cannot wax emotional over a leading character that one dislikes and therefore finds nothing in common with.

From whence derives this emotional or sentimental appeal? What brings a lump to the throat or laughter to the lips or romance to the heart? We are an idealistic people. Throughout our mores, mirrored in our popular literature, is a kind of code or list of rules, the idealized life. It matters not that it may be more often honored in the breach than in the observance. When the average reader identifies himself with hero or heroine who lives up to this code through thick and thin, his fancies and his emotions are titillated. In our mass of western fiction, for example, we accept as reality a kind of never-never land which never did exist anywhere in the west. The typical western story and motion picture horse opera have become almost as stylized as classic mythology.

The following are a few of the most typical rules and traditions of the code around which commercial writing is built: (1) that young love is the essence of living and is best fulfilled in marriage; (2) that every individual has some good in him no matter how bad he may appear superficially (the crusty unpleasant character with the heart of gold); (3) that friendship is almost the highest form of human relationship, and faithfulness to friendship is sometimes more important than love or duty; (4) that above all, no matter what occurs, a man must do his duty; (5) that true generosity is one of the most selfless and noble of human acts; (6) that renunciation—of child, wife, sweetheart, friend—in justifiable circumstances is a proper necessity for continuing to live; (7) that man is the complete master of his own fate or destiny and that those with sufficient virtue or courage or self-sacrifice can overcome all obstacles to success; (8) that the young and innocent child can often aid the confused adult; (9) that patriotism is noble and pacifism despicable unless one is a minister; (10) that home and family is the only desirable situation in life and when in imbalance must somehow be restored to balance; (11) that evil people will inevitably repent or be properly punished; (12) and finally that good must and will triumph over evil. Often combinations of these themes are used.

Damon Runyon admitted quite frankly that all his stories were based upon the Cinderella myth.

By deliberately shunning these themes of the idealized life and eliminating the traditional tricks of the trade in an effort at revealing truth and re-evaluating character, the quality writer or artist eliminates any real possibility of emotional appeal to the masses. Themes of quality stories are often deliberate refutations of the popular code; for example, that charity is often only self-egoism, that marriage may be slavery of the worst sort and that emotional love is full of snares and pitfalls, that homosexualism is proper for the artist, that childhood instead of being a happy period is often a tortured and nightmarish fantasy, that bad can and does often triumph over good, even to the eventual benefit of the human race.

The dividing line between commercial and quality is much more clear-cut in the short story than in the novel, in which the two often overlap. Many of the tremendously popular novelists of our day who are regarded critically as essentially quality writers have one or more elements in their work that make them popular reading. The underlying sentimentalism of John Steinbeck's novels is well known. Beneath the hard-boiled characters of Hemingway's short stories and novels are extremely sensitive he-men, whose code of loyalty to friends and loyalty to duty is appealing. The southern background (romantic) of the novels of William Faulkner and Erskine Caldwell, plus their blunt and specific handling of sex, have made them widely popular. Wilbur Daniel Steele has conceded enough to the market to use background effectively and contrive interesting plots. Such a writer as Willa Cather discovers popularity in her romantic settings, her graceful style, and her engrossment with religion.

On the other side of the fence, writers such as Sinclair Lewis and John Marquand use the traditional commercial devices in their novels but use a more intellectual and critical approach and serious theme.

It is interesting to observe that were Mark Twain living today he would unquestionably be a craft writer. He was in his own day. He made use of every popular device in the book in order to gain a large audience: plot, superficial character treatment, humor, love, exotic settings, sentimental appeals. He is great not because of his technique but because of the happy accidents of place and time of birth, journalistic training, and an acute sense of observation plus a keen ear for the nuances of folk speech. Henry James, whose psychological and often wordy and abstruse works went practically unread in the same period in which Mark Twain lived, could not be made popular despite the efforts of all the modern critics and college professors who are taking part in a critical revival.

To return to the young writer's problems in learning to handle the essential ingredient for commercial success. Sentiment in a story is not easily attained, but must be craftily injected—a matter requiring long practice. Nor will emotional appeal be present in a story unless the author himself has not only built it up throughout, but also experienced it within himself. He must feel in sympathy with the situation to such an extent that he may even weep as he is writing it. This is no exaggeration. The other day one of my students asked me whether I really thought that Miss So-and-So (a popular commercial writer for the women's magazines) believed the tripe she wrote and experienced those emotions. I said that certainly she did. It may be that she feels only synthetically, however; that the process of writing puts her into a kind of self-attained hypnotic trance in which all that she writes seems true at the moment, even though the next day she might say that she dashed the thing off and didn't, of course, believe a word of it. She is probably lying without realizing the lie.

All this does not mean that the craft writer's style drips with emotional, saccharine phrasings. Far from it. Careful restraint at the right moment, the situation shedding its own tears or laughing its own laughter. Extreme histrionics on the author's part in portraying emotional situations are likely to arouse contempt rather than sympathy.

Most young writers with commercial aspirations can never attain this knack of building up sentiment and emotion based on one or more of the themes of our traditional code. They remain hopeful writers.

The quality writer follows his own bents, writes what he pleases, reads what he pleases, and if he is lucky he eventually arrives somewhere and if he is unlucky he remains unknown and probably teaches English in a high school or university. For the young commercial writer in his formative stages, imitation is often of considerable value. Study the magazines you hope to write for. Read all the stories. Imitate the one you like the best in a story of your own. Or imitate a style you especially admire.

However, I do agree with Hugh McNair Kahler, fiction editor of *Ladies Home Journal*, when he said in a recent letter to me that such engrossment in market and such imitation can be carried too far: ". . . I am not sure that it is a good idea to try to tailor short stories to anybody's measure. To be sure, any issue of any magazine will give you some idea as to the kind of stories that its editors have liked enough to buy and publish, but every good editor is always looking for the good story that will be unlike all the other good stories that he has previously published. By and large I think it is pretty generally true that nobody can write for an audience to which he does not himself belong, and the best work, I firmly believe, has always been done by people who were concerned only with pleasing themselves. Given a reasonable degree of competence in the mechanics of the craft, there is an audience, large or small, for anything that any of us writes to please himself, since none of us is unique, however much our egoism tries to persuade us that we are."

In conclusion, may I point out that neither road is easy, that craft stories are in many ways more difficult to write than are the experimental or quality stories and are sometimes better stories; that for ninety-nine out of a hundred potential writers, the same brainpower and energy devoted to almost any other field of endeavor will yield them far more in cash. Those with "quality" or artistic aspirations may find poetry a more satisfying outlet for their creative instincts than prose.

Try this experiment with yourself: Determine to give up all thoughts of writing for six months. Rid yourself of the too-popular and false notion that creative writing is an easy path to fame and financial success. If during this period you find yourself contented—if you do not particularly miss writing—then fall upon your knees and thank whatever god you worship that you have escaped a trap (for writers, even successful writers, are almost invariably discontented, unhappy, slightly confused people).

If you cannot eradicate the itch for writing, if it continues to annoy you, to make you restless and irritable and dissatisfied, then you might as well accept the fact that there is no help for it, and put every faculty of yours to work to make a success of what you have chosen to do and can't help doing; or to have it from the mouth of William Saroyan: "The best way to begin being a writer is to come right out and admit that one is definitely a crackpot. After that, the going is sure to be a lot easier."

16

How to Write for the Slicks

PAUL GALLICO

Former movie critic for the *New York Daily News,* Paul Gallico was graduated from Columbia University in 1921; was a sports editor and columnist from 1924 to 1936, and served during the war as a correspondent for *Cosmopolitan Magazine.* Now a free-lance writer, Paul Gallico is the author of *Farewell to Sport* (1938); *Adventures of Hiram Holliday* (1939); *The Secret Front* (1940); *The Snow Goose* (1941); *Golf is a Friendly Game* (1942); *Confessions of a Story Writer* (1946); *The Lonely* (1949); *Small Miracle* (1952); *Trial by Terror* (1952); *Foolish Immortals* (1953); *Snowflake* (1953); and *Love of Seven Dolls* (1954). He has also written stories and articles for the *Saturday Evening Post, Cosmopolitan, Good Housekeeping, Esquire, True Magazine,* and others.

In the preceding article on the contemporary short story Mr. Summers analyzed the story market, speaking chiefly from the viewpoint of a teacher of story writing and an advisor to young writers. Mr. Gallico speaks with vigor out of his experience as a successful writer of short stories for smooth-paper magazines. He tells us who are the readers of these magazines and what they wish to read. He describes with zest and vitality, qualities which characterize his own stories, how to produce fiction which will please both editors and readers. On his way through Mr. Gallico delivers adroit side-blows at other types of stories. He presents the short story as a high form of entertainment, involving the writer in the full use of all his abilities, and forcing him into hard discipline.

Paul Gallico's article is the talk of a true storyteller, a spinner of yarns, a man with enthusiasm for his craft and also for his readers.

H. H.

How to Write for the Slicks

YOU will probably consider it presumptuous of me to try to tell you how to write short stories for the "slicks" market in a matter of a chapter of three thousand words more or less, but I can assure you that that many words actually are not needed to furnish you with the key to the mystery.

The whole thing may be summed up in a paragraph. Tell a good story. Write it in a fresh, novel, original and entertaining manner, or, if your story is sufficiently strong and enthralling, submerge yourself and the telling thereof so that the drama contained therein may be fully realized. In other words, permit it to tell itself.

Having done this, thereafter it is only a matter of negotiating with the editor, or agent on the price you have decided you wish for it.

It is really that simple. Nine out of ten rejects occur because the writer has not done this. The rest of this chapter may then be well devoted to some of the reasons *why* he or she has not done it.

To begin with, and so that we may understand one another wherever possible and avoid a confusion of terms, the word or appellation "slick," as applied to a magazine, has to do with the quality of the paper on which it is printed and not the business acumen of the publishers and editors, or the adroitness and smart aleck plot twists and turns of the story.

The texture of the paper, smooth and slippery to the touch as opposed to the rough texture of the "pulps," which again is a technical term descriptive of paper grades, is of a higher quality, gives a better print job and will take photo engraving and four color work for illustrations and advertising. It costs more, looks better, is sold for a higher price and in return is supposed to give a higher literary return in stories and articles than those printed on cheaper stock and at the same time not quite so high, depressing or obtuse as some of the tales appearing in the arty or literary magazines and printed on top quality rag or linen paper with deckle edges and hand-drawn initial letters.

This magazine then, printed on the slick or "coated" stock receptive to color work and filled with lusciously illustrated advertising, is the popular medium, which reaches the most people, the vast literate but not literary, magazine- and story-reading public of the United States which can afford to buy practically everything the advertiser makes, advertises and sells. It is for the middle and white collar classes, the businessman, the office worker, the sales people, the suburbanites, housewives, mothers, nurses, professional people, harried and harassed by the difficulty or responsibility of their jobs or the plain ordinary difficulty of everyday life and the struggle to live it, who turn to the story for surcease, entertainment, relaxation, vicarious excitement, romance, education and escape.

These are the people for whose diversion and pleasure you eventually intend the story you offer for sale to the market of such material, the slicks.

And this is why amongst other reasons, which we will go into later, you must tell them a rattling good tale, spin them a yarn they won't be able to put down after they have passed the fourth or fifth paragraph, weave an enchantment about them that will spellbind them to your saga until the last word is told.

Not wanted here is the pallid narrative of the vapors of some delicate, unreal creature, or pages of introspection into the hopelessness of human relationships, but robust and gripping dramatizations of those very relationships and all the particular Hell to which they can lead.

The episode, the anecdote, the quasi-dramatic moment buttered up with psychiatric schmaltz and presented between buns of sophisticated and almost unintelligible prose will get you by no editorial portal but *The New Yorker*, an amusing and frequently entertaining magazine which has ruined more good young student writers than you would consider possible considering the not too exciting prices it pays.

It is necessary to make the distinction here, because *The New Yorker* is unique in that it specializes in literary fragments masquerading under the guise of short stories which they are not, while the big, high-paying well-known slicks demand complete and finished tales that come fully equipped with beginning, middle and end, a theme, conflict, development and conclusion which leaves the reader, if not wholly satisfied according to his nature and temperament, at least in possession of all the facts.

Further to be borne in mind is that you may write the most exalted prose, lush description and ear-lulling dialogue in the business, but if you have a peanut brain and a peanut soul you will not succeed in selling to the slicks because for all the criticism leveled at them, they do not buy peanut stories.

The story you tell must have some importance. Behind it there must be some guts, soul, human experience and human understanding.

Then, as far as selling the slicks is concerned, there is also the matter of your own enthusiasm about and belief in your story. There have been cynical professionals, and probably always will be mimics and tricksters who after studying the type of story that appears in these publications can formularize it and in cold blood, even with considerable contempt for both the formula and the medium, reproduce it to the point where it will sell.

But I am of the opinion that the editor buys these *manque de mieux*. He always prefers it if you will bleed a little onto the page. And so if you would make a success of writing for the slicks, my counsel to you would be to write neither up nor down, but to be a little in love with your story. Better still to believe it the greatest short story of its kind ever told, to be filled with the idea and the excitement of it, to live it inwardly for days and weeks and carry your enthusiasm to the typewriter. Your inclination then will be to worry less about form than content. You may study the technique of the short story until you have long white whiskers, or your sylphlike figure has given way to middle-aged spread but there never yet has been a story successfully sold on the A-B-C formula, sine and cosine of the craft alone. If you haven't a fine story to tell and do not believe passionately in the need for your telling it, not all the text books in the world, or the gathered wisdom of ages will help you to make a sale. Never make the mistake of putting the cart before the horse. What editors buy, in exchange for cash of the realm, is flesh and blood, preferably from the rich heart region, not dehydrated brain cells or desiccated cerebral tissue.

I cannot give you THE definition for the slick magazine short story, but I can offer you mine, and be glad to lend it to you until a better one comes along, which of course may be any moment.

A short story is an important story in which important things happen to important characters who are in conflict with one another. At the end of these happenings brought about because of the situation in which the characters find themselves and how they react to it because of the kind of people they are, none of them will ever be quite the same again. They will be happy, unhappy, richer, poorer, in jail, out of jail, married or forlorn, but none of them will be as they were when the story began.

And if through your narrating of these events the reader finds himself a little moved, and perhaps a little changed too, so that because of what he has read, he too will not ever be exactly the same again as he was before he picked up your story, why then you have done yourself a job. Your check will be fat and juicy. The editor will invite you to a deadly luncheon. Even the publisher may condescend to pop into the editorial sanctum and have a word with you.

From time to time when I have imparted this prime nugget of wisdom to students their reaction has been—"But you have said and everybody says that in a short story, character *never* changes, so when you say . . ."

Yes, yes, I know. But I am not talking about character and I suppose it is best to make this plain. I am talking about the situation of the people involved.

To take as an example if one of the basic characters in your story was a miser, a chronic one with a lifetime record of miserliness, this particular characteristic could not be changed during the process of your short story. For him to reform suddenly and finish out the yarn as the soul of generosity would be unbelievable and unsalable.

However, if because conflicts arise between his miserliness of soul and his love for his family and as a result of these conflicts his wife leaves him forever and departs for South America with some more liberal friend, and further his daughter, because he will not spend the money to heat the house properly, comes into fatal contact with a pneumococcus, Type I, and dies like Mimi of a cough in a heart-rending scene which you will write most affectingly, then, it seems to me you would be justified in saying that the situation of your chief character had indeed altered as the result of the story and that while he would still be a miser he would never again be the same as he was before.

I have gone into this much detail on this subject since I find that most students, amateurs and would-be professional writers with their sights set on the gold in them thar slicks all suffer from Episoditis and frequently mistake an episode or anecdote or mere incident for a story.

These same folk are delighted when they happen on one of these ready-made happenings in everyday life, because at the drop of a Bursar's Fee, they will inform you that their main difficulty is that they cannot think up the plots and counterplots and subplots that go to make up this high-priced fiction in the *Saturday Evening Post, Collier's, Cosmopolitan, Good Housekeeping* and kindred publications.

Most people are inclined to make the whole thing too complicated for themselves. A plot is really nothing more than a set of characters, a set of circumstances and a dramatic conflict. In these conflicts we see human beings against other human beings, human beings against Fate or Nature, or the Elements, or man pitted against himself. This is the stuff out of which plots are made, outside of the standardized and easily recognizable formula plots of various types favored by certain of the magazines.

This, I think, is as good a place as any to point out to you or remind you that most of the stated difficulties with writing stories, usually referred to as plot trouble or character trouble, or beginning or ending trouble is purely fancied and wholly imaginary and is a kind of protest registered by the mind which balks at the business because it is really difficult.

Thinking up stories, working them out logically and dramatically to the point where they are so exciting and attractive that they will fetch large sums of money is hard, exhausting work. However much the mind adores the tangible results in folding-pelf, it emphatically rejects the trying processes of earning it, and because it is really so difficult to do, it writhes and twists and turns in a never-ending attempt to evade.

The mind, as you very well know, does not want ever to face reality if it can be avoided. It also does not care too much about facing up to the labors connected with creating a disciplined unreality.

Therefore it throws up every conceivable kind of obstacle and delights in giving these obstacles technical names and terms behind which the writer can hide until his conscience drives him forth into the storm once again. The mind of the writer is not his friend or his servant. It makes a sucker out of him a dozen times a day. It is his worst enemy and therefore not to be trusted for one moment.

As you must know if you have meddled with this business at all, there are usually plenty of real difficulties connected with working out a story properly (the chief one being to force yourself to think logically as well as dramatically and temper imagination with sense) but even if there weren't we would invent them just to get out of work, and most of the time we do. You have only to listen to the unconcealed joy in the voice of a writer who when you ask him how his latest opus is progressing replies—"Badly. I'm stuck right now. Can't seem to make the characters do what I want them to do," to know exactly what is going on.

The cure for all of these self-delusions is first to laugh them off as a lot of hooey and then to beat the be-Jesus out of your mind by forcing it to go to work.

If you ask me *what* kind of a story to write for the big slicks I can only advise you that you are bound only by your own experience, imagination and intellect, that the scope is unlimited, and that there are actually very few subjects that cannot be handled with sufficient tact, delicacy and understanding so as to make them not only palatable but interesting to this huge reading public.

But there is one thing of which I cannot emphasize the importance sufficiently. To succeed in the high-paying market, throw away your miniatures, your pastels, your sketch blocks. Paint on big canvases. Select big themes and depict them in bold and glowing colors. In other words you will be expected to deliver something for the money.

This may be a crude and commercial tag to place upon an art form, but there is no reason, beyond the limitations of the writer, why a story devised for, aimed at and written for a high-paying slick magazine should not be an excellent piece of literary work as well and eventually find its way into the anthologies of the best stories of the year, etc. etc.

But if you have made a study of literature and writing and great short stories in particular, you must have noted surely that never are the themes picayunish, pallid or unimportant. Big events and exciting or arresting happenings form the bases of these stories. This does not mean that every time you sit at the typewriter to concoct a story for the big commercial market that you must scheme to send an express train over a cliff, or sink a luxury liner with all hands in mid-ocean. A man, miserably and unhappily in love, debating with himself whether he will live or die presents a dilemma which, though well known, invariably commands attention.

Get used to thinking big thoughts and handling big problems involving big emotions, for that is what people pay off on in the long run. The members of the reading public in search of diversion, entertainment or rank escape want and need to read stories involving all the human emotions to which they themselves have been prey and which therefore they can understand and share vicariously. Amongst these you would include love, hate, greed, envy, vanity, ambition, jealousy, fear, loneliness, yearnings, etc.

Remember likewise that to reach your readers and get your story to them, you must first be admitted through the portal of an editor—many editors as a matter of fact since in several of the editorial offices of the high-paying magazines stories are bought on the strength of the majority vote of the senior staff.

The editor is not your enemy but your friend when he picks up your manuscript for he wishes nothing so much as to find a rattling good tale which will increase the circulation of his publication, making possible a rise in the advertising rates and a bonus for all, not to mention that he has had the satisfaction of discovering it.

Nevertheless, by virtue of his profession and the number of manuscripts he reads monthly in search of the perfect one, he must be a little jaded or, at the very least, desperately familiar with all the plot and story clichés. And so to sell an editor you must really slug him with your idea, or at the very least move him.

Remember that when your script enters the office of the editor, either via an agent or the mails it is in immediate competition with hundreds of other stories. If, let us say, the capacity of the magazine is for five short stories a month and hundreds are submitted, it may begin to dawn upon you what your chances are and how good you have to be to knock over the opposition. And remember too, that the editor has seen them all, practically, in one form or another. He knows virtually every plot and is familiar with every kind of writing. No sooner does he begin to read a story than his mind must perforce attempt to ticket it and drop it into a classification. No matter what you are attempting, he probably has read something similar before. And so to hold his attention and stir his check writing arm, you must really knock him dead. And you won't do it with a pastel or a piece of blown-up trivia.

You must move your reader and your editor emotionally. Make him or her want to cry, or laugh, leave them pleased or angry or frightened, sentimentally satisfied, or vicariously suffering the pangs of disillusionment, depressed or stimulated, but SOMETHING must happen to the person who encounters your story. If it doesn't, the failure can only lie at your door.

Never be afraid to put honest sentiment or emotion into a story aimed at the slick market. Genuine warmth and laughter with a hint of tears behind it is a priceless commodity. Not that I would recommend a writer weeping all over his pages or embarking upon emotional debauches, or chuckling appreciatively at his own wit. I just wish to make the point that if you are inhibited about emotion and sentiment and cannot let go, you will probably never make much of a writer, at least not for the magazines in search of mass readership.

The question of what to write or what not to write as far as the big slicks and their taboos are concerned can for the most part be anticipated and settled in your own mind by the use of simple common sense, judgment and good taste. If you are inherently a person of good taste and normal reaction your writing will reflect it and you need not worry about offending.

In addition to your reactions which stem from the kind of person you are, you use common sense daily in judging people, in deciding whether you approve of them as people, or their actions as they might affect you or the community. You are perfectly safe in applying the same judgment to the characters in your stories.

How to Write for the Slicks

You know what you like when you read a book or a magazine, or attend a play or a movie. A scene misplaced, or too long drawn out, soon invites your yawns. You also know how restive you become and how you yearn for escape when trapped by a bore who is engaged in telling a long, wandering, pointless story. Apply the same judgments to your own work.

The same holds for matters of good taste, and ethics. You know, or should know, what is or is not in good taste in human behavior, what annoys, or shames, or embarrasses people. Surely you have at some time or other sat in the theater or at a moving picture or in front of a radio or television set and felt yourself beginning to perspire slightly, or squirm in your seat because of what was going on. It is this apparatus you must count on to keep others from squirming and heading for the exits. The slick magazines are involved in exactly the same kind of inhibitions and taboos as the good citizens for whom they publish. Since it is you who have chosen your audience for your own commercial purposes you have no right to quibble over the reactions of this audience. And if you wish to sell to them you will be wise to study those reactions, taboos, inhibitions and credos and defer to them. There are plenty of other mediums for free, untrammeled and unlicensed writing, up to and including, if you must, the privately printed and circulated pamphlet.

You will soon learn the various individual taboos of the magazines, dictated sometimes by the audiences they reach, or quite possibly the eccentricities of editor or publisher, or both. You can buck these taboos if you want to, but it is rarely worth the effort since it is equally rare that artistic integrity actually depends upon your including them in your story.

What should really amaze you in dealing with the slicks is how much literary freedom and artistic integrity jealously guarded by the editor really exists where under the system of purchasing and publishing stories it really need not.

There is no excuse for not knowing what the slicks want and how they want it, for the magazines are on the stands every month and you have but to buy them and read them. If in the space of six months or so of such work you cannot familiarize yourself not only with the minds and viewpoints of their editors and the groups at which they are aiming, but the various recipes for stories where formula stories occur, then you have no business trying to write for them anyway, since ordinary intelligence is a necessary adjunct to the writing business. In fact it is by the exercise of this intelligence in the selection of themes on timely subjects, big events in the news that lend themselves to fiction treatment, or political or philosophical trends, that you will land many a sale over a competitor more immersed in his art and not quite so wide awake to what is going on in the world about him.

Nor should the fact that the stories you write and sell frequently have no basis of reality in terms of life as it is, upset you, for neither have the fantastic sums paid by these magazines for this type of innocent fairy tale. The market price for a story full of the bitterness and grim disillusionment of any twenty-four hours spent as a passenger aboard this planet *might* go as high as $500 in a going literary magazine, whereas the pay for maintaining the fiction that this is the best of all possible worlds is five times that amount.

And more than maintain it, you must to a certain extent believe it and entertain at least some of the more harmless illusions, for the editor is quick to smell out cynicism in your story and reject it as the work of a greedy and inept opportunist. You cannot very well do both, have your literary cake and eat it at the same time. Those few who have succeeded at it have really written on two planes or in two media to achieve their success. As an example of what I mean I can offer you Mr. J. P. Marquand, who when he wrote for the slicks chose mainly the medium of highly entertaining detective stories revolving around a character named Mr. Moto. Philip Wylie, most of whose beliefs and doomful prose couldn't get past the elevator operator in the office building of any slick publication, has for years been selling the *Saturday Evening Post* the deep-sea fishing adventures of two raffish characters named Des and Crunch who operate a charter boat out of Miami. Mr. Wylie believes passionately in deep-sea fishing. He also believes in Des and Crunch. Therefore his stories ring true and bring delight and entertainment to many who would be appalled if they read what he really thought about middle-class life in the U.S.A.

The slicks keep up with the times and are today far broader in scope and higher in standard than they were a quarter of a century ago, with, I should say, less emphasis on the formula story. Their readers have added a few years of mass intellectual maturity and occasional recognition of the adult facts of life and the periodicals who print for them reflect this. Two wars in twenty-five years have forced us to grow up a little. Careful reading of these magazines will indicate to you to what extent this has taken place. As a matter of strict fact, careful reading of them will tell you as much as anyone can about how to write for them. The editor can try to advise you, teachers of the craft will analyze and explain it in terms of patterns or formulas, but in the long run you will derive only material which you should be sufficiently alert and bright enough to determine for yourself.

17

Floating Target

WARE TORREY BUDLONG

Ware Torrey Budlong came to fiction writing by the route of newspaper work. Beginning as a syndicated feature writer, she moved on to positions as Washington correspondent for a chain of papers, book review columnist of the Associated Press, and special foreign correspondent.

Her fiction writing started with a group of mystery novels written under a pseudonym. Her short stories have been published in *Saturday Evening Post*, *Collier's*, other general magazines, women's magazines, British publications, and translated into half a dozen foreign languages.

She is married to Theodore Warren Budlong, has a son and a stepdaughter, and lives in New York City.

Ware Torrey Budlong, one of the younger writers, whose stories have appeared during the past few years in many of the popular magazines of wide circulation, writes with humor and candor of her experiences in satisfying the editors of magazines directed toward the millions of American women readers.

The title, "Floating Target," is apt. Now you see it, now you don't; now you hit it, now you miss it. Many of the comments are provocative. One question foreshadows the discussion in Mr. Allen's article later in this book. Why do magazines which have grown progressive in their articles insist upon *pigeon-hole* plots in their fiction?

Mrs. Budlong describes the limitations of these markets for short stories, and includes the occasional surprising escapes into a wider freedom. And as she says in closing, "You can always do a piece aimed at a shooting star. It might sell."

H. H.

Floating Target

WRITING short stories for American women's magazines offers a specialized set of satisfactions, and also a specialized bewilderment. To sell with any frequency in this field, you must either pick a groove and stay in it, or else expect the jouncing from satisfaction to bewilderment.

This adjustment is entirely different from the simple business of writing for general magazines. Simple, that is, not easy. You know when you plot a story for the general magazines that you are aiming at a certain blue line of excellence. If your story is original without being offensive, and hits well above that blue line, it will probably be accepted. But when you write for the women's magazines, you are taking sight on a floating target, which bobs up and down, swings without warning in a new current, and occasionally dips under the surface.

One of the satisfactions, then, is the sporting flavor of the attempt. And when you make a sale, there is the pleasant surprise of hitting a target in motion.

A more serious satisfaction in writing for women's magazines is that you can make a comment, take on a theme or, as the editors put it, say something. In contrast again, a large portion of the stories in general magazines are for entertainment only. But the women's magazines are a home from home for writers who are nagged by ideas on feminine problems. I have had a women's magazine editor stop me on the first sentence of a plot for a story, to ask "What does it say?" It's a good feeling that some editors somewhere actually want you to say something, besides spinning a story.

Provided your characters come alive and the story creates its own vitality, you can be simple and direct and lay your point on the line. Two or three of your characters get together, tackle a problem, sweat it out, and produce a gram of home-grown philosophy, or a straw to show which way some wind is blowing. And at the end you can sit back and know your story has a backbone, under what you hope is entertainment value.

An allied satisfaction, if you are a woman, may be that you have an added interest in writing for women. You are beset by the vital but less articulate sisterhood asking "Say *this* for us." You have writhed your way through variegated feminine problems of your own, and you enjoy taking a crack at them, spreading their insides out for a good look, hoping when you're done that some reader will say "That's for me."

Women's magazine readers supposedly keep an eye open for new ideas, and not just from the home-making departments. Apparently they read a story, note the heroine's attack on her problem, and say, "So that's how she handled it. Now I wonder—if I tried that, would it work on Henry?" This of course is dream-bait for authors.

Such satisfactions are obviously present for all writers in this field. The bewilderment, however, does not apply so widely. Writers for women's magazines may be divided roughly in two groups: the writers who are temperamentally suited to staying in a groove, and the writers who get claustrophobia in grooves. The claustrophobic writers are afflicted with the belief that a good story doesn't necessarily have to follow the standard pattern. If they are stubborn about this, they will encounter the special brand of bewilderment provided by the women's magazines. Before amplifying this matter of bewilderment, there are some points to be pegged down.

Naturally there are quite a few steps in the process of selling enough stories so you know a sale is not an accident. Some of these steps are too universal to comment on, and others are personal and individual. I've been asked to give here an account of my particular experience in writing for women's magazines. So the clover tops I clip off en route are my own, right or wrong. They have been tested in shop sessions with other writers, and tested again in discussions with editors. But for what they are worth, the responsibility is mine, assumed with a liberal dose of modesty about tossing off comments so flatly. The reader will kindly interpolate "in my opinion," whenever needed, from here on in.

The first story I ever sold to a major women's magazine was done by a simple formula. A writer friend told me that the whole secret of the thing was conflict. So I seized on a domestic conflict that interested me, and my unfortunate husband and wife beat their brains out in conflict from first word to last. They struggled and argued and rent their souls and suffered. For good measure, to be sure there was enough of this conflict gimmick, I threw in the hurricane of 1938. Well, it sold. But the trouble was, when I started applying that formula again, there were few conflicts providing so much spiritual gore. My conflicts would have to be watered down a little and, furthermore, I couldn't keep on leaning on the hurricane of 1938.

So I began all over again. Obviously, I would need something more than conflict, to keep going. And as a matter of fact I didn't care muoh for formulas.

The first vital step I took was to accept the fact that I couldn't write what I wanted to write, in short stories. This step took some time, it was more of a crawl.

An editor told me, "Never write for any magazine. Write a story as you see it." I did this for a while, and collected rejections. In liking my kind of story, I was a minority of one.

I wcnt away from the whole business and wrote a couple of mystery novels. This spoiled me badly, as I could even decidc about my own commas and clinch the matter in the galley margins. But finally I went back to short stories and crawled some more.

I tried a compromise. I wrote a story partly as I liked it, and partly as the magazine seemed to want it. This sold. Another sold by the same method. So I finished my first step. I couldn't write as I wanted to, but I could get some of the things I cared about under the wire.

The second thing I did was to separate story ideas for the women's magazines from those for general magazines, since the two kinds of stories were sometimes basically different and sometimes needed different treatment. So, as I got ideas for stories, I dropped them in the proper pot and set them at the back of the stove to simmer. In preparation for a different treatment. into the women's magazine pot went also a dash more emotion, more clinical details of mood, and some assorted oddments called the woman's viewpoint. Once in a while there was an upset, and a general magazine bought a supposed women's magazine story, but in the main segregation helped.

The next step in this progress was taken when I started studying the women's magazine fences. There they were, the strict taboos in barbed wire, and the other wooden fences best summarized by the editorial saying, "Well—we never use that. Unless, of course, it is an outstandingly good story." This remark is likely to send you away convinced that you will never do an outstandingly good story, and mordantly fence-shy.

There are a lot of unexpected fences. It is obvious that too much passion should be strained out of love scenes, and too much strong language from quarrels. But I was startled when an editor told me seriously that all heroes must be good looking. Or, of course, appealingly homely. After that, I found the crooked smile sneaking up on me once in a while.

Another small fence is liquid refreshment. After I watched one of my women characters have her cocktail edited into sherry, I learned. That character wasn't the sherry type. But I had walked straight into the fence that sets a double standard for drinking. From then on my women drank iced or hot coffee according to season and, at the most, a soft drink without any trade name.

There are other taboos, fences with a red blinker light attached, that warn you that you proceed at your own risk. The taboos against stories about artists, writers and Hollywood stars; against characters or plots glorifying radio; against too glamorous characters of any sort; against any kind of deformity. There is also a firm preference, a taboo in reverse, for reader identification rather than reader escape.

Everybody knows the fences, they go on and on, and become familiar. It takes a little while, however, to set them up around your typewriter.

Somewhere in this progress, I collected a check list for stories—the musts: A clear story line. Emotional intensity. Characterization that projects real people. Reader identification. Rising suspense. A pull-in, a carrot in front of the reader's nose, early in the story. A serious point made, or at least a gimmick to identify the story. Tautness. A simple style, readable without effort, with an occasional spin on a phrase when it comes naturally.

When I looked that list over in cold blood, I wondered why I ever tried to write short stories. It didn't even include a lot of things that weren't musts but that I hoped to do. But the list did help. It sometimes stopped a bad story, half written, and sometimes helped diagnose a muddled one.

I had got that far, in my own journeying, when the war got into women's magazine fiction. All of a sudden, some of the fences came down. You could stop pulling various punches. I rolled up my sleeves, plunged in and sold stories. This was fine while it lasted. But it was no help for what came later.

After the war, there was a great desert, full of sand in the eyes and general frustration. You couldn't write about the effects of the war, you couldn't write about what happened when the men came home, you couldn't write about the men still on foreign duty. The people I saw in all directions were having God's own struggle making new adjustments, but I couldn't write short stories about them. As nearly as I could make out, the editors believed that readers were so tired of war and adjustments, they didn't even want them mentioned any more.

So the old plots got dusted off, and the magazines began to come out with stories set in a vacuum. They had no relation to life at that time in America. Reading them in the midst of watching the postwar problems all around me, the stories rang phony to me. I couldn't write stories, just then, that took the premise that there had never been a war.

Gradually, I found some valid stories to write that were the same, whether the men concerned had spent the last few years fighting or in a void. The stories that mentioned the war sold in England, where for some reason the readers or editors were willing to admit there had been a war.

Coming up to date, the war is now sanctioned again in the women's magazines. In addition, I gather that readers are supposed to be slightly more broad-minded in general. And the young crop of readers is always pushing along, with a delayed but definite effect on editorial opinions. But in the main, the fiction setup is unchanged.

There is that target, bobbing and spinning. And to complicate life further, it stays inside a fixed territory. There are all those glimmering stories to write, over yonder on the horizon. But the target stays inside its set boundaries. This is a confinement more thwarting than any taboo fences.

It is bewildering that the women's magazines don't want to go outside the same old territory of stories. And it is bewildering that, even inside those fixed limits, the fiction policy is erratic.

So we are back again, with our satisfactions and bewilderment. That is, any writers like me. There is that other happy band of writers who get set in the groove, deliver skillfully and tirelessly, and apparently have no problems. But I can stay just so long in any groove, even watching the checks come in. Then I see a different idea for a story, or a story that can't be done the traditional way. I'm out of the groove again, and maybe I'll sell the story and maybe I won't, but I do it my way.

There are some editors on the women's magazines who brighten a writer's life. The editors who take the time and patience to say why, when they reject a story. The editors who add a comment with an acceptance, so you know what kind of dent that story made. The editors who help you wrestle with a piece of your literary soul over the luncheon table. The editors who say, "Keep on going your way. Don't give up."

But they can't lift the bewilderment. It is everywhere in the picture. Why must the fiction boundaries be so limited? Why do magazines, progressive enough to carry articles that cut frankly into new fields from birth control to venereal disease, hold back in their fiction from variation in theme, form or style? Again and again stories are published, which are nothing but warmed-over fiction hash with a strip of avocado on top.

I asked an editor point-blank: if you were choosing between two stories, equally well done, one with a pigeon-hole plot that has been used over and over, and the other with an original plot—which would you take? The answer was flat: *the pigeon-hole plot*. That is what I mean by bewildering.

I know some of the reasons for staying in familiar territory. I can see the circulation manager and the advertising manager peering over the fiction editor's shoulder. But the situation can't be laid entirely to the circulation manager, or the editor, or the publisher. Somewhere along the line, there also could be a lack of confidence in the readers.

Why underrate the women readers? Editors murmur about circulation troubles, advertising troubles, and playing safe. Why play safe so insistently, when using newer stuff more often might rake in more readers? One magazine offers excellent stories that are focused on the problems and interests of younger women. Are the other magazines hamstrung by their older readers? I'm not complaining, but it would help just to know the score.

In dark moments, I have a dreadful uncertainty. Maybe nobody knows what the women's magazine readers want in the way of short stories. Then I remember that the editors have their reports on reader response, their files of letters from readers.

If the women's magazines have arrived at a precise definition of their readers, couldn't they pass it along to writers? If we were convinced once and for all that the readers liked formula stuff and didn't want a more varied diet, then we could stop trying to sell individualized stories in this field. But I personally shall have a more hopeful opinion of the readers, till I am proved wrong.

In contrast to this uncertainty about what the readers of the women's slick magazines want, is the clear reader-analysis provided by a group of first-person mass-reader women's magazines. These magazines have estimated their readers by poll and letters, interviews across the country, and surveys. They have boiled down the results so they could give their writers a real understanding of the people they were writing for—an invaluable aid in beaming stories.

A story must have spontaneity, must take its own head. But it can be shaped in the plotting, and shaped again in revision, so it conveys itself best to a given type of reader. And being read, after all, is the objective.

The glimmers of editorial viewpoint on readers that do come through can be baffling. I had one story turned down on the grounds that the hero wasn't the kind of man that women's magazine readers would have a chance to marry. That's hobbling the characterization. Plotting a story for the women's magazines can seem like an obstacle race, not the least hazard of which is tripping over your own feet.

To leave the whole matter of the fixed territory of stories, and turn to the erratic movement of the target inside that territory, there are of course many understandable reasons for this lack of stability. Editors have their own fluctuating factors to cope with. There is the factor of scheduling, to get a proper balance of stories in a given issue. There is the inventory factor. There is the fact that there seems to be a cycle in the quality of stories that go to the magazines, with the result that mediocre stories are bought sometimes because there are none better available. And once again, there is the influence of the circulation and advertising departments.

But when these points are added together with due respect—the target still seems to be bobbing around more than is necessary. A fairly mild story will be rejected because it might offend the readers. And then a highly controversial story is bought, and when letters of disapproval pour in, the editor says that was expected and the story published regardless. So where are we?

Also, the unexpected shifts of current provide suspense enough for half a dozen stories. An editor approves of a theme one month, and dislikes it violently the next. Anything may have happened in between, of course, but it's unsettling.

Just about the time you despair of the target ever getting in your sights again, it pops up unexpectedly. For example, when you do a sharp and frank analysis of some women characters, and expect a firm turndown. One story of mine of this type was rejected by a general magazine with the comment, "If American women are like that, we don't want to know about it." It was published in a women's magazine.

When a few writers for women's magazines get together, there is apt sooner or later to be an agonized outcry—"But what do they *want*?" Outside of the well-worn ruts, what *do* they want? One thing is sure, it does no good reading the magazines to find out. Every so often there will come along a story so stingingly right that its claim is obvious. But reading the general run of stories, in an earnest effort to find out what is wanted, leads only to hair-tearing.

It is difficult to mention this to editors, as it looks like sour grapes because your latest effort didn't get accepted. If you bring the matter up just after an acceptance, it is more graceful, but appears to be too fixed an effort to write by rule in the future. Nevertheless, it would be a godsend if, after a certain number of acceptances, an editor would sit down with a writer and sketch roughly what his magazine is looking for in new material. And the answer isn't "good stories." It's a lot more complicated, and it varies with the magazine.

The fact of variation among the magazines themselves, incidentally, is of course to be expected and causes no special difficulty except in one instance. There is one magazine in this field that is receptive to less standardized stories, but since this attitude sets it apart from the others, a story rejected by that magazine is apt to be a misfit elsewhere. Paying this price for progress can certainly be taken philosophically.

Granted that a percentage of stories in the women's magazines must be held inside a pattern, there is always the hope that the percentage of nonpattern stories will rise. Meanwhile we try to cope.

I did a story once, about a man and woman who fell in love, though for specialized reasons they were able to meet each other only in the dark. The editorial comeback was—women don't fall in love with men they can't see. Well, maybe not. But just to confuse me again, the story sold in England. To take the modest view, this could be because of the well-known shortage of men in that country, enabling English women readers to picture themselves falling in love in more unusual circumstances. Or it could be merely because of a shortage of manuscripts that month. Anyhow, it's confusing. It probably would solve everything, just to move to England.

There is always this consolation in writing out-of-the-groove stories. They usually sell somewhere, from New Zealand to Denmark, and most frequently in England. Sometime I want to solve the mystery of the English market. Stories that I happen to be more satisfied with, that are off the beam, are a big risk in this country but usually sell in England. Somebody likes them, I tell myself. They can come alive in print. God bless England.

To make various points, I seem to have referred to a fair amount of sales. I should hastily add that I've had a chastening amount of rejections. I've learned a lot from rejections but I don't like them any better for that. If you look on writing as a gallop for self-expression, rejections are less important. But if you look upon it also as a challenging profession, then the rejections have to be added into the score.

It is sometimes said that writing for women's magazines means completely conformal writing, but that isn't so. There are the two categories, the grooved story and the free story.

There is no compulsion to write formula stories. The decision is up to you and your bank account. If you want regular checks coming in, then you stay in a groove. If you can afford to write as you choose, you will sell erratically, but you will write those stories that glint on the horizon.

It has also been said that writing for the field is a mechanical process. Once again, this is not true of the nongroove stories. A story may come all in a piece and readily, because the subconscious, or habit, or what you choose to call it, has done the selection and rejection painlessly. But a *good* women's magazine story, like any other good story, has a drive of its own, an entity of its own, and its own individual overtones. When you start to write that kind of nongroove story, your subconscious is tapped, and the story itself takes over. Then, the process is far from mechanical.

Taking a broad view, there is discipline in writing for women's magazines. There is also an opportunity to try to write toward a definite audience, which is good exercise for the subjective side of any writer.

Writing short stories for the women's magazines, in the main, means directed technique. But discipline helps, till it chafes. And there's an out. You can always climb up in the white-washed ivory tower and do a piece aimed at nothing or a shooting star. It might even sell.

18

Serials: Stepchild of the Novelist

MARGARET CULKIN BANNING

Known primarily as a writer for the women's magazines, Margaret Banning is also the author of essays, articles and books such as *The Case for Chastity* (1937); *Salud: a South American Journal* (1941); *Letters from England* (1942); *Letters to Susan* (1936) and *Mixed Marriage* (1930). Her recent works are *Give Us Our Years* (1950); *Fallen Away* (1951); and *Dowry* (1955). Born in Minnesota, she was graduated from Vassar College in 1912.

Margaret Culkin Banning has achieved the feat which Pearl Buck speaks of in her article as so difficult: the feat of writing a satisfying and readable novel which also appears as a serial in a magazine. At first blush this may not seem so remarkable—other authors have done it too. But Mrs. Banning has done it *every year* since 1920! So it is with great authority that Mrs. Banning speaks of the broadening of the serial pattern, the loosening if not destruction of the "formula" for serial writing.

Perhaps this freedom is still more "on the way" than actually accomplished. Perhaps most changes cease after a while to be advances and freeze into a new formula. But this is not true of one advance—an advance that Mrs. Banning herself has had much to do with. *Characterization* in the serial has grown ever more adult and more absorbing. And whenever this happens, the mechanical plot is doomed. For real, rounded, human figures will show it up, walk through its absurdities, and finally distort it back into reality!

As Mrs. Banning points out, the actual limitations imposed by the serial form *need* be no worse and can be as stimulating as those surrounding the drama. What the serial needs is experiment and exploitation.

E. J.

Serials: Stepchild of the Novelist

ANY appraisal of the women's magazine serial should begin and end with the attitude of writers toward this highly paid and widely read form of fiction. The contemptuous criticism of serials, coming almost always from those who never have read any of them, is sometimes annoying and often justified, but it is not very important. The fashion of lumping together all serials and crying down the lot of them as contrived, mechanical, trivial pieces of escapist fiction is as stupid and unrealistic as are most generalities.

It has always seemed unfortunate to me that serialized fiction should not have a place of greater dignity in the writing profession. But the fault has not been in the critic nor in the reader, it has been in the writer. Writers have not regarded the production of serials as an art, nor even as a highly respected craft. Serials always have been the stepchildren of the novelist.

Stepchildren are not always badly treated. There are instances when there is little difference between the feeling of a novelist toward a story which he is intending to sell serially, and another which he knows cannot be serialized. But that is the exception. A novelist usually feels that the book that he cannot or will not have serialized is his own brain child. But the story which the novelist intends primarily for serial sale and its rewards, is too often the child of the editor. The novelist only has it committed to his care to bring up and develop. This he may do with extreme scrupulousness, but if he does it without love, the serial stepchild shows the invariable results of lack of affection, careless supervision, or actual neglect.

The serial situation has changed very greatly in the last two decades and a great deal of the criticism directed at serials in women's magazines has not kept up with the times or taken cognizance of the changes. Twenty years ago most editors of magazines which were read widely by women felt that two or three serials, biting at each other's heels in the pages of their magazines, were absolutely necessary if their readers were to be held to the habit of subscription or regular buying of the periodical. These serials were standardized by individual editors both in length of installment and in the number of parts. Some editors wanted six-part serials. Some wanted four installments in a story. They also asked for, expected, and got climaxes of suspense, guaranteed to hold reader interest for thirty days at the end of each part. Life is not so evenly divided in its natural climaxes and the serial writer had to do a good deal of contriving. For this he—or more likely she—was extremely well paid.

But the picture has changed very considerably. An editor said once that there would always be a place for the four-layer-cake novel, with sugar frosting. Today that is doubtful. Some important periodicals, notably the *American Magazine*, broke the serial tradition. The *American Magazine* editors decided some years ago that their public would prefer stories that were "complete in one issue," and in that magazine, as well as in *Pictorial Review* and the *Woman's Home Companion*, the "one-shot" began to appear and to edge out the serial, partly or altogether.

The war also had a very definite effect on serial reading. Many people were traveling, constantly enroute. Women as well as men were moving about so fast that subscriptions could not keep up with them, or with their changing interests. They might read the October issue of a magazine but not be sure of getting the November issue, so serials confused or bored them. Also, reading time was limited. Many magazines cut down the number of serial stories they were in the habit of printing and found that they lost no circulation because of that. Today they publish one serial, or at the most two at a time, and if they cannot find a serial story to suit their needs, the editors get along without one.

Most interesting of all the experiments in regard to serial values was the one tried by various editors of excellent literary taste, who bought long pieces of fiction and published them over a period of weeks or months in installments, regardless of artificial climaxes or contrived suspense. They found that readers of women's magazines were quite normal readers. Their interest could be held by characterization, by beautiful prose, by fine thought, quite as firmly as by the worrying carry-over of an unfinished dramatic incident.

That four-layer-cake-serial, frosted and sweet and not too good for the mental figure, is rapidly becoming a thing of the past. Editors of women's magazines are looking as always for good stories. It is habitual now for them to buy novels that they like, break them up into installments and publish them as serials of three parts, five parts, or seven. The fiction content of all magazines is far more flexible and varying than it used to be, and improved. When the *Ladies Home Journal* publishes a story of subtle beauty like Rumer Godden's *Take Three Tenses*, or an unhurried, definitely cynical story such as John Marquand's *Point of No Return*, it proves that to say that "all continued stories in the women's magazines are trashy" is only to be uninformed.

Of course the comment is made that such serialization is almost accidental. These two stories mentioned were written "for book" and not "for serial." It is "writing for serial" which still has a stigma attached to it, not publication as a serial. But there are few novelists even in the first rank who are not vastly pleased by the sale of a story as a serial. The large lump sum payment is always welcome. More than that, it is one way to make sure that the story will have several million readers. A book publisher cannot insure that, but the editor of one of the large women's magazines can promise and deliver to the novelist a public of that size.

The publication of a great many fine novels in *McCall's Magazine*, which discovered and published James Hilton's best work, the *Ladies Home Journal*, the *Woman's Home Companion*, and *Good Housekeeping*, has made serialization in the women's magazines eminently respectable. But as yet it has not taken the bad name off "writing for serial." This is too bad, for it is entirely possible that if the serial developed a fine and individual technique, it could often be as fine an achievement as writing a good play. Why should not a five act story, dramatically told, measure up to the standard of a five act play which has reading as well as acting value? There are hundreds of young writers working on permanently unmarketable novels who might be able to write interesting serial stories if they would take their tongues out of their cheeks and the scorn out of their minds.

The thing works both ways. The serial should be more highly regarded as a form of fiction if it is to improve the standing of the writer of serials. On the other hand, or in reverse, the author should regard the serial more highly if he is to improve it as a fictional form.

Why do editors want "continued stories" in their magazines? They are more flexible than they used to be and, as I say, have found that no serial is better than a bad serial. But the editor of a woman's magazine still rejoices when he finds a really good serial already written, or can persuade a skillful writer to take on the job of writing a serial for his periodical. The editor wants serials today because he knows that continuing interest in fictional characters will make people buy his publication.

The crudest form of serialization is the comic strip, but it proves beyond any doubt the great hold of the serial on the ordinary person. A man wants his morning newspaper to see what is happening to the world, what Dorothy Thompson or Drew Pearson has to say, but also to see what Andy Gump or Dick Tracy are up to now. Nobody but a fool turns up his nose at this fact. It takes a good deal of skill to do a comic strip. It takes imagination and even some sympathy. The good strips continue indefinitely because they have created a character or two. Why have Jiggs and Maggie such a hold on the American public? Because that strip exposes and re-exposes the snob, and the human situation is so common that it is actually endearing.

I never take too seriously the statement so often made by various people, who say proudly "I never read serials." I have heard people make that declaration like an oath and then rush off to see what is happening to Orphan Annie or Skeezix, or perhaps to buy *Harper's Magazine* and go on reading a serial story by Aldous Huxley in its pages. Serial interest is merely continuing interest in a person or in the situation of a person, and is as natural as curiosity or friendliness.

A vast potential audience for the fictional serial exists. It deserves more respect than it gets and the writer is the one who must build up that respect. If he wants to write serials, capture the enormous audience, and the financial rewards, he should be willing to study the medium and give it his best effort.

There is a general belief that writing serials for women's magazines means writing under the last of limitations. This is greatly exaggerated. Of course there are limitations of space. *The Nazarene* and *Anthony Adverse* were probably too long for serial publication in a woman's magazine. It would take a couple of years to run them, or any such extremely long books, though skillful cutting has placed long books by Marcia Davenport and John Marquand before the large magazine public.

Foul and brutal language, no matter how accurately it may be recorded from life, is allowed no place in a woman's magazine. John Steinbeck's *Grapes of Wrath* would have been kept from serialization because of its vocabulary and that would be true about many fine stories by such top writers as Ernest Hemingway or James M. Cain. But very little subject matter is taboo as of today. The women's magazines no longer sugar coat their fiction. Every year both articles and fiction become more realistic and more honest.

Within the limitations of space and of vocabulary, which the magazines must impose, beauty and drama and humor and anger and even philosophy can find plenty of room to move. The statement of a writer that serial writing is too limited a medium for satisfactory work is often only an alibi for being too stubborn or too lazy to master it.

Certainly no completely undisciplined writer—if there are any such—should attempt to write a serial. He may produce a manuscript which happens to lend itself to serialization and be that much richer for his luck. But unless he is willing to realize that in a magazine he must share the honors of publication with a great many other people, and that he must show some deference to conventional speech and habits, he is wise to let the field alone.

Nor should any writer who has a contempt for the large public try to write serials, even if he does want money to go around the world or to buy a country estate. It cannot be done that way. The editor is quick to recognize condescension or a contemptuous attempt to "write down" to the woman's magazine public. To do that shows a great ignorance of the temper and education of that public, which includes millions of young women who can earn a good living, millions of women who run competent homes and bring up fine children and who can and do keep their minds oiled and running as they go about their jobs.

But a reasonably disciplined writer who believes as do most important professional artists, whether they paint, act, play the violin or write, that the largest possible public is the best mark to shoot at, will not demean himself by writing serials, if he gives them his best talent. If he regards the job as important, so will the editor and, quite probably, the public.

So far as I know, there are no tricks in serial writing. As in any other story, the subject of the story is important but the characters are much more so. Write about people is the only advice most magazine editors give an author. Make the people come true. The situations or problems, of money, or love, or alcoholism, or insanity, belong to the characters; and the serial story, like any other novel, succeeds only to the extent that its created characters march out of the pages of the magazine into the imagination of the reader. You cannot hold the interest of many readers today by tying a girl to a railroad track and leaving her there until the next issue of the magazine. But if the readers of the magazine like, or even dislike that girl enough, and she happens to get tied to a railroad track, the readers' interest probably could be held by telling them what the girl felt and thought while she lay there.

However, the story which is deliberately planned for serial is the better for the use of certain techniques. If a writer knows in advance that his story will be printed in five issues and that each part will be approximately ten thousand words, he can plan and outline his story so that it has balance, so that its beginning is not disproportionately long or its ending as abrupt as a push in the back. He can and should distribute his story well, keep it from straggling, dispense with all padding. Serial writing can be splendid exercise in literary balance and restraint. It could be that far more often than it is, if writers were more interested in their stepchildren.

Conferences with editors on projected serial stories are useful. But they should not be so frequent nor so prolonged that the writer gets the feeling of being henpecked by the editor. Also, the submission of parts of a story before the whole is finished sometimes leads an editor to expect some development which does not come. In a way the editor begins mentally to write the story himself, and when it doesn't come out his way, he is disappointed and sometimes difficult to deal with. A not-too-detailed outline of the proposed story is often proper and required. When that is submitted and accepted, the writer should take over completely until the last page of his story is finished.

Magazine editors have quite different problems from those that confront book publishers. The women's magazines are advertising mediums as well as publishers of fiction and articles on current subjects. They are fashion and marketing experts, instructors in home economics. If it affronts a writer to see his stories in such heterogeneous company, he had best avoid the serial market. But if he enters it he should realize that the woman's magazine is one of America's great influences and be proud of being part of that influence. Much of the best contemporary thought and the best contemporary fiction has appeared in women's magazines. They are good enough for anyone who likes Americans.

The honest writer sometimes finds himself in a dilemma. He wants and intends to write a book without soft pedaling any facts or scenes which are relevant to his subject. He does not want to limit himself in length or vocabulary. It will take him a year to write the book and its reception will be uncertain.

At the same time a friendly editor tells the writer that he would like to have a serial from his pen. He can use a serial of sixty thousand words. The editor will pay a top price, perhaps even forty thousand dollars for this story.

Can the writer please two masters, himself and the editor? Can he satisfy the magazine editor and do justice to his own theme? Can he give his book publishers the profound study in human values they are expecting from him, if while he writes his story he has his eye on that forty thousand dollars?

Perhaps he can get the money, enlarge his public and write a fine book that his publishers will be proud to present. It is possible. But if he does it, it will be because he does not try to serve two masters. What he should do is to make an intelligent choice. He can do one of two things. The first is to accept the serial limitations and write primarily for the magazine. He will then write that serial as if it were the best and last thing he is ever going to write, with respect for every woman who will read it. He will do a good job and earn his money.

The other thing he can do is to forget the serial entirely. He will tell the editor that when the book is finished, he will let the magazine editor read it as well as his publisher. Then he will forget about what he could do with all that money and get along as best he can without it. He will write his book because he loves it. The miracle may happen.

It may not only be a fine book but the editor of the woman's magazine may buy it, condense it and publish it.

That is the only method I can see which will take the stigma off serial writing, and make it a recognized literary craft which can be raised to almost any level of skill. Many great writers have had their work serialized. Not only Dickens, but Tolstoy. *Anna Karenina* was a newspaper serial as well as *Martin Chuzzlewit.*

What the serial needs, and is getting more and more, is the interest and devotion of writers. They can make it anything they like. The article used to be a stepchild and the essay was the distinguished piece of nonfictional prose. But good writers have made the article on contemporary affairs and problems a fine literary medium. The magazine serial, whether in a woman's or a general family magazine, needs that same treatment. It should be written by good and even great writers who respect the medium and the public which it reaches.

19

The Pulp Story

MYRON DAVID ORR

Born in Michigan of Scotch and Irish parentage, Myron David Orr, after attending the University of Michigan, was trained as a lawyer at Detroit College of Law and Columbia University. A veteran of both world wars, he is married and has one daughter. He was first published in the Port Huron *Herald* when ten years old. Fiction editor of *Capper's Michigan Farmer* for fifteen years until 1942, former editor of a weekly newspaper, he is the author of three novels, *White Gold, Cathedral of the Pines,* and *Citadel of the Lakes,* together with many short stories and articles.

Mr. Orr, out of his own successful experience as a writer of adventure and mystery stories for the pulp magazine (one of the publications which have the greatest combined circulation in the world) presents a spirited discussion of what such stories must have to satisfy their readers, and what the writers must have to produce such stories. He leaves no doubt that the writer must work with discipline, with knowledge of his craft, with sincerity and with respect for the entertainment he wishes to offer to his readers. Much of Mr. Orr's advice is good for any story writer, and suggests that good stories of any kind come from a combination of hard work, craftsmanship, and integrity of purpose.

H. H.

The Pulp Story

PEOPLE, especially writers of established reputation, think any fiction rejected by the so-called slick and quality magazines will be readily purchased by pulp magazines. This is one of the greatest fallacies that ever emerged out of ignorance.

Many established nonpulp writers think that they could write for the pulps without any effort if necessary. While it is true that many of the best writers today learned the craft of fiction writing in the pulp field, nevertheless, the great majority of nonpulp writers would receive a rejection slip from a pulp editorial staff by return mail if they attempted to break into this highly specialized type of writing.

I strongly urge those who do not believe this to try it. It might prove an interesting and valuable experiment and I am sure that the endeavor will open a new vista to the ostrich-minded writer who discusses and analyzes pulp writing glibly, but always admits when questioned that he never reads "such stuff" because it would injure his style—what style?

Pulp writing has for its basis the nucleus of all good writing. It requires a highly trained and specialized ability to present the story without fuzzy focusing. It rejects all superficialities and demands extreme clarity and sharpness in every detail. It is a great taskmaster for any writer.

During the last several years I have had the opportunity of using the lawyer's technique of cross-examination in questioning many writers and would-be-writers. One of the many things which I have learned is that opinions expressed by them concerning pulp writing are not their own original ideas, but have been cribbed from others, who when "tracked down" admit that they too were only repeating what they had "heard expressed by other persons."

I have yet to find the person who can support a single adverse criticism, based on a personal analysis of pulp writing.

No one can tell another *how* to write. I have listened to many teachers of writing as well as professional writers tell how *they* write and how other people should write if they would be successful craftsmen. I have attended seminars in which writing was discussed. I have listened to editors expound the craft of fiction writing. From these people I have extracted my style of writing.

Established writers will recognize all of the essential requirements for good writing exemplified in most pulp writing. However, there are poorly written pulp stories as well as poorly written quality and slick stories. The writing instinct and the enjoyment of writing are integral parts of the successful pulp-craftsman. Along with this he must have an intense interest in *all* people. He must not be critical of their actions; rather he must accept them *for what they are* and remember them *as they are*. He must understand human motives and be able to take people whom he knows and move them about at his will—always sure what they will do and how they will react to all circumstances and conditions in which he places them. He must have a sense of the dramatic, the comic, the ridiculous and most of all he must have a *creative imagination* and be convinced that "The external truth of the subject must depend upon the fidelity of its treatment."

A good pulp writer tells his story in such a manner that his reader immediately enters into the experience of which he is reading. To accomplish this the writer must never stand in front of his reader, but just behind him and direct his attention to the experience. He must never talk *about* his characters. Instead, he gives them movement and life and a three dimensional quality. He directs but never acts himself. He lets the reader interpret the characters through their actions and words. Nothing is more irritating to a reader of pulp fiction than to have the author "block the scene" with his interpretation of human behavior. Every reader has his own ideas about people's actions and likes to feel that he is capable of interpreting them for himself.

In addition to the above, the successful pulp writer develops a supersensitivity to the visual value of words, because words and combinations of words are the only means of communication between a writer and his readers. The success of this visual link depends upon the craftsmanship of the writer in selecting the proper words which will quickly project the reader into an illusion of reality induced by the association reaction of as many of his five sensorial faculties as possible.

Recall if you will the many stories you have read. Some of them remain with you; are a part of you—even to the point of nostalgia. Why do you remember them?

The reason why you remember them is because the writer knew how to select and combine words: words with color; words with tone; words which create the harmony of five tone unity. The pulp writer must possess a keen appreciation of the value of words because he must project the various parts of his story instantaneously into his reader's mind—he has neither time nor space to tell and retell, with different approaches, each scene and each act which will eventually create the desired reaction in his reader.

For example:

There are all types of writing as well as all types of pictures. There are sketches which carry a vivid and complete story by only a few strokes of the pen and there are paintings which can be viewed leisurely for their message. Famous cartoons are as well remembered as detailed paintings. The impact of the visual projection has the same effect—only the method of projection is different.

Whether a person likes the "old masters" or modernistic works depends upon the mental complexity of his emotional requirements. Whether he has to be conditioned by the elaboration of details or whether he is capable of assimilation without elaboration depends upon the skill of the craftsman.

The pulp craftsman has the specialized skill of doing the latter. Because of the rigid requirements of pulp writing, the writer for these magazines cannot afford to make abstract projections of human motives. He must know each one of his characters thoroughly, and the reader must be thoroughly fused into the thoughts of the characters so that he accepts everything they do without question.

Whether a reader prefers stories containing artificial cleverness, twists, gimmicks, sexual promiscuity, sordid journeys into the minds of the mentally disordered, stream of consciousness, or stories with the common denominators of simplicity, straightforwardness, homey words and phrases with no double meaning, is for him to decide. The pulp writer must anticipate all these things and train himself accordingly.

As I said before the pulp writer must create an illusion of reality, and the reader must accept it as being real if the story is to be successful. The reader must experience within himself all of the feelings and reactions of the characters. He must live the lives of the characters and accept their experiences as a logical sequence of events. A pulp reader is one of the most critical and exacting of all readers. He has no time for immaterial or irrelevant detail which does not advance the plausibility of the characters and the part they play in the story.

The pulp writer must know his writing anatomy as well as the surgeon knows his materia medica. A pulp plot is one of the best examples of a "stripped deck" construction. It never puts a fibia in the place of a femur, even though both are connected and in relative positions in the human anatomy. Only after the basic structure of the story is thoroughly inspected will the successful pulp writer proceed with the additions of his three dimensional qualities.

I have heard many people say that they never read the "pulps" because they considered such magazines beneath their level of literary style and did not care to be contaminated with such low quality of writing which had no characterizations. No doubt these literary presumptives have never heard of Perry Mason and Nero Wolfe and hundreds of other pulp-fictional characters. Only those writers who are clinging desperately to the outer fringes of the inner circle of craftsmen refuse to admit the vivid portrayal of the characters of the pulp stories. It might be a good thing for those hangers-on to de-ostrichize themselves and read the publications which have the greatest combined circulation in the world.

A good pulp story consists of fast action, a swiftly moving plot, *good characterization* and a minimum amount of elaboration. Its assembly technique is the basis for all fictional stories. People who want a story quickly told, well told, vividly told, logically resolved and satisfying, read a pulp story. There are others who prefer to suffer through the protracted illness and death of Aunt Agness—spelled with a double *s*—and enjoy all her agonies.

However, for all types of fiction writing, the writer must be endowed with a creative imagination and must be able to arrange, rearrange, construct and reconstruct his own personal experiences as well as the observed experiences of others into his story. He must have as a part of his equipment, a high degree of ability to recall, analyze and select the things that give *original* sharpness to each part of his story. He must be able to interpret clearly and intelligently everything he reads about people and things. He must be a good detective in his research work and be able to place a correct evaluation on the things he finds. He must be able to establish the difference in value between original matter and secondary matter. He must not make the mistake of writing about places or things of which he knows little or nothing. The widespread distribution of the pulps as well as the other mass circulation magazines makes this a dangerous thing to do. Readers delight in pouncing on the smallest flaw.

A pulp writer should never congest the minds of his readers with unnecessary verbiage any more than a man who sees a speeding automobile approaching him as he crosses the street should stop and philosophize about its rate of speed. The reader is a part of the story action; he is taking a journey and he wants to reach his destination in the shortest possible time.

I believe that good pulp fiction begins with an immediate and forceful impact of interest in which the first threads of suspense are interwoven and the fusing of the reader into one of the characters takes place. Next is the selection of the events in which the characters take part. The events, as they clearly and inevitably change and advance, must approximate actual experience. They must be probable and believable and like life; just as a caricature, which highlights and exaggerates some feature or weakness, is a likeness of the original. These experiences *must seem to be true* and must be accepted by the reader as a pattern of the whole.

Pulp writing must be objective. There must be a continuous and interlocking suspense throughout the story. There must be continuous movement in the dramatic. There must be human interest and intense concentration and most important there must be a high quality of cause and effect. Pulp fiction properly written, thoroughly explains the result, either actual or unexpected.

There must also be conflicts. The reader wants to know who will win and who will lose. When the villain is killed, the reader accepts the killing as inevitable and retains no feelings of sympathy for him. In order to accomplish this the writer must stir the reader's emotions to the highest degree possible so that when the end is reached the reader is left with a complete satisfaction that he has taken part in the bringing about of the desired conclusion.

I like to think of the pulp craftsman as a mirror which reflects the true object. The illusion in the mirror should be sharp and reflect into the reader's consciousness as a true image. It should not be blurred by the failure of the writer to write objectively, nor by his interruptions in order to voice his own reactions and opinions.

A story may come from many sources. It may arise from a writer's feelings toward people, ideas, things or conditions. A psychology professor asked me some time ago how I got the plots for my stories—especially my murder mysteries. I promptly told him, with a straight face, that whenever I hated a person enough actually to kill him, I relieved that impulse by putting him into a story and plotting a death commensurate with my dislike for him. I learned recently that he has been reading all my subsequent murder mysteries.

As I said before there are no set rules for writing. There are as many ideas about how to write as there are writers. However the successful writer develops his own style which contains freshness of vigor and vitality. It shows no sign of effort and has a certain clarity and ease which make the writer lose himself in the story. Dr. Johnson said of Dryden, "he appeared to have no art other than that of expressing with clearness what he thought with vigor."

In spite of the fact that an author must be thoroughly conversant with his subject, nevertheless he should avoid a pedantic presentation of his knowledge. Readers resent preaching and lecturing in fiction unless they are used to bring out the ostentatious display of learning of one of the characters for a specific purpose.

And finally a person who would be a successful fiction writer should make an intensive study of the pulps as well as all other types of magazines. He must write day after day, trying out scenes and characterizations in order to acquire the craft of fiction writing. He must create something new every day. He must dramatize everyday happenings in order to develop his imagination. He must revise and cut and rewrite until he has at last created—perhaps just one sentence, or a paragraph, or a scene which is acceptable, then put it away for a week or a month and read it again. If it is still acceptable let some other person read it. *Don't read it to him.* He must feel the reaction you want him to have without the color of your voice reading the lines as you interpret them—you do not read your story to your readers.

20

Plot or Character—Which?

LAJOS EGRI

Born in Hungary in 1893, Lajos Egri was editor of the daily newspaper *Magyar Elore* and the literary weekly magazine *Americai Kepes Folyoirat*. He has acted as correspondent for European periodicals and has produced and directed plays in both America and Europe. He has had three plays produced in New York, *Rapid Transit*, 1927; *Believe Me or Not*, 1930; and *There Will be No Performance*, 1932. In addition to his works *How to Write Plays, The Art of Dramatic Writing*, and *Your Key to Successful Writing*, he has had two collections of poems and one of short stories published here in the Hungarian language. Also published in Hungarian was *How to Direct Plays*. He is at present director of the Egri School of Writing.

The relative importance of plot and character has stirred up argument ever since men began to construct plays and write first, epics and later, novels. Aristotle may have issued the first dogmatic statement: "Character comes in as subsidiary to the action. . . . Plot is the end of a tragedy." Mr. Lajos Egri, in his *Art of Dramatic Writing*, since he is writing primarily of plays, can perhaps isolate the two elements of plot and character more easily than can a critic of novels. The novelist, with all the resources of fiction writing for his use, such as interpretation of feeling, description, passages of vivid summaries of passing years, may inveigle the reader past too harsh criticism. The play, since it is a vehicle for actors, directors, and producers, is of necessity more stripped to its essentials. But this problem of plot versus character exists in all creative writing, and Mr. Egri's comments are as pertinent for the novelist as for the playwright.

Mr. Egri's conclusion marks the difference between the classic conception of man as a puppet of the gods and the modern acceptance of man as a responsible individual. You cannot oppose plot to character because character makes plot. In any situation a man acts in accordance with his character. In play or in novel the writer works from his characters into his plot. He knows now that a *man's character is his fate.*

H. H.

Plot or Character—Which?

From *The Art of Dramatic Writing*

> What is a weed? A plant whose virtues have not yet been discovered.—*Emerson*

DESPITE the frequent quotations from Aristotle, and the work done by Freud on one of the three elements of a human being, character has not been given the penetrating analysis which scientists give the atom or the cosmic ray.

William Archer, in his *Playmaking, A Manual of Craftsmanship,* says:

> . . . To reproduce character can neither be acquired nor regulated by theoretical recommendations.

We readily agree that "theoretical recommendations" are of no use to anyone—but what of concrete recommendation? While it is true that the seemingly inanimate objects are easier to examine, the involved, ever-moving character of man must also be analyzed—and the task is organized, made simpler, by recommendations.

> Specific directions for character-drawing would be like rules for becoming six feet high. Either you have it in you, or you have it not,

says Mr. Archer. This is a sweeping, and unscientific, statement. And it has a familiar ring. It is, in essence, the answer that was given to Leeuwenhoek inventor of the microscope; to Galileo, who was almost burned as a heretic when he said the earth moved. Fulton's steamboat was received with derision. "It won't move!" the crowds shouted, and when it did move they cried, "It won't stop!"

Yet today cosmic rays are made to photograph and measure themselves.

"Either you have it in you, or you have it not," says Mr. Archer, thus admitting that one man has the ability to draw character, to penetrate the impenetrable, whereas another has not. But if one man can do it, and if we know how he did it, can we not learn from him? One man does it by observation. He is privileged to see things which others pass by. Is it that these less fortunate men cannot see the obvious? Perhaps. When we read a bad play carefully, we are struck by the author's ignorance of his characters; and when we read a good play carefully, we are struck by the wealth of information the writer displays. Then why may we not suggest to the less-privileged playwright that he train his eye to see, and his mind to understand? Why may we not recommend observation?

If the "have-not" playwright has imagination, selectivity, writing ability, he will be a better man for learning consciously what the "have" playwright knows only by instinct.

How is it that even the genius who has it within his power to be six feet tall frequently misses the mark? Why is it that the man who once knew how to draw character now only makes a fool of himself? Might it be because he relied solely upon his instinctive powers? Why shouldn't these powers work all the time? The privileged one either has the power in him or he has not.

We trust you will admit that any number of geniuses have written any number of bad plays—because they relied on an instinctive power which is, at best, a hit-or-miss affair. One is not supposed to conduct important business on a hunch, a feeling, a whim—one is supposed to *act upon knowledge.*

Mr. Archer's definition of character follows:

> . . . for the practical purposes of the dramatist it may be defined as a *complex of intellectual, emotional,* and nervous habit.

This hardly seems enough, so we turn to *Webster's International*

Dictionary. Perhaps Mr. Archer's words hold more than appeared on the surface.

> *Complex:* composed of two or more parts; composite; not simple.
> *Intellectual:* apprehensible by intellect alone; hence of a spiritual nature; perceptible only to inspired vision or by spiritual insight.
> *Emotion:* an agitation, disturbance, a tumultuous movement whether physical or social.

Now we know. It is so simple and so complex at the same time. Not much help, it's true, but refreshing, nevertheless.

It is not enough to know that a character consists of "complex intellectual, emotional, and nervous habit." We must know precisely what this "complex intellectual" means. We have found that every human being consists of three dimensions: physiological, sociological, and psychological. If we make a further breakdown of these dimensions, we shall perceive that the physical, social, and mental make-up contains the minute genes—the builder, the mover in all our actions which will motivate everything we do.

A shipbuilder knows the material he is working with, knows how well it can withstand the ravages of time, how much weight it can carry. He must know these things if he wishes to avoid disaster.

A dramatist should know the material he is working with: his characters. He should know how much weight they can carry, how well they can support his construction: the play.

There are so many conflicting ideas about character that it might be a good idea for us to review a few of them before we attempt to go further.

John Howard Lawson writes in his book, *The Theory and Technique of Playwriting*:

> People find it curiously difficult to consider a story as something which is in the process of *becoming*: confusion on this point exists in all textbooks on playwriting, and is a stumbling block to all playwrights.

Yes, it is a stumbling block, because they start to build their house from the roof down, instead of starting with premise and showing a character in relation to his environment. Lawson says as much in his introduction:

> A play is not a bundle of isolated elements: dialogue, characterization, etc., etc. It is a living thing, in which all of these elements have been fused.

This is true, but on the very next page he writes:

> We can study the form, the *outwardness* of a play, but the *inwardness*, the soul, eludes our grasp.

It will elude us forever if we fail to understand a basic principle: the so-called "inwardness," the seemingly unpredictable soul, is nothing more nor less than character.

Lawson's fundamental mistake is using dialectics upside down. He accepts Aristotle's basic error, "character is subsidiary to action," and from this springs his confusion. It is vain for him to insist on a "social framework" when he puts the cart before the horse.

We contend that character is the most interesting phenomenon anywhere. Every character represents a world of his own, and the more you know of this person, the more interested you become. We have in mind just now George Kelly's *The Show-off* and *Craig's Wife*. They are far from being well-constructed plays, but there is a conscious attempt to build character. Kelly shows us a world through the eyes of Craig's wife, a drab and monotonous world, but a real one.

George Bernard Shaw says that he is not governed by principle, but by inspiration. If any man, inspired or not, builds on character, he is going in the right direction and is employing the right principle, consciously or otherwise. The vital thing is not what the playwright says, but what he does. Every great literary work grew from character, even if the author planned the action first. As soon as his characters were created they took precedence, and the action had to be reshaped to suit them.

Let us suppose we were building a house. We started at the wrong end and it collapsed. We began again—at the top—and it collapsed. And so a third and a fourth time. But eventually we make it stand up, without the slightest idea of what change in our method was responsible for our success. Can we now, without compunction, give advice on the construction of houses? Can we honestly say: it must collapse four times before it can stand?

The great plays came down to us from men who had unlimited

patience for work. Perhaps they started their plays at the wrong end, but they fought themselves back inch by inch, until they made character the foundation of their work, although they may not have been objectively conscious that character is the only element that could serve as the foundation.

Says Lawson:

> Of course it is hard to think of situations, and this depends upon the power of the writer's "inspiration."

If we know that a character embodies in himself not only his environment, but his heredity, his likes and dislikes, even the climate of the town where he was born, we do not find it hard to think of situations. *The situations are inherent in the character.*

George P. Baker quotes Dumas the Younger:

> Before every situation that a dramatist creates, he should ask himself three questions: What should *I* do? What would *other people* do? What *ought* to be done?

Isn't it strange to ask everyone what should be done in a situation, except the character who created the situation? Why not ask him? He is in a position to know the answer better than anyone else.

John Galsworthy seems to have grasped this simple truth, for he claims that character creates plot, not vice versa. Whatever Lessing had to say about the matter, he built on character. So did Ben Jonson—in fact, Jonson sacrificed many theatrical devices to bring his characters into sharper relief. Chekhov has no story to tell, no situation to speak of, but his plays are popular and will be so in time to come, because he permits his characters to reveal themselves and the time in which they lived.

Engels says in *Anti-Duhring*:

> Every organic being is at each moment both the same and not the same; at each moment it is assimilating matter drawn from without and excreting other matter; every moment the cells of its body are dying and new ones being formed; in fact, within a longer or shorter period the matter of its body is completely removed and is replaced by other atoms of matter, so that every organic thing is at all times itself and yet something other than itself.

A character thus has the capacity to completely reverse himself under

> internal and external stimulus. Like every other organic being, he changes continuously.

If this is true, and we know it is true, how can one invent a situation, or a story, which is a static thing, and force it upon the character who is in a state of constant change?

Starting with the premise "Character is subsidiary to action," it was inevitable that the textbook writers should become confused. Baker quotes Sardou, who replied as follows to the question of how plays revealed themselves to him:

> The problem is invariable. It appears as a kind of equation from which the unknown quantity must be found. The problem gives me no peace till I have found the answer.

Perhaps Sardou and Baker have found the answer, but they have not given it to the young playwright.

Character and environment are so closely interrelated that we have to consider them as one. They react upon each other. If one is faulty, it affects the other, just as the disease of one part of the body causes the whole to suffer.

> The plot is the first consideration, and as it were, the soul of the tragedy. Character holds the second place,

writes Aristotle in his *Poetics*.

> Character comes in as subsidiary to the action. Hence the incidents and the plot are the end of a tragedy. . . . Without action there cannot be a tragedy; there may be without character. . . . The drama interests us, not predominantly by depicting of human nature, but primarily by the situations and only secondarily by the feelings of those therein involved.

After checking through volumes and volumes in search of the answer to which is more important, character or plot, we concluded that 99 per cent of the writings on this issue are confused and barely understandable.

Consider these statements by Archer, in *Playmaking*: On page twenty-two:

> A play can exist without anything that can be called character, but not without some sort of action.

But on page twenty-four:

> Action ought to exist for the sake of character: when the relationship is reversed the play may be an ingenious toy, but scarcely a vital work of art.

To find the real answer is not an academic problem. It is an answer which will make a deep impression on the future of playwriting, since it is *not* the answer which was dictated by Aristotle.

We are going to take the oldest of all plots, a trite, worn-out triangle, a vaudeville skit, to prove our point.

A husband starts on a two-day trip, but forgets something and comes back to the house. He finds his wife in another man's arms. Let us suppose that the husband is a man of five feet three. The lover is a giant. The situation hinges on the husband—what will he do? If he is free of the author's interference, he will do what his character dictates, what his physical, social, and psychological make-up tell him to do.

If he is a coward, he may apologize, beg forgiveness for his intrusion, and flee—grateful that the lover let him go unmolested.

But perhaps the husband's short stature has made him cocky, has forced him to be aggressive. He springs at the big man in a fury, unmindful that he may be the loser.

Perhaps he is a cynic, and sneers; perhaps he is imperturbable, and laughs; perhaps any number of things—depending on the character.

A coward might create a farce, a brave man might create a tragedy.

Take Hamlet, the brooding Dane, and let him—not Romeo—fall in love with Juliet. What would have happened? He might have contemplated the matter too long, muttering to himself beautiful soliloquies about the immortality of the soul and the deathlessness of love, which, like the phoenix, rises anew every spring. He might have consulted his friends, his father, to make peace with the Capulets, and while these negotiations went on, Juliet, not suspecting that Hamlet loved her, would have been safely married to Paris. Then Hamlet could have brooded still more and cursed his fate.

While Romeo runs into trouble with reckless abandon, Hamlet looks into the mechanism of his problem. While Hamlet hesitates, Romeo acts.

Obviously, their conflicts grew out of their character, and not vice versa.

If you try to force a character into a situation where he does not belong, you will be like Procrustes who cut the feet off the sleeper to make him fit the bed.

Which is more important, plot or character? Let us trade the sensitive, brooding Hamlet for a pleasure-loving prince, whose one reason for living is the privileges his princehood affords him. Would he avenge his father's death? Hardly. He would turn the tragedy to comedy.

Let us trade the naïve Nora, ignorant of money matters, forging a note for her husband, for a mature woman, aware of finance, too honest to let her love for her husband lead her astray. This new Nora would not have forged the note, and Helmer would have died then and there.

The sun, along with its other activities, creates rain. If it is true that the characters are secondary in importance, there is no reason why we should not use the moon instead of the sun. Do we get the same plot results? Emphatically: *no*!

Something will happen, however. The moon will witness the slow death of the earth, in place of the turbulent life created by the sun. We substituted only one character. This, of course, changed our premise and made a considerable alteration in the outcome of the play. With the sun: life. With the moon: death.

We should like to alter the quotation from Emerson with which we opened this chapter. For our purposes it should read:

> What is a character? A factor whose virtues have not yet been discovered.

21

Fiction: Some Personal Beliefs

CHRISTOPHER LaFARGE

After graduating from the Pennsylvania School of Architecture in 1923, Christopher LaFarge practiced architecture for eight years and then turned to writing. He has been contributing to such magazines as the *Atlantic Monthly*, *Harper's*, the *American*, and *The New Yorker* ever since. Among his many works are: *Hoxsie Sells His Acres* (1934); *Each to the Other* (1939), for which he was awarded the A. C. Benson Silver Medal from the Royal Society of Literature in England; *Poems and Portraits* (1940); *The Wilsons* (1941); *East by Southwest* (1944); *Mesa Verde* (1945); *The Sudden Guest* (1946); *All Sorts and Kinds* (1949); and *Beauty for Ashes* (1953). He was president of the Authors Guild from 1945 to 1947.

The unpretentious mastery that Christopher LaFarge exercises over the English language doesn't come merely from long practice. It comes from thought and conscious experimentation and interest in the how and the why of writing. Yet his interest in technique never impedes what he himself calls "the essential element of all good stories, the accomplished telling of the story itself." I remember one short story of his (it's called *The Three Aspects* and can be found in the O. Henry collection, *Prize Stories of 1948*), in which the same incident is retold three times by three different participants. It could have been a dreary five-finger exercise in technique. Actually, the story is constantly expanded, constantly deepened and constantly simplified, so that three pairs of eyes contribute to a unified vision of storytelling, and singleness grows out of variety.

Here from the LaFarge canon itself is an example of just how story structure, how craftsmanship and the understanding of language have made it possible for Christopher LaFarge to say proudly that he has never written down for any audience. He has never needed to. His technique has brought his audience up to him.

E. J.

Fiction: Some Personal Beliefs

ALL writers, as a matter of course, approach the problems of their craft in different ways. It is of constant interest to other writers, and of occasional interest to their readers, to see those differences defined; and it is in response to that interest that I have set down my own approach to my profession.

I wrote lately a preface to a book of my collected short stories, published under the title of *All Sorts and Kinds* in March of 1949, and much of what I am going to say here is embodied in that preface, or has been suggested by, or amplified from, that statement of belief and practice. Because that preface is, in essence, an attempt to define my own present attitude toward the writing of fiction, I believe it may generate some of the interest I have suggested above.

Let me begin with the ever-vexed and important subject of criticism; for by criticism, intelligently applied, the reader makes the story his own or rejects it. When I had collected my short stories, I wrote, to follow each one, a commentary on it, giving its origin, its purpose, and occasionally my own opinion of it, favorable or otherwise. This was, as any writer will readily see, a most interesting exercise, and I hoped it would enhance the interest in the stories. But apart from the interest in the stories themselves, I hoped also that these short commentaries might suggest to the intelligent reader an approach to true criticism, providing him with as much ammunition as possible with which to shoot at the story he had just completed.

I have held for many years that criticism should confine itself to a judgment, not of what the writer might have written, but of what he did write; and that within that compass, its function was to discover whether what was written had been successful or not. That is to say, if a story was patently written to entertain, to amuse, the object of criticism was not to bewail the fact that the author was spending his time on this, but to determine if he did in fact entertain or amuse his readers. If the author's intention was evidently a more serious one—such as to exhibit a moral truth, to propagandize, to satirize—the same rule holds good; though I conceive that the critic has a full right—and the professional critic a duty—to determine whether the author has allowed his over-all purpose to becloud and confuse, to weaken, or even to destroy, the essential element of all good stories, the accomplished telling of the story itself.

The critic, then, who concerns himself with a judgment of the *kind* of story the writer chooses to compose, can only do so profitably and justly when he considers the whole body of the writer's work, and this will hardly become apparent until near the end of the writer's days. He is a brash man indeed who shall say that a particular work, provided it has been well done (and is not patently immature), was not a proper exercise of the talent of the author. Who shall determine in advance of completion that the whole progress of the artist's life work has not been forwarded by the lightest of his efforts? "Importance" is relative, not absolute; and as we demand of the theoretically excellent man that he should be of many well-rounded qualities, we must allow to the writer the same capacity for full and total growth.

I am of those who believe that a story, of whatever length, should have a beginning, a middle, and an ending. Indeed, I have never yet begun to write a short story or a novel when I did not see in advance, with a clarity that occasionally found its expression in the actual words, the ending of that story. With this practice has gone another that is personal to me and which I do not necessarily advocate for others unless it is natural to them: it is that I have always required of myself an answer in advance of actual composition, to the question, "Why am I writing this?" The ability to give an honest answer is necessary to me, although the answers can range from a pure desire to amuse, to, for instance, the desire to glorify, and help others toward, a happy and successful marriage.

In judging stories, therefore, the reader has a full right to require that the author shall have succeeded in at least a reasonable approximation of a stated or, more usually, an implicit intent; and to require further that he see the beginning, the middle, and the end of the story that illustrates it.

Another of the functions of criticism of fiction is to determine the success or failure of characterization. However well plotted and constructed the story, however solid or tenuous its intention, however admirable its purpose, it is nothing at all unless the characters within it have a good measure of reality. That measure is generally most easily discovered by one's ability to identify oneself with the character, even though that character may be quite opposite in nature. In all of us there are two sides to each quality. Our real or potential capacity to understand evil, for instance, is in exact proportion to our real or potential goodness; our selfishness is perfectly balanced by our understanding of self-sacrifice. The greater our capacity to love, the greater as well is our capacity to hurt the object of that love, and in many instances we all, as lovers, practice that act of hurtfulness. Beyond this, for the intelligent reader, it does not require that he shall have had an experience or have a quality of character, to understand it in another; and thus the process which we call identification of ourselves with a fictional being, well created, is universally possible except to the immature and the egregiously narrow or stupid.

Each reader, therefore, can judge for himself the success, or lack of it, of the author's characterizations, and in so much as he can identify himself with the characters, can find them of a reality, by so much is the story successful for him—and in this, he is (for that story) the ultimate judge. A story has no separate existence even within the covers of a book. It comes into existence, perhaps repeatedly if it is lucky, with each recollection or reading, but only then.

Characterization to be successfully real must border forever on universality. Even the most peculiar and unusual character must have some qualities of the universal kind, though they may be the less admirable ones. No character so truly singular as to be *sui generis* (if there can exist such a thing) can hope to be wholly convincing to the reader, although one can imagine circumstances where the inclusion of a nearly unique character is justified by its capacity to heighten a desired unreality.

It is not possible to say how successful characterization is achieved beyond this generality of its universal quality. There is no rule of thumb about it. One hears, from time to time, of the author whose characters "ran away from him," as though they sprang wholly out of his subconscious and had independent life. That simply isn't true, or so rarely true as not to be important. What has happened is that the character has been created and endowed with qualities because they seemed exciting or interesting or real in themselves, but were not geared to the original intention of the author. That is to say, he has created a character to fulfill a purpose, but has endowed the character with feelings and qualities which make it wholly impossible for such a person to fulfill any such purpose. Usually when this happens, the character must be altered (which is dangerous) or the original intention must be abandoned in favor of one that is opposite to the character. The ultimate artistic failure of many stories lies in this: that the characters became unreal because of what they were forced to do against their created natures.

Obviously the most difficult hurdle any writer must get over in attempting to create character, is that of the dull and ordinary man and woman. No matter how dull or ordinary they may be, they must not bore the reader. Characterization of them, therefore, poses the question of how to give them their true characteristics of dullness and ordinariness and yet interest the reader in what happens to them, in their fate, as it were. I have often thought that the capacity to do this was one of the best measures of a good writer (if not of a truly great one). One thinks at once of Flaubert's *Madame Bovary* as an archetype of the solution of this problem.

There is another act that the competent writer may not commit, and one that is frequently committed by the beginner and the amateur. It is to *say* something is so, and not *make* it be so in the story itself. The clearest example I can give is when a character is declared to be witty and yet never, within the pages of the story, exhibits that wit; and, at its worst, makes actually dull and boring remarks. The character of goodness must really be good and do good. It is not enough to say that he or she has goodness. A more complicated example would be the creation of excitement or tension in a story. It is never created by a statement, but by a whole series of happenings and remarks and descriptions that build up to tension and excitement in the mind of the reader.

The use of the stereotyped character is an avoidance, without justification in art, of the responsibility to characterize. The salty old New England grandmother, the lovable, ignorant, rascally Negro, the gangster Italian, the avaricious Jew, the chivalrous southerner, these and all like them—and their name is legion—are inexcusable devices that continue ignorant misconceptions while they relieve the author of the necessity for that hard thinking and clear observation necessary to the creation of true types of human beings. I conceive this practice of the use of the stereotype as one to be far more harshly condemned by the critic than the use of any formula of storytelling however well worn: for within the framework of the formula story (be it short or long) may lie both the author's actual (and necessary) subsistence and the opportunity to illuminate again by excellence of characterization, no matter how old a theme. Man changes but slowly; yet within the area of his lack of change is an infinite diversity that only the conscienceless writer will avoid.

For the reader-critic I must add another point. I believe very strongly that a writer should write well, no matter what his subject. To write well is a discipline, not easily achieved. It requires, among other things, that one can write good English, know how to form sentences and paragraphs, use words exactly and correctly, have a fair working knowledge of etymology or the origin of words (or how else can overtones be achieved?), and be willing to concede that although the apt sentence, the telling phrase, occasionally arrives spontaneously on the page, it is most often bettered by examination and reworking later. This is not to say that all conversation or indeed all description or bridging (the difficult passages necessary to continuity between phases of a story) should be grammatical and pedantically correct. Pedantry has nothing to do with excellence of English composition. But to be able to be skillfully and effectively ungrammatical or colloquial is to require a full knowledge of the standard from which one departs. There is possible otherwise no *art* in writing, but only a haphazard and chancy composition.

I am constantly distressed by the amount of careless writing that is published in serious journals and books. I am not of those who feel that there can be an academic standard applied to the use of the English language, for by its very genius it must continue to grow, to change, and to borrow. Nevertheless, there are reasonable limits, and these limits are constantly exceeded. It appears that the function of the editor and his proofreader, whether of a magazine or a publishing house, has been curtailed to the extent that these gentry no longer, save in rare instances, feel it necessary to edit for good usage, even of the more flexible variety.

What is lost, of course, by this practice (or lack of it), is clarity. The misuse of a word on purpose, the distortion of a phrase, the introduction of slang, the twists of fresh metaphor: all these add vitality to writing, but only when they are done consciously and with knowledge. The ignorant misuse, the careless mistake, these merely serve to confuse the reader and often to deprive the language of a word or a grammatical usage that cannot easily be replaced.

Let me give some instances. In a brilliant article published by the *Saturday Review*, "disinterested" was used to mean "not interested." This is a misuse so common in newspapers and conversation (like "I cannot help but") that one has come to expect it there; but not in a critical journal. By this misuse, a good word is lost to us. How shall you say now that a certain opinion was given without bias because the giver of the opinion was not concerned in the success or failure of the issue? "Impartial" won't cover it; "disinterested" will. By this then a loss is suffered, through carelessness.

In *The New Yorker*, famous for the care of its editing, we find the phrase: "a very singular conversation." Can "singular" be qualified?

Again in the *Saturday Review*: "one must probe into the impenetrable recesses of a murderer's mind." Can one probe into the impenetrable?

I do not wish to be invidious in these selections, and they can, of course, be multiplied a thousandfold from books and other magazines. I use them simply as examples near to my hand.

Such errors are, to me, a sign of the carelessness of the times, and I deplore such carelessness. It represents a movement which, at heart, scorns and deprecates the craftsmanship of an art: for have we not heard, over and over again, the very word craftsmanship used either in condescension or derogation? Have we not been led to accept error, sloppiness, verbosity, tautology, as unimportant in the face of final content? Is not the book, the story, the article, to be judged so much as a whole, by its social or its moral, or its adventurous, implications, that it is considered the mean carping of a little mind to quarrel with the manner of its expression? Where, as in Faulkner, that manner rises superior to its own errors, creates an effect not otherwise to be achieved, it is the result of a talent beyond ordinary using words to a purpose. Short of such use, these little, sloppy carelessnesses are a true disservice to the art of writing, for the cost of such errors is the high one of denying to him who wishes to practice clarity the tools with which to do so. If I write now, "he was a disinterested judge," shall I not be misunderstood to mean that the judge was bored?

This is the first time since I began to write professionally in 1932 that I have set down anything about my own writing. I shall add to this article, then, that I have never once tried to write down to anyone. It has seemed to me that the most difficult, the most abstruse, the most subtle idea, could be embodied in a story if the writer were willing to write it as well and as clearly as he knew how; and if he would subject himself to the further discipline of examining his work for a true and intelligent clarity, correcting, revising, discarding, and rewriting endlessly to that purpose. It has seemed to me that if that were done, a vast number of people (in varying degrees, to be sure, since the quotient of intelligence and experience is so variable in all of us) would understand and could be moved by that story. Practice has borne out this theory. I have yet to write a story that I "angled" (that distressing word!) toward this or that audience, this or that magazine. Yet almost all of the difficult stories I have written have been sold to the magazines and frequently to those of large circulation.

It is a happy and, I hope, an encouraging thing for a writer to be able to say that he has found an audience for the very best he knew how to do, and had not to give any regard at all to the conception that a wide audience could only be had at less than his best and most natural level.

I belong to the category of writer who likes almost all kinds of writing. I am of those who wish they could more often think of stories that truly amuse. Annually I read *Uncle Fred Flits By*, by P. G. Wodehouse, and annually I laugh with it and wish there were more of that kind and quality. I conceive it to be a service to mankind to be able to write amusingly, and although I have devoted the greater part of my work to serious subjects (and sometimes disagreeable ones), I know of only one qualification I would make concerning the writing of amusing stories. It is that they shall be written with as much skill, as carefully and conscientiously—as well, in brief—as any other work that the author undertakes. Only the artistic snob considers that the subject matter of lesser importance, if it has been genuinely conceived, is beneath him; and he who writes on the subject of lesser importance, and fails to devote to it the full measure of his artistic and technical powers, has committed one of the unforgivable sins of art.

That is all I have to say now. Perhaps when I am older and wiser and have learnt to write better, I may want to alter or amend these conclusions.

I shall close with a quotation from the last of the short commentaries written to follow my collection of short stories.

". . . it is true, I believe, that we tend as a people to glorify the adolescent and youthful so much, that we have not patience for the mature. It is still interesting to me that I have been able to dispose of so many of my stories, because I realize that the magazines, with the best intentions possible, cannot mold public taste except by a slow and cautious advance; but must, to survive, reflect the taste that is current in the overwhelming majority of their readers. That taste is for youth.

"Yet the events of our day are drawing us rapidly (and I feel happily) toward a more mature conception of life. The time may not be too far distant when writers, as they grow older, will be expected, and logically, to devote their skills to the more mature subjects, and will no longer be required to spend most of their time and talents in celebrating the idiosyncracies and the simpler passions of youth."

22

The Lesson and the Secret

LIONEL TRILLING

Lionel Trilling is the author of two critical studies, *Matthew Arnold* (1939), and *E. M. Forster* (1943) and of a novel, *The Middle of the Journey* (1947); as well as *Essays on Literature and Society* (1950), *Freud and the Crises of Our Times* (1955), editor of *Selected Letters of John Keats* (1951), *The Liberal Imagination* (1953), and *The Opposing Self; Nine Essays in Criticism* (1955). He is a professor of English at Columbia University.

This story will bring a wry echo from the experience of anyone who has talked about fiction writing to a literary luncheon, a summer conference of would-be writers, or a college course in the short story. The force which impels Mr. Trilling's ladies toward story writing, and the repeated inquiry which is the one blunt tool with which they hope to unearth the secret are uncomfortably familiar. Mr. Trilling gives us a finely etched portrait of these characters who clutter up the sidelines.

"The Lesson and the Secret" is an excerpt from a draft of a novel in progress.

H. H.

The Lesson and the Secret

THE nine women of the Techniques of Creative Writing Group sat awaiting the arrival of their instructor, Vincent Hammell. He was not late but they were early and some of them were impatient. The room they sat in was beautiful and bright; its broad windows

Reprinted from *Harper's Bazaar* by permission of the author.

looked out on the little lake around which the buildings of the city's new cultural center were grouped. The women were disposed about a table of plate glass and their nine handbags lay in an archipelago upon its great lucid surface.

Mrs. Stocker said, "Mr. Hammell isn't here, it seems." There was the intention of irony in her voice—she put a querulous emphasis on the "seems."

Miss Anderson said, "Oh, but it's that we are early—because of our being at the luncheon." She glanced for confirmation at the watch on her wrist.

"Perhaps so," Mrs. Stocker said. "But you know, Constance—speaking metaphorically, Hammell is *not here*, he—is—just—not—here."

At this remark there were nods of considered agreement. Mrs. Territt said, "I think so too. I agree," and brought the palm of her hand down upon her thigh in a sharp slap of decision.

Mrs. Stocker ignored this undesirable ally. She went on, "Not really *here* at all. Oh, I grant you that he is brilliant in a theoretical sense. But those of us who come here"—she spoke tenderly, as if referring to a sacrifice in a public cause—"those of us who come here, come for practice, not for theory. You can test the matter very easily—you can test it by results. And you know as well as I do, Constance, that—there—are—just—no—results—at—all."

Miss Anderson had gone through uprisings like this every spring and she knew that there was no standing against Mrs. Stocker. Mrs. Stocker would have her own way, especially since the group that opposed her was so small and uncourageous, consisting, in addition to Miss Anderson herself, only of Mrs. Knight and Miss Wilson. Young Mrs. Knight was extremely faithful and quite successful in carrying out the class assignments and this naturally put her under suspicion of being prejudiced in favor of the instructor. Her opinion was bound to be discounted. As for Miss Wilson, her presence in the group was generally supposed to have merely the therapeutic purpose of occupying her unhappy mind. It was not a frequent presence, for she shrank from society, and now she looked miserably away from the insupportable spectacle of anyone's being blamed for anything whatsoever.

Miss Anderson said, "But surely we can't blame that all on Mr. Hammell."

"No, not all," Mrs. Stocker conceded handsomely because it was so little to concede. "I grant you it isn't *all* his fault. But I think we have the right to expect—. It isn't as if we weren't paying. And generously, too, I might add. And there's nothing to show. Not one of us has sold herself."

Mrs. Territt gave vent to an explosive snicker. At once Mrs. Stocker traced the reason for the outburst to Mrs. Territt's primitive sexual imagination and said sharply, "Not one of us has sold herself to a single magazine. Not one of us has put herself across."

Of the nine women, all were very wealthy. They made Vincent Hammell's first experience of wealth, and nothing he had learned from books had prepared him for what he found. It seemed to Vincent that only in the case of Miss Anderson had wealth been a true condition of life, shaping and marking her as nothing else could have done. She alone bore something of the imagined appearance of wealth, the serenity and disinterestedness to which wealth is supposed ideally to aspire.

Vincent supposed that either the size or the age or the nature of Miss Anderson's fortune had led her—as fortunes of a kind sometimes do—into a historical lapse, an aberration of her sense of time. For Miss Anderson, although not "old-fashioned" nor long past her youth, seemed not to inhabit quite the same present in which her friends lived. She seemed, indeed, to live in reference to certain delicate points of honor such as Edith Wharton, but few after her, would have been concerned with. Vincent assumed, for example, that some high moral decision, its meaning now obscured, accounted for the unmarried state of a woman so pleasant as Miss Anderson. It was surely to be laid to some sacrifice of herself, some service of an idea. The idea which she served would not have to be very complex or important, but still it was an idea. Perhaps this explained the historical impression she made, for to many people the present consists of things, while the past consists of ideas. Like the past, Miss Anderson was a failure. Yet in some way she continued to exist with a gentle unsought authority which perhaps came from her friends' dim response to the power of the idea and their recognition of the magical, if limited, potency of the past; she was not aggressive or competitive and it was felt that she shed a justification upon whatever groups she joined.

Now and then Miss Anderson submitted to Vincent's criticism the stories she wrote. They were elaborate and literate—well written, the class called them—but they had no relation to any reality Vincent could identify. In the world of Miss Anderson's stories, servants were old and loyal; wives hid nameless diseases from their husbands or silently bore the most torturing infidelities, or found themselves hideously in the power of depraved lovers; memories played a great part, the memories of single passionate nights or of single significant phrases, and it sometimes happened that flowers or white gloves were forever cherished. When Vincent discussed these stories with Miss Anderson, he was always surprised at the small conviction with which he spoke about their lack of reality—he almost believed, as he spoke to her, that there might actually be such a world beyond his strict modern knowledge.

The distinction which Miss Anderson had was perhaps but a weak one, yet it gave Vincent Hammell a standard by which he could fairly measure the inadequacy of her colleagues. If she did not carry the power of her position, she at least carried its tragic consciousness. Wealth and position, Vincent felt, should appear in their proper forms and add to the variety of life. He was sure that there were proper forms both of refinement and vulgarity. But these women made but a commonplace spectacle. Thus, the meager taste in dress of Mrs. Stocker quite matched the meagerness of her face, which showed the irritable energy of a person whose social self-esteem is not matched by cash in the bank. Or Mrs. Territt was so very coarse in complexion, so drab in dress and so brutally dull in manner that it was inevitable to suppose that what gentility she had was hanging by only a thread of income. Mrs. Knight was ruddy and healthy from an expensive outdoor life, but in other respects she appeared no more than merely well off. Poor Miss Wilson's truly painful nervousness and her evasive eye quite transcended the bounds of class.

Yet on the other hand, it was even more difficult to believe in the actual status of Mrs. Broughton, Mrs. Forrester and old Mrs. Pomeroy, for wealth had marked them only in the way of parody and they were all so "typical" that one had to suppose that they had been produced not so much by nature and circumstance as by certain artistic imaginations of rather limited range. Vincent felt that in the east, in cities of complex culture, wealth would surely make a better show, would impart a more firmly bottomed assurance, a truer arrogance. Then too he could suppose that these women were the failures and misfits of their class, else they would not have to meet weekly to devote themselves to literature.

"I have nothing against Hammell personally, nothing whatsoever," Mrs. Stocker said. "What I think is that we need a different *kind* of person. Hammell is very modern, but we need somebody more practical. It seems to me that if we could have a literary agent who could give us the straight dope, tell us about contacts and the right approach . . ."

Mrs. Stocker had no need to complete her conditional clause. The straight dope, the contacts and the right approach went directly to the hearts of Mrs. Territt, Mrs. Broughton, and Mrs. Forrester. They murmured a surprised approval of the firm originality of the suggestion. Even old Mrs. Pomeroy raised her eyebrows to indicate that although human nature did not change, it sometimes appeared in interesting new aspects. To all the ladies, indeed, it came as a relief that Mrs. Stocker should suggest that there was another secret than that of creation. There was a power possibly more efficacious, the secret of selling, of contacts and the right approach.

Miss Anderson said, "But aren't all the literary agents in New York?" She said it tentatively, for she was without worldly knowledge, but what she said was so sensibly true that the general enthusiasm was dampened.

"But surely," Mrs. Stocker said, and her voice was almost desperate, "but surely there must be somebody?"

Mrs. Broughton, who was staring out of the window, said, "Here he comes," whispering it like a guilty conspiratorial schoolgirl. Mrs. Forrester closed her dark expressive eyes to the group to signal "mum" and the ladies composed their faces.

Could Vincent Hammell have heard the conversation of which he was the subject, he would have been surprised by only one element in it—the lack of any response to him personally. He knew he was not succeeding with the group, but he knew, too, that none of the instructors who had come before him had succeeded any better. The university had sent its best men, professors first, then young assistants, likely to be more modern. Each autumn the new man had been received with taut feminine expectancy; each spring he had been discarded, for he had not conveyed the precious, the inconceivable secret which the women had come in hopes to receive. Yet though Hammell might understand that he was not successful, he always supposed that he was a little forgiven by reason of his sex and age. He was wrong to count on this feminine extenuation—his masculinity and youth made his case, if anything, even worse.

His failure had no doubt begun when, upon being invited to instruct the group, he had conjured up a vision of gently bred ladies, all pretty and all precisely thirty years old, gracefully filling empty days and hearts with the delicate practice of a craft humbly loved. He had not been prepared for the urgent women who were actually his pupils, nor for their grim dark worship of the potency that print conferred, nor for their belief—more intense than any coterie in metropolitan garrets could have—that they were held in bondage by a great conspiracy of editors.

Vincent Hammell was carrying his brief case, an elegant piece of luggage of excellent leather and the best bronze hardware. It had been a gift from his parents who with such gifts, useful but very fine and extravagant, kept for themselves and their son the memory and hope of better days. Vincent was glad of the brief case, for it helped to arm his youth and poverty against the wealth and years of his pupils. He laid it on the plate-glass table beneath which his own legs and the legs of the women were visible. He opened it and took out a thin folder of manuscript. Miss Anderson cleared her throat, caught the eye of member after member and brought the meeting to order. Hammell looked up and took over the class. It was only his entrance into the room that gave him trouble and now he spoke briskly and with authority.

"Two weeks ago," he said, "I asked you to write an account of some simple outdoor experience. You were to concentrate on the physical details. You remember we discussed as models a passage from *Huckleberry Finn* and a story of Ernest Hemingway's." He picked up the folder of manuscript and examined its thinness. "Some of you," he said drily, "carried out the assignment."

Mrs. Stocker moved in her seat to signalize a protest which Vincent understood—all this was elementary. "I'd like to read one example," he said.

He took a manuscript from the folder. Only three of the women had attempted the assignment, two of them dully. But he was rather proud of Mrs. Knight's little story. It was quite unpretentious, about a young wife who is left by her husband in their hunting lodge in the Canadian woods. She wakes in the night to hear a howling that can be only that of wild animals and then the creaking hinge of an unlatched door opening and closing. She is not alone, but of the two guests one is another woman and the man is incompetent. She lies still and miserable, bearing all the sad isolation of responsibility; the conflict of her emotions is not between fear of the beasts and the impulse to protect herself, but rather between fear of the beasts and fear of her husband's contempt for her lack of courage. But at last she becomes bold—and finds that though indeed the door is unlatched, the howling is only that of a high wind. It was perhaps not entirely convincing that she should have deceived herself, but something in the matter of the story was indeed convincing, her desire to seem manly to her husband and the whole impulse of the story itself to discover safety where danger had been imagined.

Vincent began to read this story aloud. Just then the door opened and two women came in. They made little gestures of greeting to their friends and politely indicated, by exhibiting how they were out of breath, that their lateness had been unavoidable. Vincent waited for them to settle and then again began to read. When he came to the end, he paused for a while and looked around the table.

"What do you think of it?" he asked.

"Very nice," Mrs. Broughton said. "Very nice indeed." Mrs. Broughton, it always seemed to Vincent, had been imagined by a radical caricaturist of rather conventional fancy. Careless of verisimilitude, concerned only with the political passions he would arouse, the artist had drawn her short and pudgy, with a face of gross and foolish pride and a bridling neck which gave an air of condescension to her remarks, many of which were in their intention really quite good-natured. Mrs. Knight was not gratified by Mrs. Broughton's praise.

"Yes, it is very nice," Mrs. Stocker said, suppressing as much as she could the condescension she felt. "Of course, it has no plot, no complication, no conflict really, but it has a kind of twist at the end, it is true to life and it has touches of realism."

"Oh, very realistic," said Mrs. Broughton.

"Well, I don't think it *is* very realistic," said Mrs. Forrester with sudden authority. As compared with the inventor of Mrs. Broughton, the imagination that had conceived Mrs. Forrester was of greater complexity—some social satirist, gifted but not profound, had projected this elegant woman, not young but still beautiful, and had endowed her with an intensity of self-regard and a sense of noblesse so petulant and shoulder-shrugging, yet so easily snubbed, that poor Mrs. Forrester lived in a constant alternation of blind attack and bewildered retreat, with the result that since her beautiful girlhood scarcely anyone had felt toward her any emotion save the various degrees of contempt. "Not at all—to me it doesn't seem at all realistic." She held her pretty head high to front the refutation which her judgments inevitably and bewilderingly provoked. "It isn't *convincing*," she said. "Now take the central problem—yes, take the central *problem*. That definitely is *not* convincing. She lies there worrying about what she should do. *Why? What for?*"—her appeal was vehement. "All she had to do was ring for the guides, and that would be *that*!" Her beautiful dark eyes flashed finality.

There was a gasp from Mrs. Knight. Her cheeks flamed. She almost rose from her chair. Her voice was choked. "It just so happens," she said with terrible scorn, "it just so happens that she couldn't ring for the guides because in our lodge—there—are—no—guides—to—ring—for."

The group was wholly with Mrs. Knight in the matter. As usual, Mrs. Forrester was silenced.

Mrs. Stocker said, "Mr. Hammell, I gather that you like that story of Mrs. Knight's. And I like it too. It has a very fresh quality, definitely fresh. But the question I want to ask is whether in your opinion a story like that has a marketable value."

There were little nods around the table as the spirit of the junta asserted itself once more, but there was a constraining sense of guilt now that Vincent Hammell was here. Mrs. Knight looked very conscious. She was humble about her writing and near enough to her college days to submit to the discipline of an assigned exercise, but she was naturally not averse to knowing whether or not she had produced a commodity.

"Now you take Constance's stories—Miss Anderson's stories, Mr. Hammell. You yourself admit that they have something. They're well thought out and they're well written, they have suspense and a twist at the end. But the editors just never take them."

Miss Anderson looked up in surprise and unhappiness. Although now and then she sent her stories to market, she seemed to feel no chagrin at their refusal.

"Now why do you think that is, Mr. Hammell?" Mrs. Stocker said. There was a silence, a degree of attention that Hammell saw the significance in. He considered how to answer. Miss Anderson looked withdrawn from the inquisition.

Mrs. Broughton broke the silence. "It's because they are refined and charming and what they want nowadays is coarse—and middle class. About miners. There was a story I read about two children who could hear each other practicing the piano through the walls of their apartment." She tossed her head in resentment. "Who cares?"

Mrs. Territt broke in and her coarse voice was injured and defensive. She said, "You all talk about selling stories. What I want to know is how to write them. That's what I came here to find out." She looked hostilely at Vincent. "All this talk about what's been done already! I came here to learn *how to do it at all*!"

Three or four women were swayed by this utterance to confess among themselves what they had never before realized. "Yes, yes," they murmured and nodded to each other. The group was now divided between those who believed that the secret lay in learning to sell and those who believed that it lay in learning to write.

"Personally," Mrs. Territt said, and her glance at Hammell was now malevolent, "personally, that is what I give up my time to come here for. And I haven't got it—*nothing*." The murmur of agreement she had won had gone to her head and she was breathing hard.

Vincent said, "Mrs. Territt, one can only learn to write by writing." For the fact was that Mrs. Territt had never yet submitted a manuscript.

She bridled. "I suppose that's very smart." She used the word *smart* not in the English sense of something clean and precise or fashionable and elegant but in the old American sense of something clever and impertinent. In the eyes of all present this declassed her.

Vincent said, "How long do you spend at your desk every day, Mrs. Territt?"

She did not answer but looked sullenly at the table before her.

"Four hours a day?" Vincent said inexorably. He could feel the solidifying interest of the group. The many handsomely shod feet seen through the top of the table looked like aquarial creatures as they shifted a little with interest.

"Three hours? Two? One solid hour every day?"

Mrs. Territt was sulking like a scolded chambermaid with an inexpressible grievance. Suddenly she flashed out, "No, why should I? When I never get any ideas?" It was a direct accusation against Hammell.

Someone snickered and no doubt the fight was won, but Hammell went on: "How long do you spend every day trying to get ideas?"

She looked at him blankly from her raging sulks.

It was necessary to bring the matter to an end. Vincent took a book from his briefcase. It was a volume of stories by a writer he much admired, Garda Thorne. "Shall we continue the class?" he said. The women nodded.

Vincent began to read aloud the story he had selected. It was about two young American girls who were visiting friends in an Austrian village. They were Catholics and they were sent by their hostess to pay a call of ceremony on the priest of the village. The priest had received them charmingly, he was very polite. He was in an especially good humor because the new wine from the grapes of his own little arbor was just ready. It stood in his tin bathtub on the floor. Just as the visit began, the priest was urgently sent for. He begged his young guests to remain until his return. They could not but agree, yet as his absence continued they sat there bored and impatient and wondering how to amuse themselves until first one and then the other took off her shoes and stockings, held her skirts high and stepped into the tub. If you stopped to think of it, it was not quite probable, but it was a wonderfully funny and charming picture, the first girl standing in the wine, then the second, then both together, elegantly dressed and with their wide straw hats on, the drops of red wine splashing up to their thighs, their white feet and ankles scarcely visible to themselves as they looked down into the roiled wine.

Then there was the scramble to get themselves decent before the priest should come home, the scrubbing with inadequate handkerchiefs, the sanding of the soapstone floor to clean off the prints of their feet. When the priest returned they had to sit there demure, with their legs still sticky under their stockings. The priest served them the wine they had bathed in and their manners were perfect as they heard him say that never had he known the wine to be so good.

As the story went on to its end, Vincent was sorry he had chosen it to read. The silence was becoming unusually intense. He had especially wanted Miss Anderson to hear the story, for he thought it might suggest to her, with its simplicity, gaiety and elegance, that there were better subjects than the unreal complexities she so feelingly conceived. But, as he read, he felt that it had been a cruel mistake to read this story to these women. As it went on through its narration of the flash of skirts and underskirts, of white stained thighs, the grave silence of the girls and then their giggles and the beautiful prints of their naked feet on the stone floor, it seemed to him that his own youth had been thoughtless to have chosen the story. He felt, too, like an intruder into feminine mysteries and the sweat came to his forehead. He dreaded the return of the priest and the end of the story when he would have to take his eyes from the book and look around. At last he finished. He did not look up but moodily sifted through the pages of the book. This had the histrionic effect of letting the story hang for a while in the air.

For a moment the silence continued. Then it was broken by Miss Anderson, crying, "Oh that was lovely, Mr. Hammell," and "lovely," "lovely," "lovely," echoed the women around the glass table, beneath whose surface there was a shifting of legs and a pulling down of skirts over knees.

Vincent Hammell now ventured to look at their faces, which were relaxed and benign. There were little half-smiles on their mouths, directed tangentially at him. It was as if he himself had been the author of the story and as if the story had celebrated the things that were their peculiar possessions, their youth, their beauty, their femininity.

In the sunlit room, in the soft spring air, there was a moment of musing silence as the quest for the precious secret was abandoned. Despite himself, Vincent Hammell experienced a sense of power, in all his months of teaching the class the first he had felt. Yet in the entrancement of the women, in their moment of brooding relaxation, there was something archaic and mythological, something latently dangerous. It was thus that the women of Thrace must have sat around Orpheus before they had had occasion to be enraged with him. He would have liked to remind them, but it was not possible, that he had merely read aloud to them the story which a woman, Garda Thorne, had written.

It was old Mrs. Pomeroy who memorialized the moment. Mrs. Pomeroy was by far a gayer creation than either Mrs. Broughton or Mrs. Forrester. Perhaps she was aware of her role, perhaps she had even had the charming wit to invent it herself—she was the old lady of widest experience and profoundest wisdom and it was impossible not to see her lengthy past of drawing rooms (at home and abroad) in which the brilliant and the famous were received. Silence and a twinkle were the evidences of Mrs. Pomeroy's breadth of culture. At certain literary names she would smile, as at the memory of old, intimate and special delights. But only once had she made vocal her feeling for the great past. On that occasion the name of Proust had been mentioned by Vincent Hammell and what Mrs. Pomeroy had said was, "And also Paul Bourget."

She had added a knowledgeable whisper of explanation, "Psychology!" And now, as her way was, she smiled sadly and wisely as she spoke. She closed her eyes and said, "Such a story makes one truly glad there is literature. We should be grateful."

She spoke so seldom and perhaps she was really wise—at her benediction upon literature and her admonition to gratitude everyone looked solemn, as if, in the moving picture, they were listening to Anatole France delivering the panegyric at Zola's funeral.

"Very excellent," said Mrs. Broughton. "Very."

And now Mrs. Stocker spoke. "What I like about the story," she said, "is that it is neither one thing nor another. I mean it isn't highbrow *or* commercial."

It was not that she wanted to bring the discussion back again to the matter which so much interested her. No doubt she as much as anyone else had been caught in the moment of contemplation, but in uttering her feeling about it she used the only language she knew. And having used that language, it was now natural for her to say, "Tell me, Mr. Hammell, does this writer sell well?"

At the question there was a noisy little murmur of agreement to its relevance as the eyes turned to Vincent Hammell to demand his answer.

23

Writing for the Younger Generation

MABEL LOUISE ROBINSON

Mabel Louise Robinson was born in Waltham, Massachusetts. Her college work was done at Radcliffe and at Columbia University from which she had her master's and doctor's degrees. She has taught at Wellesley, Constantinople, and Columbia where she has a lively and productive workshop in writing which has well over three hundred published books to its credit.

She has written many books for children and young people, including the Little Lucia books, and *Bright Island* now a classic for the teen age. She has done a biography of Louis Agassiz, *Runner of the Mountain Tops,* which is used as a model of interpretive biography in several large universities. She has produced two books on writing, *Creative Writing* (1932), and *Writing for Young People* (rev. version of *Juvenile Story Writing* (1950). Her novels include *Island Noon* (1942); *Bitter Forfeit* (1947), a *Saturday Evening Post* choice; *The Deepening Year* (1950) and *Strong Wings* (1951). In addition she has written *Back Seat Driver* (1949), *Skipper Riley the Terrier Sea-Dog* (1955) and *Riley Goes to Obedience School* (in press), as well as a world landmark book, *King Arthur and his Knights* (1953) and *All the Year Round* (1954).

Out of her varied experience as a writer and as a teacher of fiction writing at Columbia University, Miss Robinson offers a number of vigorous conclusions about the demands and the rewards in writing for young readers. Her own success and the many fine books which students in her workshops have published give authority to her comments.

Her article gives the writer of juveniles a clear view of his responsibilities and his opportunities, as well as good advice on technical problems. In fact, Miss Robinson writes with such zest about the response of this young audience that she may persuade writers of adult fiction to see what they can do for the younger generation.

H. H.

Writing for the Younger Generation

WRITING for the young people of today has to take into account some of the things we have done to them. The children who are coming along now are traveling very different paths from those their elders trod. We have opened new ways to them and they explore them with great interest. Whether they will be any better off at the end of their exploration is an open question, but they will be farther along. Just now a good many of them are farther along than those who write for them.

I have always held that there are great areas of our brain which lie dormant all our lives. The children seem to prove that theory by waking up their own brains to activity such as few of their elders have experienced. We struggled over simple laws of physics and mathematics. They handle with ease the theories of Einstein and his cohorts. Why? Because these men are putting into their hands knowledge which applies to the needs of a confused world that demands clear young thinkers to set it straight.

The first question then that faces the writer for young people is—Do you know enough? The answer to that is No, probably not. We don't know enough and we never have known enough. We have delivered over to children half-baked stories, badly written, falsely conceived in their relation to life. We have thought that because children are young they are silly. We have forgotten the blind stirrings, the reaching outward of our own youth. Those brain areas we have closed off and we want to hear no more of them.

Over and over again women and men, too, though men more rarely because they are surer of themselves, come to me saying, I don't know enough to write a book for adults, and so I'd like to try a book for children. And I tell them that when they have learned enough to write for an adult perhaps a child will listen to them.

That is my conviction, too. Writing for children is not to be taken on lightly. And by that I don't mean that you can't have a lot of fun doing it, for there is no expression of yourself which could give you more pleasure. But you should know as much as the children.

Such suggestions usually make not the slightest dent on the applicant who has an irrefutable final word. "The children always listen to my stories and call for more." They would listen if you recited the alphabet, and call for more hoping sooner or later to hear sense.

Sense to them means material which is in some way related to life. Not a bad test, by the way, to apply to adult writing, though of course it would rule out a good deal of it. Children have not been around here long enough to get bored with things as they are. On the contrary they are eager to extend their horizons which in youth seem illimitable.

Now again see what we do to these searching minds. The beginning writer invariably produces fairy tales. Good reasons lie behind this tendency. He has forgotten how interesting reality can be. He has nothing much to say about things as they are. He has been fed on adult fairy stories so long himself that he has only dulled recognition of the truth. And finally, as I have already said, he does not know enough to handle reality. As indeed, few of us do!

But we can at least try to feed and water growing ideas instead of anesthetizing them. For soon enough all these splendid strivings to grow are over. They have had their source in the variety and strength of youthful interests. Try this, try that, discard, accept, in dizzy succession, the young person is alive in every direction.

Here again we need to take into account what we have done to these rich strong interests of youth. Young persons, reaching out, try the adult story, and there they find one main interest, love in its various legal and illegal forms. As if there were nothing else on this troubled earth, every magazine story concerns itself with the troubles of sex. Every magazine explains in detail to the teen age the delights and sorrows of sex. The age limit of the heroine is pushed back so far that now at thirteen the girl is convinced that nothing is worth her attention any longer except to become skilled in baiting a male. She is not mature enough to look ahead to a future when she will need other interests to deliver her from the boredom that any such concentration inevitably brings.

The adult, having shut off his own areas of active thinking, proceeds to close one by one the good brain areas of youth. Young and old, they all feed together on a juvenile kind of daydream stuff. And it seems to have too little of a vitalizing power to produce a civilization capable of dealing with many of our problems today.

Behind the sharp interests of youth, its desire to explore all the offerings of the earth which it has come to inhabit, is the urge which always drives an alert person to use a set of fine-edged useful tools. Here, untarnished by the wear and tear of adult use, are five splendid senses alert to every passing stimulus. Since all experience can come only through the senses, youth has a tremendous advantage over age in its power to discover truth and to use it. For as we grow older, one by one we discard the functioning senses and substitute a hazy reliance upon the sense of sight.

Why not make use of the rich response of youth's active senses? All good writing depends upon the skillful use of sense detail. As you get an experience, so you give it. We are afraid to use such skill on the kind of reality which the young must find out how to face. We deny youth the privilege of sadness or tragedy unless it is located as far back as Shakespeare.

Yesterday a man who had been a major in the war told me of bodies of young men piled high like cords of wood to dispose of them. When I asked him how he could bear such a sight he said, "Oh, I couldn't feel that they had ever been alive." But they had been alive, each boy in that dreadful pile, and now they were only waste, discarded, rotting. Where is that waste to be stopped except by the young people who are coming along, and who are being fed on tales of excitement and valor until they cannot wait to have their own war?

What if the truth does make them sad, what if it haunts them? Better be saddened than dead. Give children a little of the truth about war and they will not spend all their playtime shooting off toy pistols. Nor all of their adolescence hoping for a chance to bomb an alien country. Only as we give the children the truth about life can we expect any improvement in it.

Here as in every other form of fiction writing the use of sense detail carries the truth. Fiction at its best makes the reader share the experience about which the author writes. He gives it back to the reader as he got it, through the senses. Whatever the material, gay, sad, high adventure, the writer must make his reader share it. We read over and over again news in our morning paper which would torture us if we really shared its emotional content. Note the different effect upon you of reading of an accident and seeing it happen. The good fiction writer makes you see it, and feel it, and hear it happen, until you never forget it. Suppose we try some of this skill upon matters of importance. We might get results.

If then you write for the younger generation it is your responsibility whether their horizon is extended or limited. This does not mean that you should search for strange exotic material about which you would probably know less than your readers. Such fiction only serves to fog the distances. But you must, if you have lived a fairly active life, you must have come upon places, situations, people, problems, which have roused your interest and your curiosity until you really know them and have something to say about them. If you can present a sailing story with the sharp sense of detail which gives it reality, then the child on the prairies has sailed a boat. His flat horizon reaches to the sea. If you can give the struggle of a young person against poverty so that it burns with bright truth, the child of the rich will be a little less hampered. If you know dogs, horses, or wild foxes, extend that friendly relation to young people who will share it through experience or through desire to experience it. Be encouraged that what you know so well others know not at all. Say it well enough and an eager audience always awaits you.

Action is the child's first means of self-expression. For some time it is his only means. He understands action and he likes it. His first stories are entirely concerned with it. As he grows older it is still essential to his interest.

Soon he acquires speech to make himself understood. Dialogue begins to enter his stories. He goes on talking for the rest of his life, and he continues to demand dialogue in his fiction. Next to action, dialogue becomes important to hold his interest.

Finally, and this is of course a stage which is reached only theoretically by many, he begins to be conscious of the process of thinking. He realizes that there are some things which we do not act upon or talk about, at least until we have thought. And these matters of the mind are likely to be important. Increasingly to help him understand a character, he needs to know what he is thinking about.

Because, after all, with this final demand the reader has the three keys which are needed to unlock the mystery of character. He watches the person act, he hears him talk, he learns his thoughts. Is there any better way to know a person? Is there any better way for you as a writer to give reality to your character? In the old days writers talked *about* their characters for long descriptive paragraphs which we skipped. Now we present them alive. Through the incidents where they act their way out of their difficulties, talking and thinking as they go just as we do, we know what sort of people they are just as we know the people about us. Better, because often we have no key to thought processes, which might startle us if we had.

Good action inevitably produces a plot. Try it and see. If you concern yourself in a lively enough fashion with matters of importance you are going to get plenty of action before you are through. In your story you have the advantage of focusing on one problem and seeing it through to a solution which at least sounds credible. An active existence is full of plots, all of which help to make it interesting. Plots should never be the bugbear which beginners think them.

If your story is important enough for young people you ought to have something which you want to say about it. Not a sermon, not a lesson, but an underlying idea which will hold it together. Why did you want to write about this material? What does it hold that you value, that you want to contribute? Ask yourself what you want to say about it, and when you can formulate your idea into a statement, you have a theme. This underlying idea, invisible as it is, may be the most important part of your story. It brings us back to the earlier plea that we take into account some of the things which we have done to youth. Before you write a story make up your mind what you think about the material, and whether you want the younger generation to follow you. If you have nothing to say, leave this audience alone and work off your urge on stories for adults.

If your mind is still active and able to expand into fresh areas, then turn your attention to the part of our society which is still growing and which is capable of as fine and strong a growth as we are capable of offering it. If this generation, like those before it, repeats the blunders of the past, we might possibly be to some degree at fault. Though we compete with movies, with comics, with radio, we still have a power which none of them possesses. The reader takes his book into the quiet of his mind, and there he stays with it until it has become a part of his thinking and his feeling. You have entered into him and become a source of his growth.

24

Writer's Cramp

JOEL SAYRE

After graduating from Oxford, Joel Sayre was a reporter on the *New York Herald Tribune* for city editor, Stanley Walker. He has worked as a screen writer in Hollywood and in the radio department of Time, Inc. He was a correspondent for *The New Yorker* during the war. His first book, *Rackety-Rax,* a satire on prohibition era racketeers and college football was published in 1932, and was followed by *Hizzoner the Mayor*; *Persian Gulf Command;* and *House without a Roof.* His article for *The New Yorker,* "The Man on the Ledge" was made into a motion picture.

In spite of Joel Sayre's joyfully vicious snap at the hand that feeds him, he has gone right on writing for the twenty years since this article appeared in Mencken's old *American Mercury. Rackety-Rax,* that glorious translation of college spirit to gangster-ridden Canarsie, was his first book. Most recently has appeared the moving story of an anti-Nazi German family, *House without a Roof.*

No one has ever been quite so fed-to-the-teeth with writing as Mr. Sayre's unhappy protagonist, though some have approached this state. But it is only fair to point out that the author has not drawn his satire in crayon, splashed it in paint, or molded it in clay. He wrote it down (possibly after invoking the ghost of Mark Twain). For there is always this to be said for the literary profession—like life itself, it provides its own revenges and antidotes.

E. J.

Writer's Cramp

"I CERTAINLY appreciate this little visit, Mr. Reeves," said Mr. Sturgess, the big man in the $150 suit. "All my life I've wanted to know what the inside of a lighthouse was like and now I know."

"Oh, don't mention it," said Mr. Reeves. "Anything I can do for a friend of Jimmie Calder's is a pleasure."

"Gosh, it's certainly a great place you've got here," said Sturgess. "Living room, kitchen and everything. Even a telephone. And that store room! Why it's equipped like Sears-Roebuck."

"Yes," said Reeves with intense apathy, "the Department of Commerce does pretty well by its wave-swept towers."

Sturgess looked at him curiously.

" 'Wave-swept towers,' eh?" he repeated, " 'wave-swept towers!' Why, you're quite a poet, Mr. Reeves. 'Wave-swept towers.' Hmm. Pretty good."

The lighthouse keeper blushed. He was a pale, glum-looking little man in dungarees. On his head he wore the knitted article known in the Navy as a watch cap.

"And you know so much about the lights up there," Sturgess went on. "All about the optics and everything. You certainly know a lot. I mean about the lights and everything."

" 'Nautically trained lighthouse engineer,' I believe they call it," said Reeves in a flat voice. There was a silence.

"Say," said Sturgess suddenly, "by the way. I nearly forgot. I brought out a little something here with me." He pulled a huge silver flask out of the pocket of his overcoat lying on a chair. "Some Scotch. Just off one of the big liners. And not scraped off, either. How about a snort?"

"Why not?" was the lighthouse keeper's reply.

He went below to the kitchen and presently returned with two glasses and a pitcher.

"You'll have to take it with water," he muttered. "The Department of Commerce doesn't supply club soda."

"No club soda, eh?" said Sturgess, giving him another searching look. "No club soda. What do you think of that?"

"Oh, I've been around," said Reeves bitterly.

"Oh, I didn't mean anything personal," said Sturgess, "but you will admit that this is a funny place to hear about club soda."

The lighthouse keeper was blushing once more.

"I suppose it is, really," he said. "Forget about it. Well, here's how."

The two men took long pulls at their drinks.

"Must be a great life here," said Sturgess somewhat tentatively, after a long silence.

"Simply wonderful," replied the other nastily.

There was another silence.

"How about another snort?"

"Why not?"

Sturgess poured and the two men drank again. The entire round was consumed without the aid of words.

"This is pretty good stuff, if I do say it myself," remarked Sturgess. "How about another snort?"

"Why not?"

"This is pretty good stuff if you do say it yourself," said Reeves after a while.

"Why not?" said Sturgess.

"Well, here's how," said Reeves.

"Away to the races."

"This is the sixth, or is it the seventh?"

"It's only the fifth."

"How about the lights?" asked Sturgess.

"Oh, they take care of themselves. All I've got to do is hold this old tower down on the rocks."

"All alone out here most of the time, are you?"

"All alone out here all of the time," said the lighthouse keeper, and then added feelingly, "thank God!"

Sturgess was moved to sympathy.

"I don't see how he stands it," he thought aloud. "All alone out here away from everything. Nothing but the gulls——"

"Gulls!" yelled Reeves. "Gulls! *That's* what I keep for gulls."

He pointed to a double-barrelled shot gun in the corner.

"Well, I don't mean gulls exactly. I guess I really mean signs of human habitation. I should think you'd get sick for the sight of a tree."

"Trees!" said Reeves, "I hate trees."

"Why, that's funny," said Sturgess, "I never heard of anybody hating trees before."

"Well, you're hearing about somebody now," said Reeves. "Look me over. I loathe trees. I can't stand the sight of 'em. I wish there'd be a forest fire and burn down every splinter in the world."

"All right, never mind about the birds and trees," said Sturgess placatingly. "We'll skip them. What I'm trying to get at is how it feels to be marooned here all of the time. You're a man of culture. Don't deny it. You're a man of urbanity. You can't hide it. I knew it as soon as I heard you speak. Don't try to fool me. I knew it for sure when I heard you talk about 'wave-swept towers' and club soda. What are you doing off here all by yourself? Don't you miss the good things of life? Don't you miss music? I should think you'd have a radio or a phonograph."

"Music!" said Reeves wildly. "Why, I hate music more than birds and trees put together."

"Really? Well, that's a pity . . . Excuse me, I left my lighter in my overcoat."

He walked carefully to the chair, searched in his overcoat pockets, found the lighter, lit a cigarette. He pulled a newspaper from the pocket of the coat and handed it to his host.

"Say, here's a copy of yesterday's *Leader*. I thought maybe——"

"You thought maybe I'd like to observe the trend of events"—the lighthouse keeper screwed up his face—"and view the march of world affairs. And scan the passing show. Aw, blab-blab-blab, jabber, jabber, jabber, jabber, jabber, JABBER!"

He seemed about to tear the newspaper to pieces.

"Do you hate newspapers, too?" asked Sturgess.

"Do I hate newspapers. Oh boy!" said Reeves. "And not because they're made out of trees either. They're made out of raw nerves, that's what they're made of."

He threw the paper on the floor and stamped on it.

"Oh? Did you ever work on a newspaper?"

"Did I ever work on a newspaper? You bet I worked on a newspaper, all kinds of newspapers. Hick newspapers, metropolitan newspapers, Democratic newspapers, Republican newspapers, Socialist newspapers, independent newspapers, tabloid newspapers. And do you want to know what I think of all newspapers without exception? Well, I'll tell you: They're fit only to wrap fish in. Yes, sir, fit only to wrap fish in. You could make a joke out of that. The next time there is a big publishers' dinner, you could send a telegram for the toastmaster to read, see? Have it say: 'Congratulations. We have been wrapped up in you for years.' And sign it 'The American Association of Fish Dealers.' See?"

"Ha, ha, pretty good. The fish dealers wrap up their smelts in the newspapers, eh? 'We have been wrapped up in you for years.' I get it. I get it."

II

Reeves had picked up the remains of the paper and was turning the ragged pages, indignantly scanning the headlines.

"Look at the obituaries," he said. "I used to write obituaries. Hundreds, thousands, millions. Did I write obituaries!"

"Where was that?"

"Out in Iowa, when I was a cub. I was obituary editor. I wrote a daily column. The only time I was ever a colyumist, ha, ha! Not the obituaries of the prominent citizens, mind you, but the taking-off of the smaller fry. One paragraph apiece. Do you know what I mean? God, I could quote one under water:

"'Funeral services for Frank Bananas, 47, an iron puddler, who died of complications last night at Mercy Hospital, will be held at 2:30 P.M. tomorrow at his home, 558 E. Iuka Ave. Mr. Bananas was a member of the Fervent Order of Eagles, the Improved Order of Red Men, the Loyal Order of Hoo Hoos, and the Swastika Bowling Club. Surviving are his wife, Marie; three sons, Frank, jr., Floyd and

Michael; two daughters, Rose and Pearl; and his mother, Mrs. Sadie Bananas. Burial will be in Greenlawn Cemetery by Gosnell and O'Brien, morticians.'

"Ask me if I hate undertakers!"

"Do you hate undertakers?"

"Oh, golly, he wants to know if I hate undertakers! Listen, I hate everything that pertains to funerals. Not only undertakers themselves, not only undertakers proper, but tombstone cutters, florists, compounders of embalming fluid, drivers of motor hearses, grave diggers, and even the little guy that arranges the folding chairs. And as for Chopin, I have a double-distilled hatred for him, not only because he was a musician, but because, being a musician, he wrote a funeral march."

"Here, let me sweeten up that drink."

The guest poured four of Primo Carnera's fingers into each tumbler. The host was inspecting the newspaper again.

"Look," he said, "an animal story. How I detest animals, especially pets! It reminds me of the first metropolitan paper I was on—the *Star*. The Old Man, the managing editor, was mad about animal stories. If he couldn't get one, he'd wire out of town for it. Generally out west. His favorites were bear stories, which he'd run in a box under some wild and woolly date line. This is the way they usually sounded——

"'Squeaky Moccasin, Idaho, August 13.—Old Bruin thought he would make a feast of huckleberries yesterday morning in a patch three miles north of here, but he reckoned without Trapper Sam Quimby, who was about in the early dawn, inspecting his snares. Spying Bruin, he raised his rifle and fired straight into the furry marauder's heart. Trapper Quimby had no trouble in disposing of a mess of steaks at fancy prices in the market here this morning.'

"But all too often there was plenty of local furry and finny chitchat to be written. And of course it fell to me to write it. There wasn't a baby yak born at the Zoo or a new carp in the Aquarium that I didn't have to slog out and cover. It got so bad that I couldn't look at a girl wearing a set of furs without having to turn my head away, while the mere mention of sea food, even oysters or shrimps, spoiled my whole day. Beside that, after I had been on the *Star* a year, along came a presidential election and the paper got so disgustingly partisan that

I couldn't stand it any longer. All this self-anointed smugger-mugger! It made me want to scream."

"Politics one of your *bêtes noires*, too?"

"*Bêtes noires*? Say, I never could tolerate *any* kind of politics, Republican, Democratic, or Bolshevik. I got my bellyful of 'solons,' as they call them in the hick paper headlines, those three years out in Iowa. 'Solons!' " The lighthouse keeper filled his lungs and gave forth a garland of raspberries. "Solons!" In his voice was contempt for the entire army of public servants.

"No matter what paper I worked on, its politics always made me furious," he finished.

"What about the *Dispatch*?"

"Oh, the *Dispatch* was just as bad as the *Star*. It was an opposition paper all right, as far as national politics was concerned, but it lined up solid with the City Hall crowd, principally so that the ramshackle old building the paper was put out in wouldn't be condemned by the fire and health departments. Yes, I went to the *Dispatch* from the *Star*. It was all those baskets of kittens that washed me up on the *Star*. And the spaniels that could make a fourth at bridge! And the parrots who dictated night letters! But the *Dispatch* was even worse, although I must say they weren't so keen about all the cunnin' ickle wee cockroaches Mrs. Jerome Woozendinger, of 349 Muskmelon Boulevard, found yesterday in her kitchen being raised by a mother rat."

"Gosh!" said Sturgess, twirling the liquor around in his glass, "you certainly had a tough time of it."

The lighthouse keeper was again looking at the paper.

"Oh, Lord," he groaned, "here's that old cartoon again about Junior helping Mamma in the kitchen the week before Christmas! There ought to be a law! They ought to put that cartoon on the Index Journalisticus." He ground his teeth.

"Christmas," he sneered. "Christmas! Thanksgiving! Easter! Fourth of July! Yom Kippur! The Rhamidan! St. Patrick's Day! Nothing but a lot of lousy roundups, that's what they are. Shall I tell you what I think of holidays?"

"I'd love to hear."

"All holidays are detestable because they are roundups. A roundup on a newspaper is what they call a holiday story. That's why I left the

Dispatch. I was what you might call the boss wrangler of all the holidays. The *Dispatch,* claiming to be liberal and a great respecter of all nationalities, races and creeds, specialized in roundups. You know the sort of thing:

"'Over a billion holiday makers left the city yesterday to spend Labor Day in the country and at the beaches. There were nineteen deaths from drowning, ten were killed in automobile accidents, sixty-five were injured from sitting on empty pickle bottles, eleven fell down wells, while scores were attacked by mayonnaise rash.' And so on, for a couple of furlongs, with the names of the dead and groaning in agate type. Holidays, pah!"

"All right, all right," said Sturgess, "but what's that all got to do with music?"

"It was when I was on the *Chronicle,*" the lighthouse keeper said after a gulp from his glass. "The *Chronicle* was genuinely independent and as near to being O. K. on politics as any paper I ever worked on, but its big trouble was Old Violin Makers. For some strange reason the boss had a fixation on Italian and German cobblers who built fiddles out of whatever rubbish there was lying around the shop.

"These Stradivari generally had an old O'Sullivan rubber heel for a chin rest and were strung with cast-off shoes laces. Of course they weren't always Old Violin Makers: sometimes they would be guys that had constructed full-rigged ships inside empty bottles, or maybe firemen who spent their off hours knitting Paisley shawls.

"Anyway, the protagonist of these stories was always some kind of nut, and he was almost always old. The more stewed figs and marshmallow syrup with English walnuts you could dump over the story, the better the boss liked it. And naturally, after I had written one or two he took a shine to them and issued orders that I should do them all in the future.

"First, I got sick of all stringed instruments, then of music, then of Italians and Germans, and finally of all old persons.

"I remember that during that time an uncle of mine from Indianapolis turned up and wanted me to show him the town. Such a fine old fellow he was, and very good company. He'd always been nice to me as a kid and helped me through college after my father died.

"So I went to see him at the Blackstone, but the whole visit was spoiled because I was scared to death that at any moment he'd open his suitcase and pull out a cigar box Cremona or a hip flask with a model of the *Constitution* in it. Poor old fellow! Poor dear old Uncle Roger! He died shortly after."

III

Tears were streaming down the lighthouse keeper's face.

"Oh, come, come Reeves, old fellow, don't take it so hard," said Sturgess, patting him on the shoulder. "It's a pity the old gentleman passed away, but it wasn't your fault. You didn't kill him."

"Oh, oh, poor old Uncle Roger," sobbed the lighthouse keeper. "Maybe if I'd been nicer to him he'd still be with us all yet. Oh, oh."

"Here, have another drink and tell me some more about yourself."

"Aw, nuts! What are you interested in me so much for, Burgess? Just a miserable old mess of nothing, that's all I am, a mess of nothing. Here's a toast: gentlemen, let's drink to nothing. Say, Burgess, what do you keep on wanting to know about me for?"

"Never mind about that now. Go on and tell me some more about yourself. Did you ever do any magazine work?"

The lighthouse keeper instantly became almost sober.

"Magazine work!" he croaked, "magazine work! Four years, that's all, Mr. Bridges, four years. Four years, that's all, four years."

"What sort of stuff did you do?"

"All kinds, my friend, all kinds. I'm tight now, but don't you worry. Just help me hold this old tower down on the rocks, so she won't blow away, that's all. But don't worry."

"I won't. But I'm very much interested in your magazine work. I wish you'd tell me something about it."

"Aw, nuts!"

"No, go ahead. Tell me about the first piece you ever sold."

"First piece, first piece," muttered Reeves, valiantly pulling himself together. "Let me see now. First piece?"

"Yes, your first piece. What was it about?"

"Horses," was the dark reply. The lighthouse keeper frowned and clenched his fists. " 'Horses, horses, horses, crazy over horses.' Well, that's what I am. Crazy over horses. If I were on shore this Winter, do you know what I'd do?"

"No, what?"

"I'd go around tripping up all the horses I could find, and I'd found a Society for the Promulgation of Cruelty to Animals, that's what I'd do."

"Why the hippophobia? What's the matter with horses? I think they're pretty fine animals myself."

"It doesn't matter what you think, Mr. Matches. It's what I feel that matters. Or does it? Does anything matter? Gentlemen, I give you anything."

"Go on about horses."

"Oh, hell! I don't want to go on about anything."

"Yes, go on about horses."

"Well, I finally quit the newspaper business, and decided I'd write for the magazines. So I called on a friend who was an associate editor of one. He advised me to begin with nonfiction pieces. And he sent me in to see his boss. Gosh, I don't want to talk about this, Mr. Terlet."

"Oh, please go on."

"Well, the editor was very friendly and said yes, he would be interested to look over some of my stuff. He had plenty of fiction, enough to hold him for a couple of years, as he never used more than one or two stories a month. What he wanted was articles. Did I have any ideas? No, nothing very hot.

" 'Well, what about horses?' he said. There had not been a good piece on horses for a hell of a time. Was the horse really vanishing or was that just a lot of propaganda put out by the automobile people? What about the *eohippus*, the little dawn horse of prehistoric times? What about Bucephalus? What about Mazeppa? Famous horses of history. Were there any more bucking broncos? He had recently read in some paper that a man on the East Side had been arrested by the Department of Health for keeping a horse on his roof.

" 'Just a chatty, human piece on horses,' he said. 'Always take it for granted that your reader knows nothing whatever about horses. You can almost assume that he has never seen one before. And be sure to put something in about the old horse cars.'

"We shook hands and I went out of his office walking on pillows. At last! Here I was writing for a magazine. No more lousy newspaper work for me. A regular literateer from now on, henceforth and forever more. Oh, the pity of it!

"I went to the Public Library and read Hinkel's great three volume work on 'The Horse.' I ploughed through Smools' Index, looking up every reference to horses that had ever appeared in any publication since Caxton. I interviewed a livery-stable keeper and old Vince Treanor, who knows so much about race horses he whinnies in his sleep. And finally, after two weeks, I mailed the article to the magazine."

"And then, I suppose, you received the first of a long series of rejection slips."

"No, no," groaned Reeves, "would to heaven I had! No, no. They accepted it, and ran it and paid me $200 for it. The editor, curse him, wrote me a very nice little letter saying that he found 'Is Old Dobbin Really Dying Out?' the best piece on horses he had ever read, and asking me to come in and see him about some more articles."

"And did you go?"

"Oh yes, I went all right, but to get to his office I used only the streets on which no horses were allowed. I couldn't even eat horse radish after that, and one night I tried to strangle my ten-year-old nephew in the midst of reciting 'Sheridan's Ride.' Say, do you find it stuffy in here?"

"Yes, sort of."

"Well, what do you say if we open this window?"

"Fine. So what did this editor have in mind?"

"A job of ghosting. Ghosting is what they call writing a piece signed by somebody famous, see?"

"Yes, I know."

"Well, he was so pleased with 'Is Old Dobbin Really Dying Out?' that he had decided I was the very man to ghost the memoirs of a crib-biting soprano the Metropolitan Opera was about to turn over to the Navy for target practice."

"Who was that?"

"Rosie Gorilla."

"Rosie Gorilla?"

"Oh, Mme. Rosa Gerello, but I used to call her Rosie Gorilla. What,

what a creature! She spoke the conventional *chow mein* of French, German and English, but she did her cussing in Italian, which was most of the time."

"How did you make out with her?"

"Oh, marvelously. Such fits of temperament and temper! Such sulks! Such haggling over the price the magazine had arranged to pay her! She insisted on making me personally responsible for what she considered a niggardly sum. As a matter of fact it was princely. And what a lovely time I had trying to make her recall the glamorous days when she was the slightly scorched toast of four continents. All that she could do to help was to remind me endlessly that she was a 'grrrrrande artissssste.' 'I am grrrrrande artissssste,' she would say every day, just so I wouldn't forget. 'Make sure to write dat down.' And make catty remarks about her fellow singers. According to her, Melba and Gadski and Farrar and Calvé should have stayed at home and sung in the kitchen where they belonged.

"Finally, I had to go to the *Dispatch's* library and look her up in the clips. And with those and what Bill Guard, the press agent at the Metropolitan, could remember about her I finally adzed out enough for a series of four articles. I showed them to her and she covered my pan with kisses. Oh, God!"

"Well, even so ——"

"Oh, Lord, that wasn't the half of it. She was so impressed with her greatness that she went to the editor and insisted that he should arrange to have a movie made of her life story. I happened to be in his office at the time. When he failed to rave over the idea, she went into a typhoon of temper, socked me in the chest with his inkwell, and screamed her way out. When the articles appeared under her name, she wrote letters to all the papers and denounced them as fakes and forgeries. That's one of several hundred reasons why I don't love music."

IV

"Hmm. At the same time, you know, you were pretty lucky, landing straight off with your first two efforts. Did you write more nonfiction?"

"I wrote volumes of it. I wrote shelves of it. I wrote encyclopedias of it. I wrote whole *libraries* of it." His voice had risen to a shout. "I wrote about good roads. I wrote about our beautiful shade trees. I wrote about the Vanishing Redman. I wrote about the French debt. I described the horrors of radicalism, and I jeered at the D.A.R. for a liberal weekly. I bewailed the decline of the road show and I hosannaed the rise of the movies. 'At last a really democratic and wholesome form of entertainment,' was what I wrote unblushingly. Did I write nonfiction? Give me a drink before I die!"

"What about the ghost writing?" said Sturgess, rendering succor. "Was there much more of that?"

"Much *more* of it! Ohhhh! *Bales* of it, that's what there was, *bales* of it. I was a fanatically dry senator, and after the piece was finished I destroyed the specific gravity of all the rye I could find in New York for the next two months. I was a home-run hitter and a woman tennis champion. (Any sport is just another emetic to me now.) I was Miss Totsy Delray, the star of *O. K., Aucassin,* and I was a feminist with a face like a towel swinger in a pork and bean prize fight. The feminist recalled those stirring days when she picketed the White House for suffrage and went on hunger strikes for sometimes as much as five hours at a time. I was a general and a pacifist, an ex-police commissioner and a society dowager, and, by God, I was once a pair of Siamese twins. Yes, sir, a pair of Siamese twins. Can you image how vile that was? Were you ever a pair of Siamese twins?"

"No, I can't say that I ever was. But you must have gone through the struggle all young writers do before they get over. I mean you must have got plenty of rejection slips at first."

"No, no, that was just the trouble. I never received a single rejection slip in four years. Not one! That was just the trouble. Would to God I had! It might have discouraged me, and I could have turned to some happy and useful occupation like grinding knives."

"Oh, come, come!"

"Oh, yes, yes. But instead I got sucked in by the terrible editorial maelstrom. Word flew around the magazine offices that at last here was an answer to the editor's prayer: a man who could write a good, readable nonfiction article of any length, on any subject, and get it in when he promised to. As soon as I would finish one piece, I'd find three letters in my box from editors asking me to come in and see them.

"And then after a time I realized that once I had written about some person or thing that person or thing was forever shut off as a source of interest or pleasure. The person or thing became transformed into a phobia, a complex. I've told you how I wrote myself out of enjoying music. It was the same with all the other arts. Even the lively arts. The memoirs of a famous restaurant owner which I ghosted made me sick of the taste, feel, smell, sight and sound of food."

"Sound?"

"Yes, sir, even the *sound* of food used to get on my nerves. For instance, a sack of potatoes being emptied into a bin. Or the grating of a nutmeg. Or peas being shelled. Or pop corn snapping in the popper."

"Well, well. You *were* in a state. What you probably needed was some fresh air and exercise."

"But don't you see, I had ghost written for home-run hitters, and Olympic sprinters, and heavyweight champs and channel swimmers so that the thought of exercise was even more abhorrent than that of food. And five thousand words on camping and the Red God's Call for *Out-o'-Doors* fixed me up with one of the prettiest little yens to live in a safety deposit vault ever known to psychopathology.

"And the first thing I knew I couldn't sleep. It all grew out of a long popular scientific article I had written on 'What Our Dreams Mean.' I was afraid to go to bed for fear I'd dream. And I couldn't drink black coffee because of a piece of mine on Java that appeared in a travel magazine. Tobacco was out, too, on account of a little bit of whimsey on 'The Old Southern Planters.' When I would finally drop off after two or three sleepless days I invariably had hideous nightmares full of horses that played and sang, vigillions of happy holiday makers swarming up and down the good roads and climbing our beautiful shade trees, and popular athletes, actors and politicians riding around on baby yaks and carp, while generals and pacifists, stuck together Siamese-twin fashion, fled screamingly from Vanishing Redmen. Say, is there another shot in that canister?"

"You bet!"

Sturgess passed the flask to the lighthouse keeper. The mouth of the flask beat a tattoo on the edge of the glass while the golden brown liquor gurgled out. Reeves took a long pull and then a long breath.

"But what about women? Wasn't there some girl you could turn to?"

"Oh, don't, don't!" groaned Reeves, burying his face in his hands. He burst into tears again. His shoulders shook as he groaned and sobbed. Sturgess was very embarrassed.

"I'm *terribly* sorry, old man, honestly I am," he said. "I didn't mean ——"

The lighthouse keeper suddenly raised his head.

"Fiction did it," he said fiercely, "fiction it was. Fiction wrecked my life." His fist crashed on the table. "Fiction!" He glowered darkly. "Or was it truth? Truth!" His conversation was rapidly becoming Hamletian. "Truth is mangier than fiction. Ha, ha, ha!" He laughed madly.

"Julia was her name. She was a swell girl. We were engaged. One night I told her all my troubles, and she said 'Why not write fiction?' I took up her suggestion all right. I wrote a series of confession pieces for *Nothing But the Truth* and got so sick of women and love that I suppressed the banns with a sock in the nose, and beat it out of town."

"And how did you happen to get here?"

"Well, I've spilled so much I might as well spill it all. Naturally, I wanted to change my racket. Naturally I wanted to get away from everything. I thought of joining the Royal Northwest Mounted Police, but they were so snarled up with the movies, and the great out-of-doors, and horses, and policemen and a lot of other things that gave me the horrors that I just couldn't.

"It was the same way with every occupation I could think of. The life of a trapper, while sufficiently lonely, was lived among too many trees and animals."

"What about being a sailor?"

"Didn't I tell you I was once a ship-news reporter? And anyway, I'm a martyr to sea sickness. I thought of being a night watchman, but that wouldn't have taken me away from cities. And, as far as I was concerned, a factor for the Hudson Bay Company has all the disadvantages of a trapper and a Royal Northwest mounted policeman to cope with plus constant intercourse with the Vanishing Redman.

"It got so desperate that I turned to the Encyclopaedia Britannica to search for ideas on a career. I had looked in vain through the first thirteen volumes, when one day I took up Volume XIV, the one that deals with Libi to Mary (I'll surely never forget that pair) and opened it at random. My eye fell on a small sketch of the Corduan Lighthouse, the earliest wave-swept tower extant. Underneath the sketch was the caption: 'The lighthouse was begun in 1584 and stands on a rock in the Bay of Biscay near the mouth of the river Gironde.'

"The last half of the little caption jingled pleasantly through my head:

"'And stands on a rock
In the Bay of Biscay
Near the mouth
Of the river Gironde.'

"Idly I started to read the article on lighthouses, and in the middle of the third paragraph it suddenly flashed over me—I'd be a lighthouse keeper! It was just the thing I was looking for. I could be all alone, and yet not have to slog around in the great open spaces. I could be doing something useful without the necessity of having to see politicians, opera singers, old violin makers, heavyweight champions, or Vanishing Redmen. I like the sea. Because I never wrote about it, I guess. I got in touch with the Department of Commerce, went through a course of training, and here I am. Except for those cursed gulls," he finished suddenly. A flock was wheeling by the window. He darted to the corner, seized the shotgun and fired both barrels. He missed. The gulls flurried around excitedly for a few seconds and then flew off screaming.

"How I wish I could shoot," Reeves muttered through clenched teeth. He turned to his guest. "You know, sometimes it almost makes me want to go back to shore and take a course in sharp-shooting. I've never hit one yet." He laughed bitterly. "Oh, well."

"Put your gun down and take a shot at this," said Sturgess, handing him a glass. Reeves obeyed and sat down clumsily in a chair by the fire.

V

"I suppose it hasn't occurred to you to wonder who I am," began Sturgess with a bright smile.

"Why, no," said Reeves slowly, "all Jimmie Calder said today when he brought you out in the kicker was that you were an old friend of his."

"Well, I am. I've known him ever since I was a kid. I was born over on the mainland and Jimmie and I went to school together. And he didn't tell you any more than that about me because I told him not to. As a matter of fact, I made the trip up here from New York especially to see you."

"What!"

"Now, don't get excited. Wait until I've finished talking and then you can open the flood gates. It wasn't you, yourself, I came up here to see; but the keeper of this lighthouse. And *what* a break!"

"What do you mean, 'break'?"

"That it turned out to be you. Why it's the most astounding thing I ever heard of. A perfect natural."

"*What* is?"

"Now listen, Mr. Reeves, you've told me your story and I am tremendously moved by it. I think you've gone through Hell if anybody I ever heard of has. But you're going to win out. And I can help you do it, and I'm going to. Now ——"

"Say, what in hell's this all about?"

"All right. I'll 'cut the cackle and come to the 'osses.' I'm F. Peabody Sturgess. You never heard of me, because you've been out here on these God-forsaken rocks for a couple of years. But you've heard of the *Family*, I imagine? Well, I'm the editor."

"What!" shouted the lighthouse keeper, slowly rising from his chair.

"Yes," said Sturgess. He talked faster and faster. "Yes, I'm the editor. For the last year we've been featuring the inside stories of people in unusual occupations. It's funny your mentioning the Royal Northwest Mounted Police and the Hudson's Bay Company, for we've had pieces both from an inspector of the mounties and a fur factor. Of course, we sent a staff man up to get the stuff and write it, just a little ghost job, ha, ha, but those two pieces alone brought in thousands of letters. Then we had a deep sea diver and a fire chief and a lot more. Last week in our editorial conference, somebody suggested that our readers would like to hear about the life of a lighthouse keeper, so I assigned myself to the job, as I was coming up here to spend Christmas with my mother and this is one of the biggest lighthouses in the world right here.

"But think of finding a seasoned magazine writer keeping the lighthouse! What a break. Now, I'll give you an idea of the sort of thing we want ——"

"*Unmerciful God!*" shrieked Reeves, his eyeballs rolling. And with a terrible scream he rushed across the room and dived headfirst through the open window.

VI

From the Minnescoggan *Beacon*:

> Persistently refusing to take hold of a life preserver which was repeatedly thrown to him, an unknown man in dungarees was picked up late yesterday afternoon seven miles east of Crunchett Light by the Coast Guard cutter *Sally Blossom.*
>
> The man was swimming straight out to sea when the cutter sighted him. A dinghy was lowered, after he refused to take the life preserver, and when Boatswain Harry Boards reached the mysterious swimmer a helping hand, he bit it.
>
> Forcibly lifted from the water with a boathook and taken aboard the cutter, the man resisted his rescuers so violently that he had to be subdued by Boatswain Boards. He mumbled wildly about horses and music, refused food, and would not tell his name or how he happened to be swimming straight out to sea.
>
> Physicians at St. Eulalia's Hospital, where he was taken last night, say that his condition is still delirious, though not serious.

25

Writing Biography

KATHARINE ANTHONY

After studying at the universities of Heidelberg and Freiburg in Germany, Katharine Anthony received her Ph.D. from the University of Chicago in 1905 and proceeded to teach at Wellesley College and then to do research in economics with the Russell Sage Foundation in New York. In addition to *Mothers Who Must Earn* (1914); *Feminism in Germany and Scandinavia* (1915); and *Labor Laws of New York* (1917); she is the author of several biographies including: *Margaret Fuller—A Psychological Biography* (1920); *Catherine the Great* (1925); *Queen Elizabeth* (1929); *Marie Antoinette* (1932); *Louisa May Alcott* (1938); *The Lambs* (1945); and *Dolly Madison–Her Life and Times* (1949). She is also the coauthor of *Civilization in the United States–An Inquiry by Thirty Americans* (1921) and translated the *Memoirs of Catherine the Great* (1927).

Katharine Anthony's comments on the methods and purposes of a contemporary biographical writer explain why modern biographies so frequently elbow novels into second place when readers reach for a book. We all remember the older biography, dull with facts and stiff with propriety. Modern biography is no longer limited to the record of an established figure, it is free to interpret the human being.

The biographer, as Miss Anthony displays him, combines in one person the attributes and methods of the novelist, the scholar with his patient research, and the historian with his accuracy. The novelist with his interest in background influences, in hidden motives, in the complex nature of his character, is the newcomer in this field of writing. Miss Anthony's own books give evidence of the interest and significance which result from this triple approach.

H. H.

Writing Biography

MODERN biography dates approximately from the time of the First World War. Since that time it has become a productive field, where the student of human nature may pursue his course in freedom and exploit his random discoveries for the pleasure and profit of others. Before that quickening era, biography had been a solemn and sacred preserve, hedged about by restraint and conventions which made its works correct and dull. Only the novelist was allowed to deal with characters as human; the biographer was not supposed to explore human nature in his subject. He must present an established image of a reputation or a tradition.

Of the change which took place, rather suddenly, Lloyd Morris wrote: "The Victorian mind condemned human nature whenever it significantly failed to approximate its ideals. The modern mind is surprised, not by the evidence of failure, but by the persistence of ideals and the occasional approximate success. We no longer ask that our heroes be free from human defects; instead, we are glad to be reminded that human nature, with all its defects and limitations, is capable of assuming heroic stature." This describes in a few words the new kingdom into which the writing of biography had entered. It prospered by the growth in tolerance and wisdom which had somehow and from somewhere, insidiously and effectively, found its way into literary taste and public opinion.

The veterans of the First World War were the first soldiers of tradition to admit to the experience of fear under combat. They were the first soldiers who could afford the moral luxury of speaking the truth. As the war novels came along, one after the other, culminating in *All Quiet on the Western Front*, the note of disillusionment and reality was steadily repeated. The books which have followed the second global conflict have continued the tone of realism, and even more emphatically. One needs only to mention, among them, *The Naked and the Dead* and *Toward an Unknown Station* to show the latest trend. One must conclude, from the popularity of these novels, that the reading public, to which the writer intuitively responds, has also emancipated itself from the gloss and sheen of war. The romantic atmosphere of chivalry has been replaced by a more clarified vision of the soldier's actual life. No one seems to be alarmed or horrified by the revelation. On the contrary the persons most concerned—both writers and readers—seem to be stimulated and vivified by the sensation of release.

I mention this trend in the development of war novels because it corresponds in time and character with what has happened to biography. The writers of life histories have also showed the influence of the new dispensation. They no longer feel constrained to qualify an applicant for a gallery of Olympians. They are not obliged to present a flawless hero, a faultless leader, an acclaimed transcender of mortal frailty. However notable and distinguished, however worthy of his laurels, the subject of their labors has developed his proportions through experiences fairly common to all men. His career had its origins in childhood; in parental patterns; in family environment; in educational influences; in contacts, friendships, and intimacies; in the nature and challenge of the times; and finally in luck, chance, and fate—the unpredictable elements of every human career. To trace the organization of one man's or one woman's life through the intricate developments of time and circumstance, play and counterplay, requires a considerable exercise of the imagination. It would be simpler to sketch the portrait of a mythical hero, who by definition was born, and not gradually made, great. To the biographer all lives bar none are dramatic constructions.

There is no reason why a modern biography should not be as interesting as a novel. With the trammels and evasions of so-called politeness discarded, an actual life may become a scene as exciting as a fictional existence. It offers a medium through which the author can express such insight into life as he fortunately possesses, and transcendently a medium in which he can acquire more than he already has. The novelist has an edge on him in escape and imagination, but the biographer commands an advantage all his own. A child likes his story to be exciting, but he also likes it to be true. He will ask wistfully at the end if all that really happened. The same tendency survives in adults whose curiosity about life has not been prematurely hardened and whose reach for firm reality is still normally functioning. To enjoy a truthful biography is one of the signs that the mind is still young.

Let no writer suppose, however, that truth, or even factuality, is an easy road to travel. The achievement of either is a toilsome and back-breaking labor. To array given facts in chronological order sounds rather simple; but the process involves a complex and exacting research. In the first place, the facts are not given for free but have to be earned, primarily by the strict survey of secondary sources, all of which are colored by the attitude of the authors. Sometimes a mere comparison of the various sources will drain out the color and yield the simple fact. The way-wise researcher knows how to do this. And then, beyond the area of worked-over material lies the crude ore of letters, documents, memoirs, and newspapers, which by diligence and patience can be converted into valuable metal. The cleanliness, simplicity, and rectitude of his original facts are the biographer's best assurance of the final integrity of his work.

It does not therefore follow that he will present his findings as naked as they were born. Let him strive as he will for detachment, the state of grace which his employment demands, he will be fortunate to achieve it only relatively. He is bound by the limits of his own nature. He will inevitably present his living material with a coloration of his own. The contrary is neither practicable nor desirable. But if he starts from scratch with objective data, he will be less likely to wander, later on, into the platitudinous wastes and deserts so tempting to his clan. His moralizing or philosophizing will bear the stamp of his own mind. He will at least have contributed nothing to the sum total of insincerity in his own literary field.

All writers must cope in their special way with the three classic unities: time, place, and action. The writer of biography has little trouble with time and place. The sequence and geography of the main events are already established. Devices, such as the flash back, to which the novelist resorts (often with some suggestion of desperation, as I think) are not dignified by custom in biography; certainly not yet. The literary life usually follows through the normal biological processes of real life, from "the infant, mewling and puking in the nurse's arms" to the final fated "oblivion, sans teeth, sans eyes, sans taste, sans everything." All that the writer has to do is to keep to a well-marked itinerary.

Yes; all that the writer has to do is to project his hero through the fundamental experiences of human life. He will certainly need all of his resources, imaginative and creative, for this one enterprise. In addition there are of course the incidental experiences, such as the discovery of radium, winning (or losing) the Battle of Waterloo, gaining four presidential elections in a row, the unveiling of a continent, the creation of a Hamlet, the drinking of a small glass of hemlock. If the biographer can steer us through the fundamental and unusual experiences of a notable life, vividly and convincingly, he should surely be allowed his lack of worry over the shift of scene and the march of time.

The design of a life history requires him to hew closely to the third classic unity—unity of action. This performance is by no means simple. The required design is something more than a staid progression and succession of events. The order into which the events must fall lies deeper than the chronological level that meets the eye. It will be determined by the meaning and purpose which the life history in question assumes for the writer. I do not know any way he can discover this except by so completely identifying himself with the bare facts that they sink into the area of the subconscious, to return thence when needed in the shape which his own creative depths have given them. It is not easy to identify one's self thus with alien substances; but it can be done, with sweat and effort, as a part of the personal sacrifice required for all good writing. Only when the biographer has subjected himself to this ordeal does the work growing under his hand take on the luster and gleam of real life. This is just as true for an historical as for a fictional character.

It is one of the axioms of modern biography that no life is complete without its childhood. This is not hard to believe but it is hard to practice. The art of character portrayal requires that the one and only child who could have grown into that particular adult shall be delineated. No perfunctory glance at the influences of home and mother will pass by modern and enlightened standards. Fluency of sentiment and stock generalizations about childhood will not conceal the want of specific knowledge. The real child that was must be depicted. This is the aim; and the difficulty of securing such knowledge is the stumbling block.

Few persons can relate the story of their childhood without idealizing, or distorting, or overdramatizing the facts. Great numbers of persons are lying on couches in psychiatrists' offices at this moment, trying with expert psychological aid to straighten out the record. The childhood of the famous individual is additionally hard to recover, encumbered as it is by the legends, afterthoughts, and hindsight of others.

Catherine the Great is rare among the so-called "Greats" in that she was able to report her early years with accuracy and detachment. With the same candor, she set down in her memoirs the incriminating details of her adult life. Her rare truthfulness can be traced no doubt to the influence of the French Encyclopedists, whose writings had been her staff and solace for many years and who represented for the world the most advanced realism of the age. Not many persons of heroic stature have been able, or willing, or interested enough to render a similar service to posterity. Like ordinary people, they seem to think that life began with the achievement of personal independence. They are not responsible for what went before and they are, on the whole, inclined to forget it as irrelevant and unimportant.

But the biographer must explore this terrain, striving as best he can, by judicious selection and patient research, to recover the fragments of a prehistoric age. To aid his search, however, he has a valuable and usually accessible resource. Since the lives of most children are a helpless reflection up to a point (a movable point but always still there), he will be wise to pursue the fortunes of his hero's parents with rather close attention. Those mighty exemplars, whether important or unimportant in themselves, are sometimes the key to great deeds and great thoughts that seem like miracles and stagger the world.

Still biography should attempt, and almost invariably does attempt, to be something more than convincing character study. Many readers approach it as a short cut to history. They are less concerned with the personality aspect than with the formal and historic cast of the related period. These readers have their rights; and as long as the serious historians choose to ignore the general public and write for specialists, they leave the field open to less pretentious possessors.

Most solid history emanates from academic and authoritarian authors who are noticeably absent from the otherwise heterogeneous company of the present collection. Amid all their differences and divergencies, this company admits to one guiding principle: the purpose to entertain. The academic historian (provided he is not one of the notable exceptions), who usually has a chair at stake, can acknowledge the said motive only with reservations. In the very act of becoming original the professorial hand is prudently stayed. The decorum of his profession forbids him to venture in directions where none have been before him.

As the late Charles Beard remarked of his fellow historians: "If to lovers of romance their visibility seemed low, that fact had to be ascribed to the critical spirit, and not to a lack of appreciation for creative powers." But in another connection, he spoke more directly of the limitations that prudence imposed on his profession, and quoted Henry Adams as likewise deploring them. "What shape," he quotes Adams as saying, "can be given to any science of history that would not shake to its foundations some prodigious interest?" From the attitude of these authorities it would appear that history is such a vital subject that its own professional exponents are rather afraid of it. All in all, for many reasons, including those of self-preservation and monastic caution, they have kept their visibility at a consistently safe low. The effect is disappointing not only for the lovers of romance but also for the lovers of truth. The lovers of romance can go elsewhere for satisfaction but where can the lovers of truth turn if not to history?

Thus the academic historians have resigned a whole fertile field to the biographer. This is not to imply that the little brothers of Clio's clan can proceed irresponsibly, roaming at will and with joyous abandon, where the sages have trod so carefully. The more they adhere to historical facts, the more they acquire merit and rating. As we have already said, research is a discipline which they cannot side-step, a drudgery which they must grimly embrace. They must nose along the same well-documented trail that the historian follows, scenting by the way, as he does, any new and fresh documentary material. But they are not obliged to close their eyes on the end of the trail, shushing off even the most obvious conclusion of the guaranteed facts. If a new pattern or design emerges from the mere concatenation of items, they are free to grasp the vision and endow it with language. They have nothing to lose but their reputations as trustworthy and reliable writers, their honorable fame as literary craftsmen. With these commodities only the most light-minded would gamble.

The biographer must absorb much history for which he will have no immediate use. The entire historical background of the life he is following should be mapped out in his mind, even though it does not enter directly or at great length in his narrative. No character portrait has solidity and reality which does not unite with and have its roots in its period. Persons who are born too soon or born too late seldom achieve the eminence of those who are born at the right time. They may indeed become interesting subjects from just that point of view; but the role of history, whether as protagonist or antagonist in the personal drama, is of the greatest importance. The shape of the times in which the individual plays out his part needs active and close consideration. The details may be conveyed by implication or by outright reporting—it does not matter so long as they are there. The fine artistry of Lytton Strachey consists in the fact that they are always there, though only by implication.

A fact to be borne in mind, however, is that lifelikeness of the central character is the primary aim of all life histories. The human being who actually lived, thought, acted, suffered, failed, prevailed, triumphed and molded circumstances must be brought before us in his own unique and inimitable voyage and personality. To do this by the magic of language remains the principal reason for writing a biography.

26

Articles or Stories?

FREDERICK LEWIS ALLEN

One-time assistant editor of the *Atlantic Monthly* and managing editor of *Century Magazine,* Frederick Lewis Allen was editor of *Harper's Magazine* and vice president of Harper & Brothers, Publishers. Author of *Only Yesterday* (1931); *The Lords of Creation* (1935); *Since Yesterday* (1940); *The Great Pierpont Morgan* (1949); and *The Big Change* (1952); he also wrote the text for *The American Procession* (1933); *Metropolis* (1934); and *I Remember Distinctly* (1947), with his wife, Agnes Rogers Allen.

Mr. Allen's article on what has happened to *Harper's Magazine* in its editorial policy during the last twenty-five years may well increase the apprehension already felt by fiction writers. Is the short story as a vigorous fiction form disappearing from print? Does the reading public prefer articles, turning perhaps for fiction satisfaction to the movies and currently to television? Even in the popular magazines of widest circulation articles crowd fiction off the table of contents, outshine stories in the titles featured on the covers, eclipse stories in strategic position and in display of illustrations.

Mr. Allen finds two chief causes for this threatened extinction of the short story. Intelligent American readers are intensely interested in urgent public issues, and if they read fiction at all, read novels and/or mysteries. The readers who still consume magazine fiction, short or long, prefer the nondisturbing, familiar daydream story. But he also says that except for a brief period of vitality at the end of the war, when writers set down vigorously the results of their exposure to new experience, the short stories which turn up are not as good as they should be.

Has the fiction writer of ability and serious purpose abandoned the short story for the novel, knowing that only for the book will he find

his audience? So rarely that it is an event will any publisher put out a volume of short stories, especially stories without previous magazine publication. Book buyers reject such volumes. And yet the short story of the past has been a flashlight illuminating brilliantly a small area of experience or character.

H. H.

Articles or Stories?

THE market for short stories and articles is ever changing, and the changes which take place in it are brought about by all sorts of causes. These causes range from the vagaries of public taste—and the national and world events which influence these vagaries—to other things which are not always apparent to writers, such as the jockeying for position that goes on between various magazines and groups of magazines in their endless competition for the attention and loyalty of the reading public. Let me illustrate what I mean by citing what has happened to one small sector of this market over the past twenty-five years, during all of which time I have watched its ebb and flow from a single vantage point, the editorial staff of *Harper's Magazine*.

In the early nineteen-twenties *Harper's Magazine* was in a bad way. It had a long and distinguished reputation, but for twenty years or so it had suffered from the competition of the rising mass-circulation magazines. It had been losing advertising to them; and what was more, it had been losing authors and illustrators to them, simply because it could not afford to match the prices which these new giants of the periodical publishing business could pay. At that time it was our custom to publish some five stories a month—with as many as seven in the "Midsummer Fiction Number"—and to illustrate them. In the fiction market we had certain advantages: because we were editing for a small public of comparatively intelligent readers, rather than for a mass public, some really brilliant stories came our way that might have been considered by the editors of the mass-publication magazines to be too subtle or somber or socially sophisticated or shocking for

their readers. Yet on the whole it was clear that what we were getting for the most part was a second-best assortment of fiction; other periodicals with big circulations and fat treasuries were skimming the cream. We were losing money. We were also losing prestige. Something needed to be done.

Now at this very time, as it happened, H. L. Mencken was making a lively success with his new magazine, the *American Mercury*. It was unillustrated, which meant that it didn't need to spend money for an art staff, or for pictures, or for half-tones and color plates, and that it could be printed on inexpensive paper. It used very little fiction, but concentrated on articles of ideas and opinion—mostly saucily unorthodox opinion which appealed mightily to the intellectuals among the rebellious younger generation. The success of the *Mercury* was only one of many signs of the intellectual ferment of the day. For during the nineteen-twenties a lot of people were questioning the prevailing American mores—the Victorian proprieties, the stupidities of politicians, the narrow-mindedness of clerics, and the crudities and absurdities of those American businessmen whom Sinclair Lewis had taught us to call Babbitts. In short, there was a new market for new ideas, especially among readers under forty. And so the editor-in-chief of *Harper's*, Thomas B. Wells, decided that the way to put the magazine on its feet again was to move into this new market—and incidentally to save money by so doing.

That meant a plain orange cover, well designed, which simply listed the contents of the magazine (and saved money on art work). It meant dropping illustrations (which also saved money). It meant going after articles which discussed political and social and intellectual problems from fresh points of view (and thus drew on the talents of lively minded writers who were willing to accept rather low pay if they could reach and impress an influential audience). And it also meant reducing the number of stories per issue from an average of five to an average of three or so. I think our fiction standard rose, but there was no denying that we had reduced by these changes the total size of the fiction market.

The experiment was successful. *Harper's* boomed.

But a few years later came the Depression, bringing with it both new financial problems for publishers and new shifts in public taste.

Advertisers canceled their contracts. Readers began to economize on their magazine fare. Revenue dwindled. But at the same time the widespread public bewilderment over what was happening to American business, and accordingly to the jobs and fortunes of Americans generally, brought a new and intense interest in economics and also in politics as it impinged on economics.

Pretty soon articles on the conflict between science and religion, or on divorce, or on "What Should I Tell My Child?" began to look pretty trivial and unimportant in the face of the disaster that was overtaking the country; confronted by the staggering crisis of the Depression, thoughtful readers wanted articles on the trouble with the banking system, on the problems of public relief, on the fancy new panacea called Technocracy, and so forth. These we provided. And because *Harper's* wasn't troubled, as were most of the mass-circulation magazines, by any fear of distressing its readers with uncomfortable facts, or of talking over their heads about economic affairs, it gradually became one of the liveliest forums for the discussion of this central problem of the time. Result: it got through the Depression without disaster; though it lost a lot of advertising, it kept its appeal for readers—attracting a great many new ones—and by drastic economies it managed to keep in or near the black. And it satisfied, furthermore, its editors' sense of what its role should be in such a crisis. But note another result: in the process it reduced its monthly quota of stories from three to two—and sometimes one.

Throughout the rest of the nineteen-thirties we bought fiction very meagerly at *Harper's*. Partly, I suppose, this was because we editors ourselves became absorbed in economics and politics—and, as time went on, in international affairs too—almost to the exclusion of any active interest in stories. But partly, perhaps, it was because of what was happening to the fiction output of the day. It seemed to us that while the manufacture of well-made happy-ending fiction for the mass market continued with little apparent change, much of the fiction that came to us was now of two types. First, there was the plotless narrative of the Katherine Mansfield or *New Yorker* school—a poker-faced account of some conversation or episode which came to no climax but subtly conveyed a mood. Second, there was the radical story of economic warfare, from which one might learn how sordid was life among the miserable sharecroppers, or how it took a strike, with brickbats flying, to persuade the sensitive young hero that he must cast in his lot with the workers because he too belonged to the people. Some stories of each of these types were good, and there were of course many excellent ones that did not belong in either of those categories; but on the whole we had little taste for trying to increase our fiction output. It is not much of an exaggeration to say that throughout the nineteen-thirties we bought each month what we regarded as the least bad of the stories that reached us. (It is possible, of course, that one reason why the current crop of fiction did not impress us was that we printed so little; that the best authors and agents considered us hardly worth bothering with, and passed us by.) Anyhow, during those years we editors focused our chief attention upon the adventures of the New Deal, and the economic and social condition of the United States, and the news from a Europe in which the Fascists were rising menacingly.

And that was what our readers seemed to want, too. For we could not help noticing that our best political and economic and foreign articles brought us newspaper comment, radio mention, and streams of letters of approval or disapproval, whereas our finest stories brought us almost no comment whatever. And this situation continued. I remember when Eudora Welty's story, "The Wide Net," came in, early in 1942, being vastly impressed with it and saying to someone that I thought it might win the O. Henry Prize. Well, it *did* win the O. Henry Prize (which of course is why I remember my prediction; I easily forget the predictions that aren't fulfilled). But I don't suppose it brought us more than three letters of favorable comment. Possibly our editorial policy had automatically selected for us a social-problem-minded group of readers who didn't care about first-class fiction. But there it was: our purchases of fiction remained small, and there was no pressure upon us to increase them—except from a few writers of fiction who naturally objected to our apparent negligence of the art in which they excelled. Our readers seemed to prefer articles on the problems of the day, and these they got in full measure, especially as it seemed to us that to provide such articles was to perform a public service.

Then came the war, and with it a slow change in our sector of the market. Again it is not easy to distinguish causes from effects. Now we had on our staff one or two editors who took a newly active interest in current fiction and did energetic scouting for it. Perhaps this was the chief reason why better stories began to come our way. But I think, as I look back, that something more than that was happening. For although during the first year or two of the war story-writers had had a tough time adjusting themselves to the fact that stories which mentioned the war were likely to take on the artificial aspect of propaganda, and stories which did not mention the war seemed to evade reality, before long something else began to happen. Men of different backgrounds and temperaments, thrown together in the inexorably close contacts of military life, reacted to one another in ways which were the real stuff of fiction; men who lived thus herded together for months or years on a bleak Pacific island provided fiction material at its best. And now this material began to arrive, thrown into story form by craftsmen who under the stress of war happily forgot they had ever been told that a story shouldn't have a plot. It began to look as if the short story were not a worn-out form after all: as if it still had new life in it, and could combine again within a small compass excitement, character, and subtlety. At the same time there seemed to be a corresponding new vitality in the stories written by women. We at *Harper's* were so delighted that we celebrated the apparent renaissance by often running three or four stories per issue instead of a mere one or two.

During the past year or two I have wondered whether this particular phase in the history of the American short story might not be approaching its end. Today the war stories have almost all been written; the drama of readjustment from military life to civilian life has been pretty thoroughly exploited; and the brilliant new talents which the war and the readjustment brought into the open have at least partly turned to the writing of novels and plays. Perhaps the short story renaissance is about over. And meanwhile the special audience which reads *Harper's* seems to be as intent as ever upon articles. Still our attempts to provide news and information and ideas and discussion bring us more readers and more visible prestige than our attempts to provide fiction, whether as art or as entertainment. And so we have got down again to an average of two stories a month.

Perhaps, as I suggested a moment ago, this may mean nothing more than that on the whole our editorial staff does better, temperamentally, at article-hunting than at fiction-hunting. Perhaps so many magazines today are policy ridden and therefore inhospitable to the serious discussion of ideas, which do not fit into any given pattern of policy, that we get a disproportionate number of effective articles from writers who wouldn't know where else to send them, whereas the market for good fiction is somewhat less restricted and we at *Harper's* thus find ourselves in direct competition for good fiction with other magazines which can pay more than we can. But I am inclined to think that there is a little more to it than that.

I am inclined to think that today the public which takes a definite and intelligent interest in short fiction of high quality is not very large. There is a tiny band of highbrows, distributed largely in our big cities and college towns, whose standards for fiction are so very special that they could not believe that any "commercial" magazine, or any magazine with a circulation larger than that of, say, the *Partisan Review*, could possibly produce much that would interest them. From this select group we derive no measurable support; if they write us at all, it is usually to excoriate us for our alleged disservices to culture, or possibly to ask whether we might be interested in a definitive critical essay on T. S. Eliot or Kafka. The professional writer who might hope to get support and encouragement from this group is likely to be disappointed, especially if he has the good fortune to be well paid for his work. There is another and much larger group of intelligent American readers who are intensely interested in public issues but either are indifferent to fiction or confine their fiction-reading to novels and/or detective stories. And there is of course another and much larger group who consume fiction, long and short, in considerable amounts but would be repelled by stories which do not have happy endings or which make undue demands upon their imagination; these people would scarcely be interested in *Harper's*, or in any other magazine which concerns itself primarily with quality.

I remember once being told by an exceptionally astute editor that he wondered whether a really great story might not be published in a leading magazine and win no acclaim at all, because nobody whose critical judgment would count for anything would happen to see it. That was in the days before Edward J. O'Brien began his indefatigable annual surveys, and before there was any O. Henry Prize. But in a sense this is still true, I believe; perhaps truer than it was then. For my guess is that since about 1930 we have been living in an era when most keen-minded readers, most men and women of sharp curiosity and discrimination, are interested primarily in facts and especially facts about public affairs; and that our magazines half-unconsciously shape themselves to this situation. The editor who thirty years ago dreamed of introducing a new genius in the art of literature is likely today to dream of introducing an article that will turn the course of history.

The world being in the state that it is today, this is probably just as well; the course of history needs considerable changing. But it means that the market for excellent short stories is not likely to become larger and more eager until a good many thousand intelligent readers decide that the thing that they want most to read is good short fiction, and that they will not only pay to get it, but will debate, criticize, and applaud it.

There will, I trust, always be a market for the story which combines high distinction with pace and excitement. There may also be a market for the story whose distinction is not combined with these other more marketable qualities. But if this goes on being true, it will be primarily because there are a good many editors whose enthusiasm for the best is so great that they are willing to publish it whether they have public encouragement or not. Today such public encouragement is lacking—and sorely needed.

27

On Science and Creative Art

WILLIAM L. LAURENCE

Born in Lithuania in 1888, William Laurence became an American citizen in 1913 and is now one of the country's top-ranking journalists in the scientific field. A free-lance writer and play adapter from 1921 to 1926, he has been a science news reporter for the *New York Times* since 1930 and was awarded the Pulitzer Prize in 1937 for reporting the Harvard Tercentenary Conference of Arts and Sciences held that year. He was the exclusive reporter of the discovery that uranium 235 held the key to utilization of atomic energy, and was selected by the heads of the atomic bomb project to visit secret war plants and to write a series of reports to be released following the use of the bomb on Japan. For this work he won the first annual award of the Society of Silurians for the best editorial staff achievement of 1945 by a New York City newspaperman. He is the author of: *Hypothesis for Use of Avidin in Malignancy* (1941) *Dawn Over Zero: The Story of the Atomic Bomb* (1946); and *Hell Bomb* (1951).

Science has always walked well in advance of daily living, usually with ordinary men feeling no concern about the gap. Suppose a scientist said the surface of the earth was round, not flat. The ground still felt flat enough beneath the common man's foot, flat enough for him to plow and sow, nor did he slip off any earth curve when he went after his mate. The cog wheels revolved slowly drawing men and their lives and their knowledge abreast of scientific discoveries.

Today the gap between science and the daily life of most men is far greater than ever before, and for the first time men are uneasy. The reverberations of the atom bomb have shaken them; in small, trivial ways the results of science in their daily living stir some curiosity, at times some fear. Men know the world is changing, however stubbornly they pretend to cling to old ways and ideas. They long to know more. The new knowledge which they need is technical and highly specialized, a matter of symbols, formulae, equations which are a foreign language requiring an interpreter.

Mr. Laurence's article is brilliant witness of his skill as such an interpreter. He shares the scientist's excitement in his conclusions and discoveries, and he translates the abstractions into meaning more intelligible to the average man. He has in many articles led the reader to glimpses of the new world.

Here in "On Science and Creative Art" he issues a challenge to creative writers. His premise, that nothing exists in the intellect which has not previously been experienced by the senses, is of course the basic principle of all art. His final paragraphs offer a stimulating and demanding future to the writer.

H. H.

On Science and Creative Art

THE first three days of the Harvard Tercentenary Conference on the Arts and Sciences, devoted as they were exclusively to higher mathematics, appeared on the surface as a newspaperman's no-man's land in which he dare not venture, yet to me personally it constituted a challenge I could not afford to ignore. Aware of the dictum that "mathematicians were the only ones privileged not to know what they were talking about," I entered Emerson Hall in the Harvard Yard, hallowed by memories of William James, Josiah Royce and George Santayana, with the air of one embarking on an adventure from which there may be no return, yet, as I took my seat in surroundings familiar to me since my undergraduate days, I could almost hear Santayana lecturing on that very same rostrum on Locke's concept of the origin of ideas. *"Nihil est in intellectu quod non antea fuerit in sensu,"* I could hear Santayana quote in his soft Latin voice. Nothing exists in the intellect that had not previously been experienced by the senses. If mathematicians did not know what they were talking about, it must be because they had forgotten that all intellectual activity, no matter how high the level, how abstruse the content, and how far from its origins, had its deep roots in sense perception, from which it must constantly draw its nourishment if it is to have any meaning as objective truth. The topmost leaves of a two-thousand-year-old Sequoia tree, if they had the capacity to think, I said to myself, may not have any inkling of the existence of the sturdy roots deep down in the moist soil several hundred feet below, but the very fact that the leaves had physical reality would most certainly be proof of the existence of the invisible roots that keep them alive through a long-distance system of suckling at nature's breast.

As I sat there listening without comprehension to one presentation after another by a number of the world's outstanding mathematicians, gaining a measure of satisfaction from my observation that many a face among the distinguished gathering of professionals in the field revealed varying degrees of bewilderment, I began composing in my mind my report to the lay world on my explorations in the intellectual jungle of higher mathematics, and the strange jabberwocklike beasts I had encountered therein. It was to be a tale of parallel lines that, according to non-Euclidian geometry, meet in infinity, and the adventures that befell them on the way before the climactic clinch in non-Euclidian space, after successfully eluding all the traps laid for them by monstrous Euclidian villains determined that no respectable parallel lines must ever meet. It was to be touch and go on two narrow parallel roads, all the way until their final escape from the conventional three-dimensional world of Euclidian space to the infinite stretches of Elysian fields in the blessed four-dimensional continuum. The major villain in the piece, disguised until the last minute as the friend of the young lovers, was to have been a creature named Square Root of Minus One, Einstein's mathematical symbol for the fourth dimension, alias Time, sworn enemy of man in general and of all young lovers in particular. And remembering the words of Royce in that very same Emerson Hall that "while the Good always triumphs, its triumph is always a tragic one," my tale of adventure in the mathematical wonderland was also to have its inevitable tragic ending. For a little consideration makes its obvious that parallel lines can retain their identity, and hence their very existence, only as long as they do not meet, namely, only as long as they remain in Euclidian three-dimensional space. Once they meet they are no longer parallel lines, and are thus "dead" in the real world as we know it, mere "ghosts" in the four-dimensional "hereafter."

I never did write that story, not because it did not fit into the accepted pattern of a "news" story, for I was confident then that my editors would have welcomed it as a tour de force affording the hurried and uninitiated newspaper reader a sniff of the rarefied atmosphere breathed by the dwellers in the fourth dimension. The reason it was not written either on that day in August 1936, or on the two succeeding days during which the invited scholars occupied themselves exclusively with higher mathematics, was that on each of the three days something more tangible, and hence more newsworthy, came along that required more immediate coverage. On that very first day, for example, Professor Edward Kasner, famed Columbia mathematician, came along with a solution, after 2,500 years of futile efforts by his predecessors, to the vexing problem of the horn angle, which, in case you don't know (as I didn't at the time), is the angle formed at the tip of a horn, or the juncture of any two curved lines. It appeared that this type of angle was a geometrical anarchist that refused to behave in the orderly and predictable manner of the nice, well-mannered straight-line angles. It had defied the efforts at solution by all the great geometers in history, including the great Newton himself, and it threatened to go down as one of the unsolved riddles of the cosmos, when along came genial Dr. Kasner (whose fascinating book, *Mathematics and the Imagination*, is hereby commended to all creative writers) and cleared up the mystery. That was "news," as the solution of any mystery always is, and, to add to the excitement, it turned out that the sum of the parts of a horn angle was greater than the whole. The story appeared with a double-column head on page one of the *Times* the following morning and marked the first time, to the best of my knowledge, that any story dealing with pure mathematics received such prominent display in any newspaper.

My second day of exploration in the intellectual jungle was a dilly. Perusal of the program and questioning of those in the know revealed that an epoch-making high-altitude flight in the upper mathematical stratosphere was to be made late that afternoon by one of the world's top-flight (no pun intended) mathematicians, the illustrious Joseph

Eli Cartan of the Sorbonne in Paris, who was to deliver an hour-long address, in French, on something he called "non-affine geometry." Never having heard before of even "affine" geometry, I naturally had no inkling of what "non-affine" geometry might be, and I became even more apprehensive on perusing the text of the lecture, which members of the Harvard mathematics faculty, aided by the French faculty, had gone to considerable pains to translate in advance. My best bet was the late Professor George D. Birkhoff, head of the Harvard mathematics faculty and one of the world's outstanding mathematicians, and so I called on him bright and early that morning for help.

"This is way over my head," I told him.

"It's over my head, too," came the startling reply.

Here, indeed, was a fine how-do-you-do. "There must be someone in this great galaxy who would know something about it," I protested.

"Perhaps Einstein would," he said, "but, unfortunately, he couldn't come. There are, however, two of his assistants here. Maybe they could help."

It was unthinkable to beard the lion himself, particularly since he spoke no English. So off we went in search of the two Einstein associates, who turned out to be two very amiable young men. They would be very glad, indeed, to help all they could, but could I wait at least two hours while they studied the text? Luckily, it was still several hours before my deadline and a few hours before the great Cartan was scheduled to deliver his paper. So we arranged to meet at Professor Birkhoff's office at three that afternoon.

At 2:45 Dr. Birkhoff called me on the telephone. "Sorry," he said, "they have just informed me that it is over their heads, too."

Here we were, non-affine geometry and I, the same two parallel lines that could not meet in three-dimensional space. The only hope left was to go to the great man himself at the close of his lecture at about 5:30, too close to the deadline for comfort. Professor Birkhoff, who by this time had himself become highly intrigued, offered his expert services as a Socratic midwife.

The old gentleman did his best to convince both Dr. Birkhoff and me that here at last was one mathematician who actually knew what he was talking about, but, at least as far as I was concerned, the more he talked the deeper I felt myself sinking into a nightmarish quagmire, with the Square Root of Minus One about to do me in. In desperation I decided on one simple question. The two pillars on which modern science rests are the relativity and the quantum theories. One deals with the cosmic forces operating within the universe at large, while the other deals with the forces holding together the nuclei of the atoms of which the universe is constituted. Yet between these two mighty pillars, supporting the whole structure of man's understanding of his world, there was a seemingly unbridgeable gulf that no one had succeeded in crossing, eluding the lifetime efforts of the master "universe-builder"—Einstein—and creating the anomalous situation in which the whole, and the parts of which it is composed, were, intellectually speaking, not interrelated, the sum total of the parts not making up the whole, while the whole could not be explained in terms of its parts. "Could it be," I asked in faltering French, "that Professor Cartan's non-affine geometry might provide the missing link between the relativity and quantum theories?"

"Oui!" said the great man with a light in his eye.

That *oui* was the tiny needle in the huge haystack I had been rummaging in all day. I must have startled the professor when, after a mumbled *"merci beaucoup,"* I made a dash for my typewriter. Here was "news" with a capital N. One of the world's greatest mathematicians had at last found the key for putting the Humpty-Dumpty of the cosmos together again. At last a universe in which the parts fitted into the whole, and the whole was understandable in terms of its parts. Before I became aware of it I had stretched that little *oui* into two columns and was well into the third, handing my copy to a relay of Western Union messengers in "takes," when one of the boys handed me a message from the editor in charge.

"Be less emotional and more factual," it read. "Send new lead!"

I handed the message to my wife, who knew of the hectic time I had had, and that all the "facts" I had to go on was just that one wee-bit of a *oui*. She roared and I joined her. I then wrote a "less emotional," though hardly more factual, lead paragraph, handed it to the messenger, and proceeded to finish the third column. It must have satisfied the editor, for he again played the story on page one, thereby establishing a record of two page-one stories on pure mathematics on two successive days. When I ran into Professor Cartan that morning in the Harvard Yard he was all smiles. "*Oui, oui!*" he beamed.

I dwell on these two episodes at length because they illustrate what is to my mind the most important fact in the writing of a scientific article. *Nihil est in intellectu quod non antea fuerit in sensu.* Since all intellectual activity, including the purest type, has its roots deep in the senses, it can be as dramatic and exciting, at times more so, as any activity arising from the senses, and requires the same approach and treatment as any other subject in the field of creative endeavor. To do so effectively one must always remember the roots buried deep in the senses nourishing the intellectual leaves and blossoms on top. It is not generally recognized that a concept in higher mathematics can be, and is, to those who understand it, as aesthetically satisfying, and as capable of producing an overwhelming emotional experience, as any musical composition, painting, drama, or any other form of creative expression. When Einstein completed the structure of his relativity theory, described by Bertrand Russell as "the greatest intellectual synthesis of all time," he was so emotionally overcome that he was confined to his bed with a fever for two weeks.

After I got over my first shock at my editor's message I realized that he had actually paid me a high compliment. If I could get emotional over a new development in higher mathematics and succeeded in conveying that emotional reaction to a hard-boiled editor interested in "factual" reporting, as, by the way, he should be, then I must have attained a measure of success in extending the reader's horizons by stimulating both his imagination and his intellect through the avenue of his emotions and his senses. Any writing on science that does not meet this primary objective misses the mark, as it fails to arouse the reader's interest.

Unfortunately, science writing today is still largely of the purely "factual" variety and it is bound to remain so until men and women with creative ability come to realize that in science, and the effect of science on society and the individual, and its vast implications for the future of man and his relationship to nature and to his fellows, lies a new rich continent for the exploration of the creative mind, just as the mythology of the ancient Greeks, the Christian theology of the Middle Ages, and the combination of the two during the Renaissance, served as the fountainheads for the poets, dramatists, sculptors, painters and architects of those Golden Ages in man's history. Olympus, Zeus, and the rest of the gods and goddesses were vitally real to Homer and the Greek dramatists, architects and sculptors, as were Heaven, Hell and Purgatory to Dante. Leonardo, Michelangelo, Raphael, and the builders of the Gothic cathedrals, as well as Shakespeare and Milton, were all at home in the world in which they lived and an intimate part of it, and this fact made it possible for them to interpret it and re-create it in their own image in the greatest creative outpourings of man's mind and spirit. In the eighteenth century, man worshiped Reason, and since he still had something to worship he still felt at home in his world, though somewhat ill at ease, haunted as he was by ghosts of the past. This left us the great legacy of the music and literature of the eighteenth century, the creative spirit of which, sparked by reason, found expression in the early part of the nineteenth through Beethoven and Heine, Shelley, Keats and Byron.

Then, some time in the middle of the nineteenth century, something happened. Man had lost his home, evicted, as it were, by the Landlord for nonpayment of rent or default on the mortgage. What happened was that science, a spark, smoldering through the ages ever since Prometheus, suddenly catching fire, had changed both the world and the dwellers therein, while the tenants kept on living in the delusion that they were still inhabiting a world that was no longer there, not realizing that what they imagined themselves to be were mere ghosts of a world of yesterday. In this respect man of today resembles the first land creatures as they first emerged from the sea, who very likely kept floundering along at first in the delusion that the world they lived in was made of water.

So we have had during the past century a literature and an art that reflected a dead world, and men attempting to breathe through gills and move with fins instead of walking erect in the sun. The results were at best glorious failures, of which James Joyce may be cited as the most tragic example. Here was a giant who, had he lived in another age, would no doubt have left works that would have ranked with the greatest of all time. His tragedy, the tragedy of all his contemporaries, was that the world he was most at home in (he was really not at home in any world) was a dead world of ghosts, a lost world of pagan mythology and medieval theology, superimposed by the naïve early eighteenth-century philosophy of Vico, according to which society repeatedly passed through four eternally recurring cycles, democracy always inevitably being followed by chaos and the "annihilisation of the etym." Had he really been at home in the world he lived in, a world profoundly transformed not only by man's ability "to shatter it to bits" but also to "remould it nearer to the heart's desire," he would have been able to create new Homeric epics that in themselves would have played a major role in fashioning the shape of that world still in the making, just as Leonardo and Dante, and all creative spirits throughout the ages, not only re-created their world but also shaped its course and profoundly influenced its destinies.

We are living in a new heroic age, greater than any of the past, and the reason that it has not yet produced a Homer, a Phidias, a Leonardo, is because our eyes are still turned backward. The age-old struggle of man against the gods is raging full force in a thousand laboratories throughout the land, and in other lands as well. Instead of one Olympus there is a range of much higher mountains on which the battle is going on, every laboratory a super-Olympus, on which the most formidable citadels of nature are being stormed by mortals, whose principal weapons are the naked intellect sparked by the vision of a new revelation. Here is the raw material for the Homers and Dantes of today and tomorrow, if they only became aware of it, instead of leaving the rich field to squatters and scavengers, comic strips, "astounding" fiction, and "factual" reporting in which the forest gets lost among the trees and fallen leaves.

I could cite scores of episodes of Homeric proportions from my own experience, did space permit, without even resorting to tales of the greatest epic of all time—the bringing into being of the Atomic Age—the raw materials for which one may find in *Dawn Over Zero*. There comes to mind, for example, the time I visited a laboratory where a group of young men—principals of a new Iliad—had erected two mighty towers, topped with two gigantic spheres of highly polished chromium steel, for smashing the atom with a force of millions of volts. The towers were so high that the only place that could house them was an abandoned hangar originally built for huge dirigibles. The success of the assault on the atomic citadel depended on the absolute spotlessness of the polished spheres. But then came a hitch on the new Olympus. A flock of pesky pigeons found the spheres a very desirable resting place, and every time the young scientists would get ready to fire their multimillion volt projectiles against the cosmic forces within the atom the pigeons would fire projectiles of an entirely different kind to befoul the works of man. Was it man against pigeons or man against the gods? Whatever it was, there was Homeric laughter and considerable of Dantesque Divine Comedy there for lasting literature.

Then there was the episode of the speck of dust that was blown in through the open window of Sir Alexander Fleming's laboratory, carrying on it the invisible mold that yielded penicillin, which gave, and still gives, life to countless millions; of the sick chicken from whose throat was isolated the organism that gave us streptomycin, the first effective drug against tuberculosis; of the chickens scratching in the litter on the henhouse floor, who brought to the surface a new substance that may increase manyfold the food supply for the world's hungry millions, as well as the long missing liver factor for keeping pernicious anemia under control. All these are bound to influence profoundly, directly and indirectly, the life of man on earth. Our new knowledge of nutrition, of the functioning of the glands, and of the aging process, is leading to the emergence of a new type of old-young men and women, younger in outlook, in personality, and in their emotional and intellectual capacity than men and women of corresponding ages in the recent past. All these are but forerunners of still greater things to come. The point of all this is that the creative mind should attune itself to the new world being created and to help in shaping it. The new world in the process of being born, and the new species of homo sapiens now in the process of evolution, needs a midwife.

I remember a conversation in 1945 with the Lutheran chaplain on Tinian, then our top-secret atomic-bomb base in the Marianas, following the bombing of Hiroshima and Nagasaki. I told him of an experiment I had seen in the laboratories of Dr. Oscar Riddle, of the Carnegie Institution of Washington, in which he first injected the hormone that produces milk in the breasts of nursing mothers into the bloodstream of starved virgin rats and then introduced newly hatched squabs into their cages. Instead of devouring the luscious meal placed before them, the starved virgin animals acted as tender foster mothers to the helpless creatures. Since the wild instinct to devour could thus be transformed into mother love by the injection of a chemical, I asked the chaplain, who had offered a fervent prayer for the success of the atomic bomb mission ("Most blasphemous thing I ever heard of!" Sir Henry Dale, Nobel laureate, said to me after reading my account of it in *Dawn Over Zero*) whether it would not be a good idea for the Church to call on biochemistry for a little assistance.

"Just think of it," I said, "the world might have been saved the most stupendous tragedy in its history if only someone could have persuaded Hitler's doctor to slip regular injections of mother-love hormone in his arm. And since nearly two thousand years of Christianity have failed to bring about the universal acceptance of the Golden Rule, it may be well to try to introduce Christianity by means of a shot in the arm. The world would then become one big brotherhood overnight!"

That this is not literally possible, from the purely scientific point of view, is because, unfortunately, there is not enough of the mother-love hormone (named prolactin) to go around. But it illustrates the fascinating, and terrifying, possibilities that science holds in store for the future, and provides a sample of the treasurehouse of material which the creative mind of today could fashion into works of art and literature that would in themselves help to shape the new world, and the new men and women in it, now in the process of becoming.

All the creative urges of man stem ultimately from the fact that he is by nature circumscribed by time and space. The greatest promise, as well as the greatest threat, that his scientific achievements hold for him spring from the very fact that he has now gained for the first time a large measure of control, greater than he ever had before, over the limitations of space and time. This he has achieved, on the one hand, by contracting space, through the airplane, radio, television, and such, which enable him to crowd into any given time an infinity of experiences that would have taken several lifetimes in earlier generations; and, on the other hand, by stretching time, through the lengthening of his lifespan as the result of new knowledge of fundamental living processes which is still snowballing. This could not help but produce profound psychological changes, radically affecting the personality of the individual and of the society in which he lives. If the supreme expression of art is to be man's spiritual relationship with nature and his fellow men, then he must inevitably learn to adapt himself, and make himself at home once more, in the new world he has fashioned. He must learn to readjust himself to the fact that the frames of reference in which he had lived, space and time, have undergone a profound change, in the course of which he has evolved, and is still evolving, into a new being, living in an entirely new frame of reference.

Having profoundly modified space and time, and become, in turn, modified by them, we are gradually evolving from three-dimensional, Euclidian beings into dwellers of the four-dimensional, non-Euclidian, space-time universe of Dr. Einstein. We are parallel lines approaching infinity. Those who make themselves at home in this new universe will be the Homers, Dantes, Leonardos and Michelangelos of tomorrow.

28

Article Writing

HENRY F. PRINGLE

After being graduated from Cornell University in 1920, Henry Pringle worked as a newspaper reporter for the *New York Sun,* the *New York Globe* and the *New York World*; became an associate editor of *The Outlook* in 1929 and, later, a professor of journalism at Columbia. Since 1927 he has been a free-lance article writer, contributing to the *American Mercury, The New Yorker, Collier's* and *Harper's,* and is the author of: *Alfred E. Smith, a Critical Study* (1927); *Big Frogs* (1928); *Industrial Explorers* (with Maurice Holland) (1928); *Theodore Roosevelt, a Biography* (1931); *The Life and Times of William Howard Taft* (1939); and was the winner of the Pulitzer Prize for biography in 1931.

Mr. Pringle agrees with Frederick Lewis Allen about the importance of the article in contemporary magazines. He calls articles "the backbone of today's magazines." Out of his wide successful experience as an article writer he offers advice so clear and practical that he may persuade some fiction writers who are gasping for survival to try their typewriters on this popular form of writing.

Mr. Pringle takes up the chief problems which perplex the writer who wishes to try articles and does not know how to begin. He also disposes effectively of the common fears and misconceptions which beset the novice. His article will help the would-be article writer to solve all his problems except the final two, which belong to the professional as well as to the amateur: first, finding good article ideas; and second, doing the work necessary to collect the material.

H. H.

Article Writing

THE essential stock-in-trade of the writer of magazine articles is ideas. If he has good ones, which does not mean that they must be sensational, editorial doors everywhere will swing open to him.

The reason is simple enough. Nearly all currently successful magazines have staff writers. In addition they usually buy regularly from a group of established free-lance writers. When an editor has an idea for an article he is likely to assign it to a member of his staff who is eating up the publishing company's substance by being on the weekly pay roll. At intervals, often because it is a special subject, the editor will hand an idea to one of his free-lance contributors.

Quite a lot is always being said about the slim chances of the young writer breaking into the big magazines—the so-called slicks. I honestly don't think this is true and I cite the experience of Samuel Lubell, who has written for most of them. Sam had just graduated from the journalism school at Columbia University and planned a trip around the country. He intended to finance it by writing pieces for the magazines and came to me with a list of suggested topics. Nearly all were excellent. As far as I can remember he sold all of them. And at the time when he started out he didn't know a single editor personally.

It is absurd to suggest, of course, that the young beginner will make a strike the first time he tries. But articles are the backbone of today's magazines, whatever my fiction friends may say. This is particularly true of the national weeklies. The *Saturday Evening Post* normally prints eight articles a week which means that four hundred subjects a year, not counting those which do not work out, must be dug up somewhere. *Collier's* runs about the same number.

Let's get rid of the notion at the start that the staff of any reputable magazine will steal an idea, from a beginner or anybody else. I have known only one editor who ever did so, and he is no longer in the business. The editors I know will invariably give a new writer a chance to develop an idea. The most careful records are kept to prevent misunderstandings. If the beginner fails and, at some later date, the same topic is presented by an established contributor, on the other hand, an editor may feel free to tell the veteran to go ahead.

Why does the beginner frequently fail? The principal reason is because he does not understand the difference between a newspaper feature story and a magazine piece. Any good reporter can do a feature in a day or two, including the writing. A magazine article takes weeks, even months sometimes, of laborious research. It probably involves travel. Then comes the job of reducing a staggering amount of material to five thousand words. But the author is, of course, paid in proportion; probably five hundred dollars to the beginner and anywhere up to three thousand dollars or more to regular contributors. For reasons I have never been able to comprehend writers are reluctant to disclose what they are paid. I would make a guess, though, that the average article price to an established writer would be $1,000 to $1,500.

The problem for the beginner is to learn where ideas can be found. The first thing to do is to make a very careful study of the magazines that look as though they might be possible markets. And I mean study. The novice should go to the nearest library and look at issues for at least a year back. He should critically examine the types of articles which have been printed, the way they are written and their length. I am inclined to think he will find that the articles in the big magazines do not differ very much. But he will also learn that some editors have prejudices against certain kinds of ideas—the travel or the historical article, for instance.

Where, then, to find ideas? They won't be uncovered just by wandering around with your eyes open, any more than exists the mythical reporter with a "nose for news" who chances up an alley just as a crime is perpetrated. The best way to get ideas for magazine articles is by reading such newspapers as the *New York Times* or the *New York Herald-Tribune*, especially the Sunday editions. Read the obscure items; many and many an idea has lurked in a stick or two of type. Read the columns on education and on the developments in the world of science. Scan carefully the dispatches from various parts of the country. Look for new personalities in the news.

The weekly news magazines as well as *The Nation* and the *New Republic* are fertile sources for ideas. Of particular value are the departments on education, science, religion and other subjects in *Time*. It is also a good notion to read technical journals, but this depends on whether the aspiring writer thinks he can handle scientific subjects. If he can make technical subjects vivid and clear to the lay reader he is fairly certain of a successful free-lance career. In this atomic age nearly all editors are receptive to scientific articles, and few writers handle them well. The same thing applies to medical science. Maxine Davis, to cite an example, writes a monthly article on medical topics for *Good Housekeeping*. Her work, because of its clarity, is in such demand that she frequently does a second medical piece, under a pseudonym, for another monthly.

The ambitious free-lance writer will do well to attend the newsreel theater, if such exists in his community, fairly regularly. Camera men roam the nation. They often shoot events which are ignored by the newspapers. Of particular value are the documentary films frequently shown; also the shots which have been turned on odd personalities in various sections of the country or which explain scientific developments.

An idea is not necessarily barred because it lacks the new or the fresh. To an increasing extent, happily, magazines are becoming interested in careful reappraisal and in purely historical subjects as well. *Holiday*, the new and extremely successful Curtis Publishing Company monthly, has printed articles on American cities and on such shrines as Mount Vernon which have been written about repeatedly. The *Saturday Evening Post* has bought pieces about the National Archives, the Court of Claims in Washington, the Empire Theater in New York, Philips Andover Academy in Massachusetts and Howard University. Its lengthy series on American cities has been a circulation puller which astonished the editors.

I'm willing to gamble that there is a magazine story in Grant's Tomb in New York, in the Kansas City, Missouri, war memorial and in the Alamo in Texas. The point is that the idea may be old, but the presentation of it must be fresh. That is where the long hours of digging come in. An article on an old subject must be so authoritative and so interesting that nobody will do a piece about it again for decades to come.

Today's magazines offer considerable variety in the kinds of articles which may be written. *Harper's* and the *Atlantic Monthly* are open to "think pieces" on the problems of the day. These monthlies, by the way, are exceedingly important to the beginner. He won't be paid much, probably three hundred dollars for a full-length article, but the magazines are read by nearly all editors. And they are, perhaps, a degree more willing to consider the work of the unknown writer.

The beginner would be wise to stay away from historical ideas for a time despite the fact, as I have said, that magazines are publishing more historical material. A fertile field is the personality piece. The greatly mourned old *American Mercury*, as it was brilliantly edited by H. L. Mencken, started a new vogue in the personality article. He made his authors be bitingly objective. *The New Yorker* profiles, equally honest, are so well known as to need no examination here. The subject of this kind of nonfiction is nearly always a national figure. But I think I can discern a trend away from this rule. So look for the unusual figure, it might be a politician or a merchant or a housewife, in your home town.

Travel articles are a good bet. The *National Geographic* clings to its ancient rule of permitting nothing unpleasant to be said, but other magazines will insist, as in the personality piece, on objectivity. It is no longer enough to describe Charleston, South Carolina, in terms of old houses, lavender and lace. The author must explain Charleston in terms of its economics and tell about its faults. Travel pieces, by the way, need not be about distant lands. Americans travel far more in their own country than abroad. Possible travel subjects might lie in some camping trip through the Rockies or in a voyage along the inland waterway to Florida.

Most magazines are interested in exposés. J. C. Furnas's vivid account of automobile accidents, *And Sudden Death*, was unquestionably the most successful article ever published by *The Reader's Digest*. *The Woman's Home Companion* has recently been running an exposé almost every month; on bad water supplies, insane asylums, abuse of nurses in hospital training schools and on other subjects regarding which the women's clubs of the nation might be stimulated to take some action. The beginning writer who digs up an idea for an exposé may find it his entering wedge to the big markets. But a word of caution is in order. He must have absolute proof of everything he writes. No magazine is going to risk a libel suit from the work of an unknown. Editors have trouble enough with suits which arise from so-called established authors.

So now you have an article idea—I hope—and you would like to know how to sell it. The free-lancer who lives within striking distance of New York or Philadelphia has an enormous advantage. Most editorial offices, but not all, are located in those two cities and the ultimate goal of the free-lancer is somehow to achieve personal contact with editors. Distance fom the eastern seaboard is a serious handicap, but it need not be fatal. Frank Taylor lives on the Pacific coast and yet is one of the most successful writers in the business.

Establishing personal contact with an editor will not be easy, at first. This will come without too much trouble after the first article has been sold. But how to sell that first piece? The best plan is to expand your idea into a brief outline—about a page of typewriting. Select the magazine to which it is best suited and then mail it to the editor whose name you know, of course. Or do you? It is on the magazine's mast head. It is permissible to send three or four idea outlines at the same time, if you have that many good ones. But never, never write a story in full—I refer to nonfiction obviously—and peddle it around. To do so stamps the author as an amateur. Besides, you have no way of knowing whether the magazine does not have somebody else already at work on the subject.

I wish I could tell you that all editors will give you a quick answer. The Authors Guild has been working on this problem for a long time without much progress. Some editors are prompt, with the staff of the *Saturday Evening Post* as the best example. Others, unfortunately, are slow. So the beginner will do well to submit ideas which are not too timely. Occasionally a free-lance writer with a timely idea makes the mistake of submitting it in duplicate to a number of magazines at the same time. But this can lead only to trouble. The possibility exists that two editors will accept it, and then what is he to do? Editors will not, incidentally, give a specific order for an article. This rule applies, with few exceptions, to the veteran just as much as to the new writer. About the most that can be hoped for is a letter saying "your idea is promising; we would be glad to see the article."

The best way to sell articles is, of course, through personal interviews with the editor. Such talks, as I have suggested, will come in time. By means of them ideas can be examined carefully. Often some rather completely different article will emerge as a result of them. Then there is the agent. The young writer will have trouble finding an agent who will handle his stuff. But it is decidedly to his advantage if he can get a reputable agent. No agent who asks more than 10 percent as commission is honest.

This is not a treatise on writing. I am assuming that anybody who wants to make a living through magazine articles can write literate, simple English. But maybe a hint or two will be of some value. When an editor has said that an idea has possibilities, the first thing to do is to read everything that has already been written on the subject. Consult the Guide to Periodical Literature, going back at least ten years. Skim through the index to the *New York Times*. From such sources can be found the people it is necessary to interview. A personality article may require talks with as many as 50 people who know your victim, who are either fond of him or dislike him. In addition you must read all the books, speeches and statements—if any—that he has made.

If I may offer a final scrap of advice, it is that the man or woman starting a free-lance career should have some other source of income for the first year or two. I am certain that more incipient careers have been ruined because of financial worries than for any other reason. If the rent, the baby's supper or payments on the mortgage depend on selling a specific article—then, in all likelihood, the article will bounce back. I don't know why this is so. Perhaps the writer is so worried over the outcome that he does not do a good job.

So have a regular source of income.

29

The Ghost Talks

THE GHOST

Here is a real inside-the-inside story—How to Be a Ghost, by a factual, funny, and lifelike wraith. It has always been this editor's opinion that ghost writing is not as bad as it's cracked up to be; that, for instance, vast audiences have been spared hours of unspeakable boredom because political ghosts have worked on a great man's speeches. But never before has the positive value of the ghost-writers' profession been explained so simply: it is through the ghost that the great gift of knowledge which the inarticulate have for the world can be made available.

The role of scribe for the illiterate was long an honored profession. The ghost writers have gone a step further and become co-ordinators, coherence-inducers and organizers of the wealth of wisdom stored up in the memories of people who have all kinds of talents except that for words. More power to them! For the world needs all the knowledge it can get.

E. J.

The Ghost Talks

A WRITER who is a part-time Ghost has a hard time keeping shady. Let out the merest hint that you have been ghosting and there follows a barrage of inquiry,

"How can you write another man's book for him? Who has the ideas? Who pays you, the man or the publisher? If he can't write, how do you get anything out of him?"

"It's all a matter of picking his brains," I reply, which is sufficiently ghoulish to be satisfactory. "I pick 'em and then chew on what I find until it begins to take form."

"I don't get it."

"Well, suppose a great engineer wants to write about the time he mined diamonds in South Africa. I know little of diamonds and nothing of South Africa. So I ask questions for hours and hours and listen while he answers. When I can get no more I go away and try to put what I have into outline. The outline is full of gaps. I hie me to the library and read about diamonds and South Africa and fill in as many of the gaps as I can. Then I take the outline to him and he answers more questions. I try to persuade him to write something, anything, under such of the chapter headings as I have been able to make. If he cannot write at all, we *talk* the book over chapter by chapter and I take notes and write the chapters later. As each chapter comes to life I get him to read it. He is full of contradictions and suggestions. I make notes of them, tear the chapter to pieces, get them all in and write it all over again. After some months of this he may have a book."

"It sounds fascinating." The queer part of it is that it *is* fascinating, no end. Before I became a Ghost I had an idea it would be the dullest kind of work. I was a *Writer*. I had notions of my own, and thought highly of them. After I had ghosted a bit I found that I had added new worlds to my experience, worlds I hadn't even dreamed of. They were not *my* worlds, but I had been a part of them for a time, and I reveled in them. To dig stories of those new worlds out of reluctant, inhibited minds that wanted to bring them into the open, but just couldn't, was absorbing. Those people hadn't the foggiest notion of how to get their stories into words and how to mold and knead and spank those words into shape so that they could appear on a printed page and so convey the story to others. That power was mine and as a Ghost I have haunted my employers with a right good will, determined to extract the last iota of golden material and so add glory to the finished story. Secret glory for me. Hardly a man or woman who wants a name on a book is willing to share any of the kudos that come after publication.

There is just one kind of Writer who becomes a Ghost, that is the Writer who needs cash. There are two kinds of people who employ Ghosts, those successful enough to have some cash and the vested rich who have always had cash. The dull years of the depression found many able and well known Writers hard up and panicky. At the same time people with money who had stories in their systems, shared the panic by wanting to see their stories in print before the whole world went to pieces. They scurried to Publishers and told their stories. Publishers sent for Writers who might be willing to be Ghosts, for cash, from either the Publisher or the would-be storyteller. In the little band of Writer-Ghosts I know, one Ghost has given this would-be storyteller a fitting title which most of us have secretly adopted. He is our *Mummy*! Encased within himself he carries a precious jewel of a yarn, never to be brought to the light of day unless an explorer breaks in.

Add to the Mummies, who cannot write, a second kind of Ghost employer. He is a *Writer* who is so popular he cannot fill the orders he receives and so engages Ghosts to do a part of the work for him. This bird is fairly rare. But when you hear of a man who is on the radio daily, television occasionally, writes a couple of magazine articles a month, gets out some movies, and about a book a year, you can be certain that in the background are Ghosts who assist him. An unusual Ghost, who haunts a little world all his own, specializes in popular clergymen. A preacher has a tough job trying to write and deliver fifty to a hundred sermons a year, plus parish visits. But books by popular preachers sell well. This Ghost has done six of them for five different preachers. He also helps out with speeches and sermons. The books are successful but the Ghost has never seen his name in print. I asked him why he did not strike out for himself. He shrugged his shoulders.

"My subject is philosophy. At thirty-two I am still too young to hope to get anywhere with that. These dignitaries I work for have names. For years they have spoken with authority. When I came out of college I might have starved if I had not become a Ghost. After the first book it was easy and I ate regularly. Now I am saving money."

That the ghosted book is a living lie seems to trouble no one, Ghost, Mummy, or the reading public. From the Pharaohs on, ghosting has a long and dishonorable history. Several of Julius Caesar's secretaries acted as his Ghosts. One of them is credited with the deathless *Veni, Vidi, Vici.* Seneca wrote Nero's speeches. Washington's *Farewell Address* is supposed to be the work of Alexander Hamilton; Mark Twain is said to have written *The Autobiography of Ulysses S. Grant.* Franklin Delano Roosevelt's first *Fireside Chat* was reported to be the work of Arthur Ballantine. After the death of Frank Harris, Frank Scully printed a "confession" which seemed to prove that the biography of G. Bernard Shaw which carries Harris's name on the title page, was written by Scully. Babe Ruth and Paul Whiteman, Queen Marie of Rumania, Charles Lindbergh, all popular idols for a time, used Ghosts. The Roosevelt administration developed the biggest flock of Ghosts ever seen in Washington, D.C., which has always had a large Ghost population. It took three men to write Harry Hopkins' little book *Spending to Save.* Charley Michelson, miracle writer, ghosted John Garner, Joe Robinson, Pat Harrison, and at least once, General Hugh Johnson.

Three thousand miles across country from Washington lies the second Ghost stronghold, Hollywood. Practically all articles signed by movie stars are the work of Ghosts. I have acted as Shade to a number of the most luminous. It took Hollywood to develop a Ghost of a Ghost. Lola, a lovely star of the first magnitude, suddenly developed literary ambitions. She and her publicity woman Miss V., came east and signed up for Lola's life story in ten installments at $1,500 each. On the way back Miss V. fell to calculating. Lola had asked her to ghost the series for half the money. Miss V. realized that she was already working sixteen hours a day so she asked Lola if she as a Ghost might have a Ghost working for her. Lola did not care. She had tired of the whole thing. As soon as she got back she quarreled with her husband, who was also her producer and manager, and fell in love with a new and handsome actor just arrived from Europe. She would have shunted the series altogether only she wanted the money to buy the new man a nice car. With infinite labor the two Ghosts got together the first four articles and sent them east. The producer-husband was used to Lola's fancies but he became aware that this last one looked serious. The fifth number of the series would begin his romance with Lola and it would be awkward if it should come out after she eloped. So he staged a scene. He had the mail watched and when the double check for Lola and Miss V. arrived he burst in on them, denied having sanctioned the articles, accused Miss V. of taking double pay and threatened to publicize the whole affair unless Miss V. returned three thousand dollars within twenty-four hours. Lola wept and so did Miss V. The husband vanished. Lola rose, wiped her mascara daintily and patted Miss V.

"Don't you worry, dear. I'll see you stay paid for your hard work. K. will just have to wait for his car. I'll get the money." And get it she did. On the morrow the astounded husband-producer received a check for three thousand dollars from Miss V., together with her resignation, and Lola's lawyers served him with papers in a suit for divorce. The articles stopped, Lola gave both Ghosts a bonus. K. never got his car. By the time Lola got her divorce there was another man. The public was then reading four articles signed by Lola written by the Ghost of a Ghost. It sounds, and is, crazy. But the public must be a bit crazy, too. Readers want to be just as intimate as they can with their gods, be they prizefighters, ball players, politicians or actors. Readers do not like double signatures; every attempt to put them over as a general practice, has failed. Readers want to believe that they are enjoying just what their idols wrote, in an intimacy as close as they can achieve. And readers get what they want.

They are the only people satisfied with results. For the relation between Ghost and Mummy is a trying one and becomes increasingly strained as the work progresses. This is deep stuff and it would take a psychiatrist to analyze it. You start out, all enthusiasm, to act as Ghost to a particular Mummy. And as you write you get yourself on every page. The Mummy reads and knows that something is wrong, although he does not realize that he is seeing you in the book and not himself. So he begins to fret about your pet words and phrases, which somehow have crept in. You take them all out and replace them with his—although they are not nearly as good—which appeases him somewhat. You begin to feel sorry for him because he is obviously having such a hard time, and in schoolteacher fashion you fall to praising all the good things he brings to you. That has an excellent effect and you pile it on. You try to tune in with your Mummy, reminding yourself that you are his interpreter and that you are not writing a book of your own. Many times you are guiltily conscious that you have come to regard the book as yours, which keeps your work at its best, but is hard on your Mummy. You know quite well that as an ethical Ghost you must be prepared to outdo Voltaire.

"I do not agree with a single word you say, but I will defend to the death your right to say it," is a noble sentiment. But a Ghost does much more than defend what he disagrees with. He *says* it—for his Mummy of course—and *he painstakingly says it in the way he believes his Mummy would say it if the Mummy were articulate.* The Ghost is a freer of speech and a liberator of thought. Farther than this no man can go.

By the time two thirds of the book is complete the Ghost becomes honestly confused as to which parts are his and which are the Mummy's. Fortunately the Mummy is still more confused, which is a tribute to the good work of the Ghost—but which has its perils. For from this time on the Mummy believes that he has done almost all the work—the Ghost didn't know a word about the matter until he was called in—and the Mummy wants to get rid of the Ghost. Many a book is broken off at this crisis and a few of them are never finished. If a Ghost is wise he prepares for this contingency by getting a signed contract with his Mummy before he begins. Even then he has to fight it out and there is hell to pay.

One Mummy of mine is a man of great distinction and many honors, a man accustomed to having his own way. He tried to go on without me and got stuck. At last he wired me and I flew out to his summer home. He was in a terrific emotional state, pitying himself one minute, and in a rage the next. I told him frankly that he was incapable of completing the book alone, and he ordered me to clear out.

"See here," I said. "Unless you call the police, I stay. You have begun a fine book. I've worked hard on it. Yes, I know I've been paid, but there is more than money to this game. I believe in what we have done and I am going to stick it out."

He turned purple and yelled,

"But this is MY book."

"It might be," I agreed, "but it isn't a book yet. And if you send me off it never will be." He flung out of the house and was gone for hours. When he came back I handed him some chapters I had gone over and we got to work. The book sells well. He and I are friends—I hope for life.

Public interest in health has increased to the point where doctors rush to engage Ghosts to do books and articles for them. Ghosts are agreed that the material is great stuff but that doctors are the most disagreeable of all Mummies. The contempt a medico feels for a layman is deeper than any well. Four doctors with whom I worked laughed at my mistakes in technical matters, sneered at me and in the main treated me as feebleminded. Doctors are spoiled. They lay down the law to their patients without fear of contradiction. They have no idea how to delegate work and they are fiercely jealous of all credit. In a Ghost-Mummy collaboration the Mummy is really the patient and the Ghost the technical expert. But no doctor I ever worked with believed that.

Businessmen are much easier on the ghostly system. The chief trouble with them is that they have no idea how much time writing takes and they become impatient before it is all over and want to call it off. One of my assignments was the life history of a railroad president who had won his spurs in a day when might meant right. He roared with laughter as he told a yarn of early days. A rival road had laid tracks on a disputed right of way. He and his gang stole there by night, ripped up the tracks and laid their own. The rivals came just as the job was done and a free-for-all fight ensued in which he and his gang won. The coveted way is still in possession of his road. When he saw the tale in print he got cold feet.

"See here. The X magazine engaged you to do this. How much will they pay you?"

"Six hundred an article." His eyes popped.

"You mean to say you pump me and they pay six hundred a story—why you pirate. You buccaneer!"

"There's the little matter of putting the stories into writing," I retorted. "And you should feel flattered by the price. I am supposed to be good. As for piracy and buccaneering, well let's read over that last chapter." He chuckled.

"You must be good. You win. I was going to buy you off. But you cost too much. Come on, I guess I can stand it." And he was game to the end.

Male Mummies outnumber female ones by a big margin. Actresses, society women and wives of great men are the main females, and all of them are hard to keep at work. I took on a job for one western society woman in her seventies who would drop off to sleep without notice, even while being interviewed. That hundred and ten pound old lady was sheer grit. She forced herself to work and while she was at it she worked hard. But she was suspicious lest I steal her stuff. Every day I was called to meet visiting relatives and friends who asked question after question. They were unanimous in believing that the book stood no chance of being published and that I was just a gyp. I stayed in the old lady's home a month and we did the rest by mail. In time the book was published and she became a prophet with honor in her home town and state. I am sure that no other investment of the two thousand dollars she paid me, plus expenses, could have brought her so much joy and satisfaction. Some of the money came back to her in royalties, how much I never knew.

Ghosting seems a sexless job, for Ghosts of both sexes work for Mummies of either. Male actors from Europe or Central or South America usually demand female Ghosts. One well-known female Ghost reeled into my apartment gasping,

"A drink and quick." She never drinks when working and she is a temperate person at all times. When I supplied the necessary she was holding her head in both hands.

"I've got to do the life of D——— that young Austrian star. I've been with him four hours. That boy is under thirty, and according to him Casanova is a piker. D——— strings along women like beads on an endless chain. He has been insisting upon telling me ALL to minute details. And he expects that to get into print! When I argued that carnal moments did not appear in print in this country, at least in the lives of movie stars, he was outraged.

"'Vat,' he roared. 'I cannot tell how I make luf? But people want to know how I make luf! They come to see me make luf!' All afternoon I've been swimming in the deep purple. And the Producer and of course the Johnston office want a nice, clean, romantic story."

"Maybe he wanted to add you to his bead chain?" She grinned.

"He can't be very particular, but I am too fastidious. No I'll just have to make him a model of chivalry." And he was, when the story appeared. In all probability he never read it.

How much money does a Ghost make? Magazines pay from $50 to $1500 for ghosted articles signed by Mummies. A book brings five hundred to five thousand dollars sometimes paid by the publisher, but more often by the Mummy who retains all rights to the book. There is a general idea that Mummies want to be Writers. They do not. They want the prestige and acclaim that come to Writers. No Mummy would face the years of drudgery a writer lives through before he attains a moderate success. Mummies have been successful at something. As authors they expect to begin where they stand—at the top. They are willing to pay someone to do the dirty work for them; they are used to paying for that. The Ghost must charge them for his time, his ability and his experience. And a written contract is his only protection. If the Mummy wants bargain rates the Ghost can refer him to one of the Ghosting Bureaus or Associations. Recently the morning papers reported the arrest of the head of one of these organizations. The arrest was the result of a plant. A police official, in disguise, had applied for a thesis, price five hundred dollars, to be done in a hurry. When the thesis was turned over the Ghost was arrested as a violator of a state law that makes writing a thesis for a college student an offense. The case has not been settled. Meanwhile the practice of Ghosting theses goes right on. One man boasts that he makes ten thousand a year out of college students. His charges run from ten dollars for a short paper to seven hundred dollars for a Ph.D. thesis. Another Ghost haunt claims that it has two hundred professional writers on call. The manager acts as middleman. He refuses nothing, even a paper to be read at an afternoon woman's club.

Any Ghost worth his salt will turn down a book he is unfitted to write. A prosperous manufacturer in the textile business brought me a gangster story. He said frankly that he wanted the prestige of being a writer and was willing to pay for it. I read the yarn. It had a good plot but action and dialogue were impossible. I have no gangster vocabulary so I turned him over to a fellow Ghost who finished the book.

Last year I turned down ten offers to be a partner in a book venture with half-royalties as payment. Usually a Ghost demands a down payment of five hundred dollars or more and a percentage of the royalties. It takes a year or longer to write most books, more months before publication and another half-year after the book appears before the first royalties are paid, a long, long time to wait—for another fellow. Your own work is a different story. Ghosting on a cash basis means payment at once, often as weekly income, and many a writer has used the cash to tide him over while he has completed his half-finished book.

As a Ghost I ask neither gratitude nor appreciation. But no Mummy can stop me from feeling a pride in a jewel of a yarn I have dug out of him. I know that some of the books I have ghosted are as good as my own and one is much better. It does not worry me that my name has never been connected with that book. Nor does it concern me that it will never be connected with this article. When I Ghost, I Ghost and when I write on my own I am a Writer. And if I did sign this I would never get another Ghosting job!

30

Poetry at the Mid-Century

BABETTE DEUTSCH

Babette Deutsch has written a number of novels and juveniles and has edited and translated *Modern Russian Poetry* (1921); *Contemporary German Poetry* (1923); *Russian Poetry* (1927); *The Steel Flea by Leskov* (1943), all with her husband; and *Crocodile* by K. Chukovsky (1931); as well as poems of Pushkin and Rilke. But her major work is as a poet. In 1929 she was awarded the National Poetry Prize and, in 1941, the Julia Ellsworth Ford Foundation Prize. Her poetical works include: *Banners* (1919); *Honey out of the Rock* (1925); *Fire for the Night* (1930); *Epistle to Prometheus* (1931); *One Part Love* (1939); *Take Them, Stranger* (1944); and *Animal, Vegetable, Mineral* (1954).

In this nadir of poetic repute, when the only verse that most people read from one year's end to the next is what appears on greeting cards, it is well for us to stop and consider our poets. There are not many of them. There never have been, but in the past, as Babette Deutsch reminds us, they have sometimes had to be limited by law and weeded out by examinations, so popular has the profession been. It is not such measures that thin the ranks of the poets today, but sheer economic necessity. For no one who could possibly bear to do anything else would involve himself in the thankless job of whittling out unread verses nowadays. There's no percentage in it, as they say. Thus, though we do not have many poets, we certainly have more than we deserve, for we deserve none at all.

It is ourselves that we are hurting by our stupidity and ignorance of poetry, much more than the poets. Poets are the leaven in the lump of civilization. But our sodden and lumpish society prefers to lie unleavened and unchanged by the ferment of poetry. Poets like Babette Deutsch and those she celebrates here will go on writing; they can't help it, though the silence about them will kill some of them. But what of us who exist in that silence? Are we going to begin to listen? Or are our ears and our minds dead already?

E. J.

Poetry at the Mid-Century

WHEN the lights of Europe were hidden under the bushel of medieval scholasticism, China was living in the glow of a golden age. The arts flourished, and the writing of poetry was high among them. Indeed, it was part of the training of every government official. The few who attained the highest posts were those who, having passed an examination held at the palace, became members of the Imperial Academy, which was known as the Forest of Pencils. We have, of course, got beyond all that, and no such requirements are made of the men who head our congressional committees, or even of the President and the members of his cabinet.

In a period reputedly blinder than the Dark Ages, in a misty island north of Europe, the druid bards were subjected to even more rigorous training than the Chinese officials of the T'ang dynasty, and were held in yet greater honor. The bard who was poet and philosopher, as distinguished from the one associated with the law giver or with the priest, spent twelve years getting instruction in the elements of poetry, and when he was ordained received the right to wear a mantle of crimson bird feathers and to carry a golden branch as his wand of office, being next to the king in power. It is refreshing to realize that no such tiresome training, ending in absurd ceremonies and unmerited deference, is accorded the contemporary poet. As one recently and supremely distinguished by the receipt of the Nobel Prize observed, ". . . fools' approval stings, and honour stains." Poets today are not largely subject to these stings, nor need they go far out of their way to avoid such stains. Their lot is rather that described by a half-literate boy who died in a charity hospital:

I live in an age where the age lives alone,
And lonesome doth it rage
Where the bard dare not come.

Samuel Greenberg, whose mother tongue was Yiddish, seems to have had a tenuous spiritual kinship with another God-intoxicated Jew, but Greenberg got drunk on the dictionary. He received posthumous recognition, having involuntarily contributed to the work of a contemporary who also died young. But this poet, Hart Crane, even more deeply stricken by the raging lonesomeness of the age, committed suicide.

Crane's major work, "The Bridge," was an attempt to compose the Great American Epic, and, in a different way, as superb a failure as Ezra Pound's unfinished "Cantos." The poem, which runs to fifty pages, is in effect a more ecstatic, far more ambitious and ambiguous version of Whitman's well-known lines on "Crossing Brooklyn Ferry." Not the least interest of Crane's work is the devoirs that it pays to the chief Ancestors of American poetry. If one excepts Melville, who wrote his greatest poem in prose, these were Walt Whitman, Edgar Allan Poe, and Emily Dickinson. During their lifetime two of them were abused and all of them neglected. Yet within the present century the diverse influences of these three, moving however coyly and deviously, have become part of the substance of American writing.

To a large extent, the poetic renaissance that coincided roughly with World War I might have been taken as a response to Whitman's challenge to the "poets to come":

Not to-day is to justify me and answer what I am for,
But you, a new brood, native, athletic, continental, greater than before known,
Arouse! for you must justify me.

Whitman's delight in what he called the divine average, and in the rich variety of the American scene, his hurrah for positive science, were the fiber of the work of those who explored the landscape and the folkways north of Boston, in the neighborhood of Spoon River, on the Chicago streets and the western prairies. His free strophes, his discovery upon the peaks of the Rockies of the law of his own poems were later to be echoed in the more savage attestations to cosmic consciousness of Robinson Jeffers. All this is clear enough. But, astonishingly, when the Battle of Imagism was no mere footnote to literary history, its major general was making a pact with Whitman. He had detested him, but came to him now, he said, as might a grown child to a pig-headed father. "It was you that broke the new wood," said Pound to Walt. "Now is a time for carving." It was not more than three years ago that Eliot, who has several times publicly acknowledged his immense debt to Pound, first spoke respectfully of Whitman. Yet without Whitman's pioneer work in extending the subject matter of poetry to include the details of urban and industrial life, and in liberating verse and vocabulary, it is doubtful if the more careful craftsmen of a latter generation could have carved out the "Cantos" and "The Waste Land." It has even been suggested that poets seemingly as remote from Whitman in their approach as Marianne Moore and e e cummings would not have achieved, the one, her meticulous notations on small reptiles, large mammals, and delicate museum pieces, the other, his idiosyncratic evocations of grasshoppers and locomotives, if they had never known *Leaves of Grass*.

When Emily Dickinson was asked if she knew Whitman, she replied that she had not read his book, but that she had heard it was disgraceful. One imagines that if she had read it, she might have responded as did the Victorian Jesuit poet, Gerard Manley Hopkins, who reluctantly admitted that he knew Whitman's mind to be more like his own than that of any other living man, a pity, because the American was a blackguard. Miss Dickinson's intense concern for the unique and the particular, her thrifty accuracy, have nothing Whitmanesque about them. Yet her use of metaphors taken from the kitchen and the law courts, even more than her dreadless delight in the natural world, bespeaks her kinship with the disgraceful, the blackguardly man. Both were forerunners of those compatriots who returned poetry to its roots in common experience and the language of daily converse. But Miss Dickinson was able to view that experience and to use that language with a fine sense of irony, a fact that places such penetrating young practitioners as Elizabeth Bishop and Jean Garrigue in direct line of descent from the witty recluse of Amherst.

If Whitman's all-embracing celebration of these states fostered regionalist poetry, and if Miss Dickinson's work was exemplary for its concentration on particulars as pointers to general truths, then that most loyal of Americans, William Carlos Williams, carries a dual inheritance. He is pre-eminently the poet of his neighborhood: the suburbs of the eastern seaboard. And he has always been alert to what might be called the Thinginess of things. There is about his work no trace of moldy sentiment. He writes what presents itself to him immediately, a piece of green glass among cinders, the gay pompoms on his wife's new bedroom slippers, an old woman greedily munching plums from a paper bag, a tree, a dish mop, a sea lion. Above all, he gets at the essence of reality as apprehended not *behind* but *by means of* the phenomenon. He has, too, an ear for the speech of his time and place as sharp as any American's, not excluding Frost.

One of the chief themes in his long, yet uncompleted poem, "Patterson," is the difficulty of finding a language in which to formulate experience. That of science is too abstract and bloodless. Common speech has been devitalized in another way by the highest paid publicity man and the lowest paid English teacher, as well as by the creators of those sad pages known as comics. Where will the poet find a language? Williams gives an answer that harks back to the cry of the imagists for directness, concreteness, and economy: "Say it, no ideas but in things." To get the full weight of this is to know what St. Augustine meant when he spoke of the world as God's poem, "arranged, as it were, by an eloquence not of words but of things."

But the poet's job is, after all, to translate God's poem (or is it the Fiend's?) into words. For those who look back to Poe, the words must be chosen to give pleasure rather than to exhibit truth, but an indefinite pleasure, of which the inextricable element is music. The effect of Poe's theories on the poetry of his compatriots was as powerful as it was slow and indirect. As Whitman discovered in the wild grandeur of nature the law of his own poems, so Baudelaire found in the works of Poe the unachieved creations of his own brain. Baudelaire himself is the acknowledged father of French symbolism, of which one of the chief representatives was Mallarmé, who has had some small effect on modern poetry in English. In "Little Gidding," the fourth and last of Eliot's *Quartets*, there is a passage in which the poet addresses a stranger encountered on the street in "the waning dusk" before dawn, a stranger in whose features he catches the look of "some dead master" half-recalled, being "Both one and many." The identity of this mysterious "compound ghost" is never clearly revealed. He seems to have about him something of the Provençal troubadour, Arnaut Daniel, something of Dante, but, unmistakably, he is one with Mallarmé. Upon being questioned, he says to the Anglo-American poet that

> . . . our concern was speech and speech impelled us
> To purify the dialect of the tribe . . .

In the poem that Mallarmé entitled "*Le Tombeau de Edgar Poe*" he spoke of Poe as one who sought, in the phrase that Eliot translates: "*Donner un sens plus pur aux mots de la tribu.*"

The labor of purification did not, however, involve clarification, or did so only in a very special sense. Poe and Baudelaire, Mallarmé and the author of the *Quartets*, all alike have given us suggestive poetry, incantatory poetry, based on the logic not of the intellect but of the emotions, poetry in which what Eliot calls the "auditory imagination" is darkly yet evocatively at work. There are, of course, as Edmund Wilson long ago pointed out, at least two groups of symbolists: the serious-aesthetic and the conversational-ironic. The former, following Poe's lead, were concerned with giving musical expression to an ineffable reality guessed behind appearances; the latter, witty and ironic, tried to present the aura of the transient moment. This second group was particularly congenial to a generation that enjoyed the conversational and ironic lyrics of John Donne, with whom, one fancies, Miss Dickinson too would have felt an affinity.

Irony was an acceptable weapon to those returning from no-man's land after World War I to the Waste Land that was their world. Yet, as Hart Crane felt, after "this perfection of death" the only motion possible was one of resurrection. Curiously enough, it came during an economic disaster of such proportions that it took on the aspect of what is euphemistically called an act of God. There sprang up a younger generation of poets (already, alas, they are going grey) who joyfully summoned and aggressively embraced the Muse of Marx. But their transports were soon interrupted and silenced by the Spanish dress rehearsal for World War II, the petrifaction of the Russian revolution into a hideous caricature of its promise, the war itself, and the moral bankruptcy that everywhere accompanied it. Poets who had neither been diverted by revolutionary utopias nor muted by Gorgonheaded revolutions continued to write in the styles to which they had accustomed their small public. (Who, except the poets, reads poetry?)

Allen Tate went on with his lapidary work of polishing the dark crystals of his lyrics. John Crowe Ransom carefully winnowed his exquisite thin sheaf. Their disciples issued small, often privately printed, volumes. So too did the fastidious blue guitarist, Wallace Stevens. Cummings parenthetically damned the unworld of notpeople while singing wonderful 1 x 1 with the voice of a surprised child. Frost, when he was not rewriting Scripture in the sly idiom of New England, was making more tender and equally homely lyrics. Pound, even after incarceration in his Pisan prison, kept on with the "Cantos." The poet who began with "Preludes" about lonely men in shirt sleeves composed *Quartets* about first and last things. Until a few days before his death, just when Barcelona fell, William Butler Yeats, to whom all poets writing in English owe an incalculable debt, went on with the heroic work of trying to hold in one thought reality and justice.

The poets were among the first to realize the hollowness of a world in which love is made to seem as standardized as plumbing, and death is actually a mechanized industry (we can get it for you wholesale). They felt increasingly the want of a view of the universe that would enable them to give an order to experience. The hunger for myth, which makes such ordering possible, is as real as physical famine, and the poet who lacks a unifying faith or philosophy seems compelled to search for or to build one. Yeats created such a construct, a *Vision* that had all the faults of a homemade thing, but that stood him in good stead. Lesser poets, among them the virtuoso whom America got from England in exchange for Eliot, and the latest and finest poet of his name: Robert Lowell, have run to the maternal arms of the Church. Others, including such pithy lyricists as the Canadian, Patrick Anderson, and the Scotchman who prefers to be known by his pseudonym, Hugh McDiarmid, have accepted, though apparently on their own terms, the Communist faith. Poets as different in background and performance as the aristocrat, Edith Sitwell, who seems to envision herself as another Ceres, and the wild Welshman, Dylan Thomas, whose dreams are those of a half-pagan, half-Christianized Freudian, have alike come to a religious affirmation of a sunlit world where sense and spirit dance together.

An American poet who, while a shrewd critic of Auden, has learned much from his technique, wrote an *Essay on Rime* in loose couplets that have something to say on this subject. Having discussed the confusions in prosody and in language that beset the contemporary poet, the *Essay* takes up the confusion in belief of which he is the victim. As a matter of fact, the confusions are related. In the first part of his *Essay* Karl Shapiro remarked that

> The measure of prosody is the current speech,
> The cadences inherent in the voice
> Of one particular generation.

In the second part he acknowledged that "The great survive the idiom of their time." At the close he asked desperately at what point in the history of art such a cleavage had existed between poet and audience. It is a problem that haunts the poet, as even the most obscure among them attest. Wallace Stevens affirms that

> The poem goes from the poet's gibberish to
> The gibberish of the vulgate and back again.

But he is himself too much the sensuous arbiter elegantiarum or the abstruse aesthetician to say much to the vulgus. Similarly, Eliot exalts the poem in which every phrase and every sentence is right, and every word at home:

> The common word exact without vulgarity,
> The formal word precise but not pedantic . . .

But in an earlier, more explicit and most moving passage he speaks of having had twenty years, "Twenty years largely wasted . . . Trying to learn to use words," and dwells dismally on the poet's

> . . . fight to recover what has been lost
> And found and lost again and again: and now, under conditions
> That seem unpropitious.

Williams, more acutely conscious of the inarticulate many of and for whom, if not to whom, he writes, laments those who die incommunicado, and cries out again: "the language . . . the language!" And Dylan Thomas, in a like mood, declares that it is "Not for ambition or bread" or "the proud man apart" or

. . . the towering dead
With their nightingales and psalms

that he exercises his craft or sullen art,

But for the lovers, their arms
Round the griefs of the ages,
Who pay no praise or wages
Nor heed my craft or art.

It is not astonishing that in this lonesomely raging age, when civilization is closer to barbarism than it has ever been, the poet frankly writes for those who will not listen but who alone could understand him. For, like the lover, he is a person unable to reconcile what he knows with what he feels. His peculiarity is that he is under a certain compulsion to do so. And he is apt to turn his bewilderment over the estate of man into rather bewildering poetry. Even those who are capable of the religious exaltation that so many seek are stricken by a more than antarctic cold, the Cold "in the heart of Man." The poet looks at the world with something of the fascinated terror that Poe felt for machinery. Miss Dickinson observed mechanical progress with a child's delighted wonder. Whitman differed from both in expecting it to prove man's deliverer. If that was a mistaken intuition, it is because we have failed to use with respect to the practical life what the impractical poet lives by—imagination.

But science and poetry are not so far apart as they seem. Some years ago the mathematician, Henri Poincaré, pointed out that science moves toward unity and simplicity: it seems to move toward variety and complication. This is true of poetry. It imposes on writer and reader alike the task of living imaginatively. There is none more difficult, as the Chinese emperors and the druid kings once knew. There is at this moment no task more necessary. And there is no greater joy.

31

On the Teaching of Poetry

LEONORA SPEYER

Leonora Speyer (Mrs. Edgar Speyer) was born in Washington, D.C. After a successful career as concert violinist, she turned to poetry. With her second book, *Fiddler's Farewell* (1926), she won the Pulitzer award. *Naked Heel* followed in 1931 and *Slow Wall* in 1936. The latter work, expanded to include a section of new poems, was reissued in 1946 by Alfred A. Knopf, Inc., a firm that published her three previous books.

Mrs. Speyer is a member of Phi Beta Kappa (honorary) of William and Mary College. For two terms (1932-34) she served as president of the Poetry Society of America; she was also an honorary vice-president of this society and was awarded its gold medal in 1955. Until a few years before her death in 1956, Mrs. Speyer conducted classes in verse writing and literary criticism at Columbia University.

Leonora Speyer, gracious and distinguished poet, for a number of years taught the writing of poetry at Columbia University, conducting at first one, and then two workshops. There are people—critics, occasional writers, members of the public at large—who insist that writing cannot be taught. Usually they refer to fiction, slurring classes in story writing and books on the novel. Any kind of creative writing. They probably include poetry as one of the unteachables. Let them listen to Leonora Speyer as she talks of her experience with these groups of men and women who wish to write poetry. She shares with them her knowledge of the craft of poetry, her wisdom, her quickened response to all poetry, and her own sensitive skill. Like Robert Frost, she is "not a teacher, but an awakener," and her students are fortunate.

H. H.

On the Teaching of Poetry

A LEARNED man, Sir Herbert Grierson, once said to me, "There is too much talking about poetry, too much theorizing. Poetry suffers from the mere approach of prose; the more it is discussed, the more it is robbed of its magic," adding mournfully, "and no one, probably, has talked about it more than I have." And yet, it must be talked about, thought about, and discussed, if we are to read it with true understanding and delight, and certainly if we are to write it or teach it. For it is an art, and like all arts it must be learned. (I think it is unpremeditated only to the lark.)

I am sometimes asked with a fine irony, "What—can you teach poetry?" My answer to that, and rather tartly given, is that I cannot teach the student talent, no amount of study will contrive a talent, that being God's affair; but having the gift, "through Grace," as John Masefield says, it must be developed, the art must be learned. To quote Siegfried Sassoon, "A man may be a born poet, but he has to make himself an artist as well. He must master the instrument."

The actual process of poetry writing, the knowledge of the forms and patterns, the terms, the play, the infinite devices; the traditions; the immense variety of words, their world of synonyms, their color, harmony, counterpoint; in fact, the English language, prosody, imposing and enthralling; these can indeed be, must be, learned. What Alice Meynell calls "The Laws of Verse"—

> Dear Laws, be wings to me!
> The feather merely floats, O be it heard
> Through weight of life—the skylark's gravity—
> That I am not a feather, but a bird!

—learn the laws! Once mastered, free yourself from their too trammeling influences, by all means; stray from them as often as you please, but know *where* to stray, and *how*. The written word: someone, surely a poet, though his name is not remembered, wrote this, centuries ago:

> The written word
> Should be clean as bone,
> Clear as light,
> Firm as stone.
> Two words are not
> As good as one.

(The eloquent implication!) Of course you can teach, and learn, poetry. Yeats studied all his life. What a lesson is in that significant comment of his:

> I said a line will take us hours maybe,
> Yet if it does not seem a moment's thought,
> The stitching and unstitching has been naught.

There is not much stitching and unstitching in some of the hasty and cocksure writing of today. I advised a friend, "You ought to work over that poem, perhaps rewrite it entirely." "I know," he replied, rather dolefully, "but I might be writing a new poem while I was mulling over this one." I believe in "mulling over" a poem; in "stitching and unstitching." Edward Arlington Robinson once told me it had taken him three years to get a certain sonnet "into shape." (That master of the sonnet.) "How shall I learn to know what to write about?" a student once asked me. "How indeed?" was my not very illuminating reply. Elizabeth Drew's reflection is more satisfactory: "How poetry comes to the poet is a mystery." And I remember Kahlil Gibran telling me, "I do not write my poems. They write me."

Robert Frost declared to a class of students, "I am not a teacher, but an awakener." And speaking of metaphors, he observed, "I would be willing to throw away everything else for metaphor," and he added, "I do not think anybody ever knows the use of metaphor unless he has been properly educated in poetry."

It is eight years since I was suddenly and rather agitatedly called to the telephone by Audrey Wurdemann, Joseph Auslander's wife. Joe lay with a broken leg. Would I take charge of his poetry class at Columbia for the rest of the semester, the while Joe mended? Little did I surmise, foresee, what that small, if intimidating, act of service to a friend would mean in my life. For Joseph, healed and nimble again, betook himself shortly after to the Library of Congress at Washington, and I more or less automatically inherited the class. There was little that was automatic about it, unless the exhilaration of a congenial job, much work, and ardor ever increasing can be thus described; and a class increasing in size and poetic fluency. Oh, yes, and decidedly, I found that one "could teach poetry."

How? That is another question I am frequently asked. How do I conduct my "Poet's Workshop"—for this engaging little nickname became its more or less official title, finding its way to the Registrar's Office and the registration slips required by the applicants to my class.

The Workshop really seems to conduct itself, together with the active co-operation of student and teacher—and that magic other thing, the "bequest of wings," as only Emily herself could name it, the study of verse. The poems of my students are first read, marked, learned, and inwardly digested, by me; then read aloud and discussed in class. Perhaps the criticism of a sonnet will lead to a fuller talk on sonnet writing, and the reading of a group of poems in that exalted form, to illustrate a point—and how more poignantly and convincingly? The room is hushed as the poems of the class are read—how intent is every listener—and I am reminded of a group of medical students gathered around an operating table. The decision of the scalpel is not more important, it would seem, than the word concerning the welfare of the poem. "I repeat," says Siegfried Sassoon, "without clarified construction and technical control, no poetical communication can be effective."

The Laws of Verse. And after the laws are fairly mastered, if they ever are, what then? Perhaps not much. Surely something. If nothing else, a clearer and a happier sense of what verse really is; and why. The perception of the more equipped surges forward; the less receptive, the humbler, will nevertheless be the richer in understanding; the poetry lover will love it the more, accepting in time the mournful fact that poetry writing is not for him or her. And that indeed is something. There are thousands of boys and girls learning to play a beloved chosen musical instrument. Few of them will attain the concert platform. All of them are well aware of why the eminent artist is justly eminent. They will appreciate every triumphant note; they *know* that sonata; they have played it themselves. The student of verse will be closer to the poem, will appreciate more intimately and deeply the ineffable line. He also senses, a little wistfully perhaps, why the sonnet he is reading is the imperishable thing it is; he has studied verse writing, he has written sonnets himself.

Nor is it necessary, in my class, to bring a poem (or a sheaf of poems) each week—although they usually do. I urge a rewritten, better-written poem in preference to a newer one, on the principle of there being more rejoicing in heaven over a poem that repenteth; I recommend the "mulling over;" and I tell my listeners of a remark of Padraic Colum's: "Do not let your poem walk too soon on the page, lest it get bandy legs." There are too many bowlegged poems running about. Nor, when I pronounce a poem "good," does it signify that it is ready for the editorial staff of a leading magazine. It only means that it is excellent class work and that I am pleased. Occasionally I ask for a copy of the poem, "to keep." This is considered a distinction, and I intend it to be. The Workshop is a lighthearted and slightly unpredictable little group, though none the less earnest and diligent. One bright young man brings me an apple and lays it genially on my desk. Another asks "where the rose is," it being my habit to pin on a flower.

"The architecture of verse," as Louis Untermeyer calls it, is studied and stressed: patterns, forms, rhythms; rhyme and its many variations, and how the expert poet employs, and enjoys, these; the French and the Italian forms and how they are used in English. "Death to the adjective!" cried Robert Louis Stevenson, meaning of course its *over*-use, one of the more blatant faults of the inexperienced writer. "Nouns and verbs are almost pure metal," is the wise comment of Marie Gilchrist; "adjectives are cheaper ore," she adds. (And adverbs, I insist, that adjective of the verb.) But the adjective can be pure metal too, and I recall a few; Yeats's "man's own resinous heart," Browning's "flash of the brush," the "mild and magnificent eye" of Wordsworth, and Dorothy Wellesley's donkey's "immoderate ears;" Keats's "alien corn," Marvell's "curious peach."

There is so much to talk about in the Workshop, punctuation and grammar become impassioned, spelling seems a graceful thing; to be exact has naught to do with pedantry or dogma, surely, nor the stern exclusion of inversion and other tenets and characteristics of old "poetic" language—what I call the *"ah me!* school." I often bring a new poet to class, I mean, his "slender volume," or a forgotten, too long-neglected, older poet. Or I bring an anthology, for a brief glimpse into the hearts, the flights, of a group of poets. I believe in anthologies, although I know they offer only a glimpse. And we read the published letters of poets, always absorbing, often revealing as regards their own verse; and sometimes I bring edifying and witty reviews, and books of poetic criticism written by brilliant contemporary men and women of letters. I quote from them—I quote a good deal in my talks—I have sought to suppress the tendency in these pages (more or less successfully); indeed I admit I do like to call upon my radiant cloud of witnesses to back me up, saying the thing I would say, and saying it so much more eloquently. And I urge my class to *read* more verse both classic and modern; I believe they do read some of the books we have nibbled at together—I see them making copious notes—and I tell them of one exceedingly prolific young poet who remarked loftily that "he hadn't time to read—he *wrote*:" having admitted with complete detachment that he did not recall the author of "Dover Beach," which had somehow loomed into the conversation. "I *write*," he repeated, that being his contribution toward literature—and sufficient. "So did the other fellow," was the succinct comment of a bespectacled little man standing by.

The obscure versus the profound, the cliché and the overrare word, clarity as opposed to the commonplace. Aristotle said it, so long ago—but I refrain, though with difficulty, from quoting his superb summing up of this highly controversial topic, seething apparently among the poets of his far day, as in ours. And the class writes its poems; sometimes really writes! I do not praise inordinately, but I do not think that too severe comment is good teaching. I remember what that master-pedagogue, Leopold Auer, once said to me: "Do not send a pupil away discouraged. Break the violin over his head! Tear his music to shreds! But send him away saying, 'I was bad today, yes; but I will be good next lesson!' That is teaching." A friend tells me of a happening in his English class at Harvard. "Barlow," remarks Professor L———, "you have written a pretty good poem—a *pretty* good poem" —Barlow sits up—"but remember, Barlow, always remember, that a pretty good poem is like a pretty good egg."

On the Teaching of Poetry

What is this impelling thing, this force, that is bringing so many hundreds of the returning service men to the universities, to the classes of English? They flock to Columbia. They have invaded my quiet little corner, my Workshop runneth over—I have two workshops now. They "started writing," these young men tell me, at the front; in the jungles, on the beaches, during the night watches on ships. In hospitals. A great deal of what they bring me is only emotional release, what I call "private poems," but some of it is more. Occasionally I am startled to find among the welter of words a fire smoldering, a true flame. And none of it is "ivory tower" verse. These men are writing about something they were living. Bleeding. And I am glad to be close to it, involved in it. And how serenely they take my criticism, not all of it indulgent. They do not seem to mind. They know what they are writing about, at least what they are writing about, at least what they want to say. One Seabee, after quite a dressing-down, looks at me with positive admiration. "Gee," he remarks, as if to himself, "that's *swell.*" And I am curiously abashed; he has lived the poem, I can only suggest how he can tell it—a little more glibly. And I remember a story of a poet-friend: she had been reading some verses of the pretty-good-egg variety; she had been too kind to the quivering young author at her side. "I couldn't tell him," she whispered to me in a corner, "it would be like stepping on a kitten." (Beloved Rose O'Neill.) But these kittens are very tough, very resilient. I have never felt a bone give away; their nine lives are all of nine in the classroom. They can take it. And profit by it. And so, it occurs to me, can I.

Swinging from my strap in the subway, returning from Columbia, books slithering from my grasp, I reflect: "What wondrous life is this I lead! Ripe apples drop about my head . . ." "What did that woman say?" a girl swaying next to me asks her friend. "Something about apples—" and they look at me . . . well, poetry is meant to be read aloud.

32

A Ballad of Anthologies

PHYLLIS McGINLEY

A former copy writer for an advertising agency and an assistant editor of *Town and Country*, Phyllis McGinley is primarily known as a writer of verse, much of which is printed in *The New Yorker*, the *Saturday Evening Post*, *Atlantic Monthly*, and the *Saturday Review of Literature*. Collections of her verse include: *On the Contrary* (1934); *One More Manhattan* (1937); *Pocketful of Wry* (1940); *Husbands are Difficult* (1941); *Stones from a Glass House* (1946); *The Plain Princess* (1945); *A Short Walk from the Station* (1951); and *Love Letters of Phyllis McGinley* (1954).

Any comment on the little gem of art which follows would be superfluous. The editors wish to point out, however (this being in some sort an anthology), that the only name on the royalty sheets from Harpers for this volume is that of the Authors Guild. As long as mixed grills and combination salads are popular, anthologies will undoubtedly continue in favor. But O, authors! Heed Miss McGinley, the poet's aged father, and the Anthology Committee of the Authors Guild! Get your name down for a hunk of royalties and not for a flat fee when that flattering offer comes to immortalize your work in a new edition of the Greatest Short Anecdotes on Life, Love, Baseball and the French Horn, edited by Fritto Misto, published by the Ephemerides Press. Or you'll be sorry.

E. J.

A Ballad of Anthologies

An urchin at his father's knee
  Sat scribbling on his slate,
And "Dearest father," quavered he,
"When I grow up I long to be
  A writer, rich and great."
That parent gently laid his hand
  Upon the curly head,
And in a voice of deep command
  He sorrowfully said:

"Oh, shun, lad, the life of an author.
  It's nothing but worry and waste.
Avoid that utensil,
The laboring pencil,
  And pick up the scissors and paste.
For authors wear hand-me-down suits, lad;
  Their cuffs, they are frayed at the wrist.
But castles and riches
And custom-made britches
  Belong to the anthologist,
My boy,
  Await on the anthologist."

"Now, father dear," the youth replied,
  "Mere wealth, I am above it.
It is the reputation wide,
The playwright's pomp, the poet's pride,
  That eagerly I covet."
Then wrath lit up his elder's face,
  And in an accent burning

He shouted, "From your mind erase
  Such vain creative yearning!

"You'd better compile a collection
  Of words that another has wrote.
It's the shears and the glue
Which will compensate you
  And fashion a person of note.
For poets have common companions.
  Their fame is a wraith in the mist.
But the critics all quarrel
To garland with laurel
  The brow of the anthologist,
My son,
  The brow of the anthologist."

Years passed. To heed, that urchin failed,
  What his papa had hinted.
Not thinking what the act entailed,
To magazines his lines he mailed
  And often got them printed.
But when reviewers passed him by
  For books he'd helped adorn,
"I wish I'd listened," he would sigh,
  "When father used to warn:

"'Oh, shun, lad, the life of an author.
  It's a road unrewarding and vile.
For the miracle's wrought
With a mucilage pot
  And a feasible reference file.
Forever that Ode on the Urn, sir,
  Has headed the publishers' list.
But the name isn't Keats
On the royalty sheets
  That go out to the anthologist,
My lad,
  The sedulous anthologist.'"

33

Writing for the Screen

NIVEN BUSCH

Former associate editor of *Time Magazine* and *The New Yorker,* Niven Busch is now primarily active as a novelist and screen writer, and has worked with Warner Brothers, 20th-Century Fox, Goldwyn, Paramount and Universal Studios. In 1937, he was nominated for the Academy of Motion Picture Arts and Sciences award for the best original screen play, *In Old Chicago.* His published works include: *Twenty-One Americans* (1930); *The Carrington Incident* (1941); *Duel in the Sun* (1944); *They Dream of Home* (1944); *Day of the Conquerors* (1946); *Furies* (1948); *Hate Merchant* (1952); and *Actor* (1955).

Mr. Busch has tackled two questions which would naturally come first in the inquiring mind of anyone who wished to write for the screen or anyone who hoped to find good entertainment in a motion picture theater. The first question comes from hopeful writers and concerns technique. How does writing for the screen differ from story or novel writing? Mr. Busch sums up the visual and objective requirements of screen writing forcefully enough to convince the would-be writer that he must learn a new way of looking at his material. Mr. Busch also suggests an increasing flexibility in the use of the camera which has promise for future experimenting.

The second question may come from writers as well as from motion picture audiences. What's happening in Hollywood, what kind of pictures are we going to have next year and the years after? That question Mr. Busch answers with a summary of present difficulties. He ends with more hope than shines through the quoted advertisement of a screen writer.

H. H.

Writing for the Screen

"I DIDN'T know that there was any writing to it," the lady said, "I thought that they just acted out a story. You mean you write the words they say?"

After all, screen actors and actresses are national idols—gods, in fact, to many. Why should some shoddy interloper be called in to concoct the words that pour from their lips so naturally and movingly? What in heck do they need writers for?

Maybe we'd better not go too far with that. It might turn out that they don't need writers and I would get myself into hot water with the Screen Writers Guild, too many of whose members are unemployed. For the moment let's assume that writers are needed, or at any rate that they are customarily involved in film making—an assumption which will enable me to get on with describing what they are supposed to do, including but not restricted to the job of putting down "the words they say . . ."

Basically, writing for the screen is a simple craft. To qualify for it you don't need much in the way of aptitude, ambition, or education, but you do require a minor physical replacement. You trade your brain for an eye. Behind this, locked in synchronized sprockets turned by electricity, shrouded in darkness and lit with a soft changing flow of images, is your new brain—a nitro cellulose emulsion, sensitive to light. This whole contrivance—magazines, blimp, lens, and operating parts—is known as the camera head. It corresponds roughly to your own head, and will correspond to it as long as you continue to practice your new trade. Underneath the head is a mechanical neck of gears balanced on a tripod in such a way that by a slight manual adjustment, eye and brain sweep up or down or left and right, a process known as "panning." When required there is also a carriage and a set of tracks collectively known as a dolly by means of which you—as the new organ that is now part of you—can roll up close to the most intimate movements in the lives of people.

For the moment, you are static—a restrictive situation for a writer, but one which we will modify later. Modify; not remove. Though you can only write *what shows*, this flat, objective point of view which irritates you now will later prove to be a source of strength. Instead of confining you it will give you freedom; it will provide the area for your greatest victories. Just as you are part camera man, the camera man is also part writer; he will bring to your concoctions a shading and perhaps even a substance which you never foresaw. Yes, he is part writer and so is the director, so are the players and the heads of the technical departments. These people are now your collaborators. You will learn to set high value on their work. Without them you could not function, for picture making is first and foremost a community operation.

So now you have an eye, a brain, a new neck and a set of wheels. What are you going to do with all this equipment? Sir, you are going to do with it everything that a man of talent can accomplish in his library, blessed with pen and ink and a few sheets of paper and entirely without the elaborate and expensive handicap which you have just acquired. And yet, in spite of the handicap you soon will soar with Pegasus, you will thunder with Homer and squeak with Mickey Mouse—for look, a miracle has happened. Your eye, your head, and the army of skilled craftsmen now enlisted in your service have supplied you with powers of presentation surpassing those of the greatest pen-and-ink writers that ever lived. Do you want a race horse in your story? Tolstoy did well enough with Count Vronsky's steeplechaser in *Anna Karenina*; you can do better. No need to tell about the animal's height, weight, and conformation—his silky coat, his tapering bones, his eager spirit. Only mention him, and there he is before you, in the flesh or its convincing simulacrum, a real horse, complete and alive. Do you want to take the audience to King Arthur's court? Just write "*Interior Main Hall, the Palace*"—and you've done it, down to the last heraldic traceries. What else? A battleship? I think of Marcus Goodrich's wonderful portrait of the ship *Delilah* on page one, chapter one of the book bearing that title.

> She was very slim and light. She was always tense, often atremble, and never failed to give the impression of a mass of almost terrible power wrapped in a thin and fragile blue-grey skin . . .

and so forth, for three hundred words of nautical description as fine as anything in modern literature. Before me is a script adapted from the book—someday, I hope, to be produced. Mr. Goodrich's introduction of his heroine has been boiled down to seven words which will, I assure you, fill the bill quite amply:

LONG SHOT—DESTROYER steaming through the waves.

Very well then. A burden of description has been lifted from you. You no longer have to tell what things look like. Perhaps you have spent twenty years learning how to bear this burden with distinction: no matter. You are well rid of it. But before you get too happy about this, let me advise you that in compensation for this minor relief you have bound yourself to a major obligation: you still have to *characterize.* The importance of your task in this department has doubled, while the instruments for performing it have been reduced in number. Remember, you have only an eye; you cannot pop inside the heads of your *dramatis personae.* Your pen is gone and you are naked and alone: even your new collaborators, the technical departments that can sometimes do so much, are powerless to help you now. What are you going to do?

This brings us to a definition, helpful in all fields of craftsmanship but a must in writing for the screen: CHARACTER IS ACTION. I must add hastily that the term action is not what we have come to accept in the other crafts, where the slight forward pressure of a story pattern is enough to hold the interest. In motion pictures action is greatly compressed and hence stepped up to a potentiality far higher than in the short story, the novel, or the spoken drama. Part of this compression comes from time—the foreshortening imposed by the eighty-five to one-hundred-minute length of the standard commercial feature picture. Because experience has proved that it is dangerous, except in the rarest instances, to tamper with this length, most screen writers load their nerves with a time chart in terms of film and pages: eight reels to a finished job, at eleven minutes per reel. They seldom have to consult this chart; the phantom reel spins in their heads as they write and when the tied end comes loose from the spool they find that the script is finished and that it is between 120 and 130 pages long.

The more story that must pass through our ninety-minute bottleneck, the greater the compression. But there is another, less substantial but equally potent factor in action compression, namely, the nerves of audiences. All audiences, to be sure, are not the same in their conditioning; they differ in different states and countries; the audiences in Europe, for instance, still being in a retarded or lethargic era of development, permit a more leisured story technique. Alfred Hitchcock illustrates this difference with a story about clouds. In Europe, he says, a director using clouds to establish a mood has a good deal of license. He can dissolve from one cloud formation to another and even a third without resistance from the spectators. In the United States, the audience will hold still for one shot. If a second is used, it is no good unless a plane appears. For Shot Number Three the plane has to burst into flames.

Very well. With time and high-tension nerves compressing your narratives, there is no opportunity for the ordinary character-building devices used by novelists and short-story writers. The problem of making people come alive must be solved on the run. What is your current problem on a job of work? Have you, let's say, a grifter in a city railroad station, to be established in a flick of film? This grifter, in the next twelve seconds of film, has to meet the star, Miss Ginger Rogers, and the ensuing scene falls flat unless you know what manner of man he is; a bustling aspirant to petty larceny, keeping himself in coffee and shoeshines by preying on the innocence of travelers. You have no time for stream-of-consciousness—no film to spare for a capsule biography, documentary research, or expositional scenes in which two other people talk about this hombre. Instead, you make him tell about himself by means of a piece of business. First, you start him moving toward Miss Rogers. He has to pass a line of telephone booths and as he strolls along he reaches out and without stopping sticks his finger in the coin slot of each. By the time he has reached the end of his walk and the start of his scene he has adequately been pigeon-holed as a man who will reach for a dollar or any part of that sum.

Charles Brackett and Billy Wilder, who won an Academy Award for their version of Jim Cain's *Double Indemnity*, had the grifter problem

I've described in a picture called *The Major and The Minor*, and they handled it in the manner outlined. At the time they made the picture the two men were functioning as screen writers and also, respectively, as producer and director of their own productions and it would have been within the power of either, for example, to inject an idea which had never been written in the script. However, unless a writer finds himself in the same fortunate situation, he had better see to it that the script contains everything he is able to contribute to the picture, without dependence on the talents of those who will work on it later (except as contributors to its pictorial values, as described earlier). He can't always be sure of getting a director who will add values—most writers feel they are doing all right if the director doesn't take anything away—nor are all producers gifted with creative talent nor all technicians inspired with the ingenuity for instance, of the famous Chinese camera man, James Wong Howe, who, to photograph the prize-fight sequences in the John Garfield picture *Body and Soul*, got in the ring and worked with a hand-held Eymo camera while he circled around the actors on roller skates.

I've mentioned the wonders that can be brought out by studio research, set design, and prop departments. Such wonders, again, are pictorial. Where historical research, to use an example, affects the plotting or characterizations of a story, a writer must stand on his own. He must also keep his fists up and obey the referee's instruction to protect himself at all times. As an illustration of the hazards to be run in this direction, there is the sad case of the professor who had been seduced from a faculty chair in history to become technical adviser on a 20th-Century Fox film of which the central character was Cardinal Richelieu. An outline of the story had already been prepared and when he read it the historian became perturbed. He complained to studio Boss Darryl Zanuck that the actions of the Cardinal as depicted in the script did not check with recorded fact. Mr. Zanuck expressed another point of view.

"You have to remember that as far as the audience is concerned, Richelieu is Rasputin!"

We've been considering the treatment of objective surfaces. Conditions become altered when the eye-brain becomes a brain-eye and exercises its capacity for subjective as well as objective portrayal. For instance, the writer can call for a deliberate distortion in the photography of objects or people when such distortion is convenient to present the point of view of a single observer who is drunk or injured or under some powerful stress. Again, the camera itself can become a character with the other characters speaking directly into it, shrinking from it, even making love to it, or aiming shots at it—as in the picture *Lady of the Lake* directed by Robert Montgomery. In this tour de force, a mystery-melodrama, Mr. Montgomery enacted one of the principal roles; his voice was used on the sound track to describe the action, yet he himself was not seen by the audience, having been replaced by the camera. Another means of turning the eye-brain inward is by "indirect narration": a character relates the story in the first person, making a sound track which will be used in the film in conjunction with a silent depiction of the action described, thus putting the audience inside the nervous system of the person telling the tale.

All in all, with the possible exception of music and epic poetry, the cinema provides as much freedom for the creator as any other known medium of expression; every year its technical limitations are whittled down, approaching a foreseeable moment when they will be nonexistent.

The forces inhibiting a writer for the screen are not inherent in the medium itself but are brought to bear upon him through economic and sociological channels: particularly censorship, and the present high cost of film making.

Personally, I feel that the first is the lesser of the two evils. In every age all artists have been limited by censorship of some kind or another, if only by the unwritten mores of their periods. Novels and plays are censored by public opinion, by fashion, and at times by the rulings of magistrates and of the post office department. With more money at stake, motion picture producers have to know at the outset whether or not their product will be judged fit for public acceptance. Most of them would rather abide by the censorship code of the Motion Picture Producers Association than risk having their creations cut to pieces by state censor boards. Only the long-haired zealot of art with a capital A, or the professional social rebel, can object to a reasonable propriety in treating sex, crime and those special subjects which, crudely exploited, can touch off racial and political hatreds.

Far more damaging to film craftsmen are minority groups which stand forever ready to pounce on Hollywood and its product for offenses perceptible only to the group in question, and whose influence, although not great, is just enough to make timid producers knuckle under. How much the protests of such groups can mean in the aggregate and to what limits of exasperation they can drive a writer may be seen from an advertisement printed a year ago in the *Screen Writer*, a trade journal once published by the Screen Writers Guild, and recently read into the record at *Life's* Round Table on Hollywood:

> WANTED, An Idea: Established writer would like a good uptodate idea for a motion picture which avoids politics, sex, religion, divorce, double beds, drugs, disease, poverty, liquor, senators, bankers, wealth, cigarettes, Congress, race, economics, art, death, crime, childbirth and accidents (whether by airplane or public carrier); also the villian must not be an American, European, South American, African, Asiatic, Australian, New Zealander or Eskimo. Noncontroversial even amongst critics, if possible. No dogs allowed. Apply P.O. Box 13, Patton, Calif.

In *Life's* report on the meeting at which this was read, I find the note "at this point there was laughter . . ."

Laughing at censorship is an old Hollywood custom but there's no laughter at all among film pundits when they discuss the real bottleneck of their business: the matter of costs.

For the last two years Hollywood has been fighting a losing battle for economic survival, the alibis for defeat being:

(1) Loss of European markets.
(2) Competition of television.
(3) Bad pictures, with consequent loss of audience revenue.
(4) The demands of labor unions upping the cost of production.
(5) Operational inefficiency upping the cost of production.

Every one of these regrettable conditions limits the opportunities of screen writers to practice their trade. A producer's risk in staking a million dollars to make a picture now becomes so great that the search for a "universal" story is intensified, and with this search the emphasis on formulas that have proved "universal" in the past. At the major studios bureaucratic reins are tightened; budgets are hammered down; story material is passed through planning committees and cost committees and editorial subcommittees until every facet of strength and originality has been rubbed off. Timidity breeds caution and caution breeds bad pictures—for show business, always a gamble, comes to grief as soon as pussy-footing sets in. Needless to say the difficulties of creation, always great, are multiplied in an atmosphere of depression and jitters, with the result that men of talent turn for an outlet to other fields.

This is the situation which writers for the screen face at the current moment in the summer of 1949. Recently I heard an executive of the Producers Association, administrators of the Code, state that in his opinion no relief was in sight—that for the future the screen writer would find opportunity for free expression only in Europe where costs are low enough to permit the making of experimental, nonuniversal pictures.

Against this view is one important fact: in the United States in 1948 there were produced, as there have always been in Hollywood's history, even the blackest, a number of pictures which combined box-office returns with artistic merit. Among these we may list: *The Snake Pit, Johnny Belinda, Red River, Command Decision, Treasure of the Sierra Madre, Boy with Green Hair*, and even such audience-grooved productions as *Sitting Pretty, Easter Parade, Key Largo, Down to the Sea in Ships*, and *Wake of the Red Witch.*

Not a long list, perhaps, but long enough to leave the seeds of hope in it. Next year the list may well be larger. A new era in picture making is about to begin, inaugurated by the government's antitrust suits, ordering the divorcement of production and theater ownership, to be effected by the end of 1950. Psychologically, the edict has undoubtedly added to Hollywood's jitters; the nation's 2,500 biggest and shiniest theaters are controlled by the big board corporations which also own the major studios. Since theaters are vastly more profitable than studios —often, in fact, operating at a profit when studios are in the red—the big board companies have wailed that the antitrust suits will bring them to ruin. This I doubt. What the separation of production from exhibition may really accomplish is the creation of an open market for products in which each film must stand on its own merits. If the separation becomes an accomplished fact, rather than a bookkeeping charade, bad pictures can no longer be booked into preferred playing time in the big chains, with products of superior merit playing the lower half of the bill or not playing in those chains at all. Major studios which survive the new deal will do so by revising their costs downward, approaching the European scale; majors which don't make the grade will be revamped into rental studios where independent companies can obtain facilities and partial financing, thus opening to writers an infinite number of small, enterprising markets to replace the half-dozen large but ham-strung markets now existing. Best of all, a writer with a good story will not always have to sell it: if he has some know-how and is not too ivory towered to get into the marts of trade and bargain for actors, hire directors, cutters, and budgeteers, he can do easily what it has been possible to do in the past only under almost insuperable difficulties, namely, become his own producer, not as a studio employee, but as partner in a company of which he is part owner. If and when this day arrives the writer for the screen will not only be a prosperous gentleman indeed—he will also have defeated, I hope finally, the economic bugaboos which now inhibit the practice of an otherwise potent and fascinating craft.

34

Writing for the (Sightless) Radio

ERIK BARNOUW

Born in Holland in 1908, Erik Barnouw came to this country when eleven years of age, was graduated from Princeton in 1929 and, after work in advertising, has been since 1937 a free-lance writer, mainly in the field of educational radio. An instructor in radio writing at Columbia since 1937, he has been in charge of radio courses there since 1946. Editor and writer for the CBS series, *Pursuit of Happiness* (1939-40), creator and supervisor of *Words at War* (1943-44), he has authored programs which, in subject and technique, have set precedent in the radio industry. He was commentator for the OWI Overseas Branch (1943-44) and worked with the Armed Forces Radio Service of the War Department in charge of educational programs broadcast to troops overseas until 1945. Member of the Authors League and president of its Radio Writers Guild, he is the author of *Handbook of Radio Writing*.

Erik Barnouw speaks up for radio—radio without television as we are beginning to have to call it. It would be sad indeed if the excitement of television were to stunt and stultify radio writing. Let us hope that instead the two fields will continue in helpful and stimulating competition. Better a fight between vaudeville and soap opera than a suds-swept universe with no competition at all!

E. J.

Writing for the (Sightless) Radio

ONE of the questions asked by the editor was, "Why do you write for radio?" As with many writers who went into radio early, it was largely an accident. In the early days of radio few people saw it as a possible medium for writers. David Sarnoff envisioned radio as a new kind of music box, supplied with music from outside the home.

In a speakeasy in the early depression I ran into a girl I had known in college. She introduced me to her husband who, she said, was a radio executive for an advertising agency. The agency had just won the Camel account and was about to launch a big new network series. When she told him I had written the book for a college musical show, he showed immediate interest. Next morning he called me up and hired me to direct the new Camel series. That day I bought a radio, my first, listened to it all week end, and came to work Monday full of ideas. This fantastic episode was not untypical of 1931. There was no reserve of people with a knowledge of radio, and radio executives had to grab where they could.

A year or two later, while directing a dramatic series, there was a script emergency during which I simply couldn't find a radio writer, and therefore did some writing myself. In similar fashion, many entered radio writing via acting, advertising, newspaper work, or other more or less related occupations. One early radio writer, Irving Reis, originator of the *Columbia Workshop* series, was a studio engineer. Twirling the dials, he gradually became interested in the possibilities of the medium, and decided to do some writing for it.

Thus radio, totally unlike television, was a sleeper. Its possible power and influence, its ability to excite the human imagination, the eventual scope of its audience, were long unsuspected by most writers. As a result radio drew few writers from other media, and instead developed its own.

Now, as this article is written, television is suddenly on us. Its early story is very different from radio's. Instead of being ignored, it is besieged. Many writers from stage, screen and radio converge on the new medium. Some assume that it will sweep other media aside. This seems a good time to have a reappraising look at sightless radio. Is it an interesting medium for the writer? What chance does it have against television?

I don't want to make any predictions about whether television will or will not do away with radio. But I do want to say that if it does, I shall be sorry. I like radio.

The fact that one works, in radio, in "only one dimension" is apt to seem a handicap to a dramatist or screen writer. But this is also what gives radio power and freedom. Is the novelist handicapped because he can't use sound? Of course not.

The man who works with the printed page really has the most flexible of all media. He is asking his reader to imagine a story. What the reader is enjoying is the story as it happens in his own imagination. The scope of his imagination and the writer's ability to stir it into the desired kind of activity are about the only limiting factors. Of all writers, the writer in print has the greatest freedom of movement in time and place. His stories can go anywhere at any time, and in and out of people's minds, with a freedom no other kind of writer enjoys.

Radio-without-sight has something of the same kind of freedom. The listener's imagination is called on to do much of the work; he imagines the final story. But one part is supplied to him: the sound of the events. This makes for an extra excitement, but it also introduces limitations. The writer suddenly has various technical problems to worry about. He can't move about with quite the same freedom. Still, he has a freedom of form which makes his job, in many ways, more like that of the writer for the printed page than of the writer for stage, screen or television.

These writers are in the business of demonstrating a story. This gives them all sorts of added ways to excite the senses and convey information, but at the same time it cuts down on their freedom. Their freedom of movement is limited by many practical, technical considerations.

The advent of television has made radio writers do a lot of thinking about their medium, not only about their own feelings toward it, but about the sort of satisfaction it gives the listener. Does it give any satisfaction which television cannot provide better?

Here we must recognize that two very different kinds of satisfaction are involved. To enjoy, simultaneously, stimuli to practically all the senses, as one can in watching a play, is one kind of audience satisfaction. On the other hand, to be stirred by mere suggestion into a great deal of thinking and feeling, is another kind. Both kinds have a strong hold over us. Neither seems likely to supplant the other.

We like photographs because they tell us so much, so exactly, in so much detail. We like cartoons for a very different reason: giving only a hint, they leave the rest to the imagination. The photograph has not done away with the cartoon.

Similarly, people still read books, and do not insist that they have pictures in them. And people still like symphonies, and generally prefer them without the sort of visual accompaniment provided by Disney in *Fantasia.* Thus the various media provide different kinds of satisfaction, and radio belongs with those that work by suggestion—with poetry, music, cartooning, etc.

This is an aspect of radio that has always interested me. And that is why I hope that after television has fully established itself, broadcasting of words and sounds and music, without pictures, will still exist.

35

Writing for Television

MAX EHRLICH

Trained as a newspaper reporter and feature writer, Max Ehrlich, radio and television writer, is the author of more than twenty-two well-known programs. Among these are *The Aldrich Family, Nick Carter, Mr. and Mrs. North,* and *The Shadow;* and such documentaries as *That They Might Live, Words at War* (Winner of Writers' War Board Award); *Main Street, USA;* and many others for such organizations as the American Red Cross, the OWI, War Production Board and American Cancer Society. His novels include *The Big Eye, Spin the Glass Web,* and *First Train to Babylon.*

Mr. Ehrlich's practical piece is full of an emotion that has been unfamiliar too long in radio and screen writing. It is full of joy at the opportunity of creating not just new twists to old plots, new techniques, in an old art—but of working creatively in a new medium.

E. J.

Writing for Television

WHEN the Authors Guild asked me to do an article on "Writing for Television" I agreed only with certain reservations, and I want to pass them on to you.

First of all, I don't want to set myself up as an authority on television writing. True, like some others, I have had a considerable amount of experience, but at this stage of the game, there are few who can call themselves authorities. Television is no longer new, but it is still moving fast and it is still experimental. Many forms and procedures have begun to jell and become routine, but strictly speaking, there are no *veteran* television writers as yet.

In a sense, all of us, no matter what our professional background, are still *young* television writers.

Second, this article must be written with a hedge around it. Some of the observations I may make here, based on my own experience, may be obsolete a year from now. Anyone who is dogmatic about anything in television is sticking his neck out. For example, it was dogma in the beginning that no writer should write a television scene with more than three, or at the most, four actors in one camera shot. The video screen, it was asserted, was too small to take any more. But since then, several top-flight directors have, through good grouping, and by expert use of cameras and lenses, used many more actors effectively in the same picture.

Third, this is not intended to be an article on the technique of television writing. That would require a textbook. All I hope to do here is outline the writer's approach to the medium, his place in it, and his future with it.

The two general types of television today are "film" or "live."

There are those in the industry who predict that most television of the future, at least in the dramatic play category, will be done on film. This shift is already well underway. A number of independent film producers, particularly in Hollywood, have been making dramatic films exclusively for television, and using film writers to write the shooting scripts. Although this kind of production was at first prohibitively expensive, the film producers have managed to shave down their budgets to a point where sponsors can buy the product.

At the present time, the bulk of television seems to be "live." And the categories definitely follow the pattern of radio. There are dramatic shows, originals and adaptations. There are mysteries, documentaries, comedies, gag, situation, and family. There are kid shows, round table forums, amateur and talent shows, music and news.

Any similarity of television programming to radio is purely logical.

The fact is that the radio writer, for example, is still doing business at the same old stand when he enters television. He is dealing with the networks, the clients, the advertising agencies, and the independent package producers as before. Same old faces in the same old offices, with the same old approaches and same old taboos. Same old program format for the dramatic show. It should be an hour, or a half-hour, in over-all length, no more, no less. And of course, a commercial at the beginning, at the middle break, and at the end.

In other words, television writers today are for the most part working for those who bought in the radio market. By the very nature of his proximity to Boxtop Boulevard, and his familiarity with its agency and network personnel, the radio writer, realistically speaking, has the best chance to get into the television setup . . . now.

Whatever happens, whatever the market, the television writer will not be just an ex-radio writer. He might be an ex-screen writer, an ex-dramatist, or even an ex-novelist. Television writing is not radio writing, nor stage writing, nor screen writing, nor novel writing.

It is, as I see it, a new technique of writing, with the elements of all these crafts embodied in it. It is creating now, and it will create, an expert and highly skilled group of craftsmen, the television writers. They will do a tough, exacting, expert and exhausting job, and their services should and will come high to the producer who wants a good product.

Let us, for the moment, examine the future of writers in television.

In my opinion, television will open up a tremendous new market for the products of writers.

First, consider existing literary properties, in the form of novels, short stories, plays, and original radio scripts.

At first, the dramatic shows on the video screen were, for the most part, adaptations of already existing literary properties. But so voracious has been the demand for new material, on a week-to-week basis, that researchers are already scraping the barrel for material lending itself to television adaptation. One- or two-set plays, short stories with interior locales, novels where the main action can be confined to limited space and cast, are grist for the mill.

But the existing literary properties suitable for television cannot last forever, and television will have to turn to original material written especially for the medium. This means that the television writer will start with his own plot, write his own treatment or outline, and finally the shooting script itself, with all its elements: dialogue, music, sound, sets, action, cameras, characters.

Like the radio writer, he will create the material, and see it through till the finished script goes on before the cameras. But whereas the professional and facile radio writer can and does turn out a full half-hour script, or five fifteen-minute scripts a week, or more, the television writer, in my opinion, will find this a murderous schedule, almost impossible to maintain.

In effect, this demand would be equivalent to a Broadway producer asking a playwright to give him a full three act play every three weeks, or fourteen full plays a year!

The point I am trying to make here is that television will require large numbers of writers to create enough material to fill television time on a radio programming basis. This applies to film television, as well as live.

I believe writers can be optimistic about television, and can welcome it with open arms. Of all the branches of show business, television has given the best break to the writers. Actors who are not visual types, or have no stage experience and who have hidden in comfortable anonymity behind the radio microphone, are worried about the encroachment of television. Producers without money are worried about it, because television is expensive, because so far it has been a big money operation. Directors without theater background are worried about it.

As of today, television is not a gold mine for writers, considering the time and effort invested. Fees are low, too low. But they are gradually beginning to rise, and they will go higher as the television networks spread across the United States, creating wider markets and giving the advertisers more coverage for their television dollar. Writers have had to sell off money in return for experience, for learning how. But those who are learning how today will certainly capitalize on their experience tomorrow.

Let us examine, now, the function of the television writer in the general program setup.

To begin with, the television writer cannot efficiently retire to an ivory tower and turn out a shooting script ready to go before the camera. Not if he is working on a dramatic show, with a reasonably elaborate production setup. Unlike the dramatist or the novelist, he cannot retire to some remote hideaway and bring in his product, and then let the producer or publisher worry about financing the product.

Like the screen writer and the radio writer, he must write *within* a set budget, already determined.

To illustrate:

You are John Smith, a television writer. One fine day you get a phone call from a producer or an advertising agency. Will you write a television show for him?

You will, providing . . .

You go to see him at his office. Suppose he has the format of the show, the idea, the star, etc. You are to provide a plot, a story, and finally, the shooting script itself. You agree on price and terms, and then you start to ask him a few questions.

First, how much money is in the budget? How many characters in the cast? How many sets? How many cameras? Will he, or will he not, use film inserts? What about music? Will these be full sets, or just flats?

These are legitimate questions, and important. If the producer can give you the answers, if he has an intelligent idea of where he wants to put his money, if he knows what his costs are, and the limits within which you can write an intelligent script, that's fine. You're in business. You can sit down with him, get out pencil and paper, break down a story into scenes, into a working blueprint within the budget allotted.

But if the producer is vague, if he just tells you to go home and write a shooting script, and worry about budget later, think it over carefully. This producer doesn't know his own mind, and if you accept the assignment, you are giving him the luxury of changing his mind later. This can be pleasant for him, but an expensive operation for you. You may go overboard on sets, characters, etc. and come in with a champagne production when your producer was really thinking of a low-cost beer budget program all the time. This means that you will have to go home and write the script all over again.

And that isn't just a trifle, to be sluffed off in a couple of hours. A half-hour dramatic show, with audio on the left and video on the right, runs from forty to sixty pages.

In short, the producer must know what he wants, and how much he has to spend. Then you can write within those limits. That means a long and careful conference on set details, cast, and whatnot before you write a word. It may mean a scene breakdown of your story, set by set, and a check of each scene, against the cost of production.

The television writer must be dollar-wise in every line and in every scene he writes. And in order to save himself unnecessary toil, he must nail the producer down to a definite budget.

To reduce the area of speculation, I'm in favor of writing a treatment, or a blueprint of the television show before the actual shooting script itself. To my mind, this is the soundest kind of insurance against that old devil, rewrite.

The television writer, to sum up, must in a sense be a producer himself, because the lines he writes and the action he portrays all depend on whether they can be done technically and financially, and as a hard matter of business. The more he knows about production and direction, the more efficiently he can write.

Let's assume you're a writer, and you know the form of the other media, but you've never written a television script, that is, a shooting script.

How then, can you learn?

Obviously, the first thing to do is see a number of television shows, not only on your video screen at home or in some bar, but also on the floor and in the control room of a TV studio. Getting into a television studio as an observer is not easy, and if you just walk in cold and tell someone you're just looking around, it's very likely that you'll be asked to leave.

However, if you have a friend at court, or know someone in television, it can be arranged. This kind of experience is invaluable in writing for television. Watching the cameras work, studying the work of the director, the technical director, the floor man and the other personnel, is a real and graphic education. If you get the script of any particular show, and follow it, line by line and scene by scene as the show progresses, that's even better.

The best possible way to learn television, however, is to write your first show in collaboration with an experienced television director. This happened to be the way I started, and I was extremely fortunate in getting this chance. When I was called in to do my first television script, no one in the producing unit knew much about television except the director. In my case, I sat down with David Lewis, a fine and imaginative television director, and we wrote the first three shows of the series together. I wrote the originals in a kind of one-act play form, to lay out the story line, construction and dialogue. Then we worked together on the shooting script.

To myself, the sound, music, dialogue, and action were familiar enough, as story elements. But it was about cameras that I was in complete ignorance, and I mean television cameras, not movie cameras. From Mr. Lewis, I learned how every line was intimately tied up with a camera shot, whether a camera was free and clear to move to the next shot, and notably what can be done and what can't be done with television cameras in limited studio space. Television writing, I learned, was writing for intimate and small pictures, connected and related and blended together by logical transitions.

After three scripts with the director, I was on my own, and thereafter wrote the shooting scripts myself.

Like the screen writer, the television writer must think in pictures, but *small* pictures. And with each line of dialogue, or each bit of action, he must constantly ask, where are the cameras? If Number One camera is on the two actors in the scene, and Number Two is set for a blowup of a newspaper headline, is Number Three available to swing to the next set almost immediately?

And what about the actors? If Joe and Mary are in Scene Two, and they must also appear in Scene Three immediately afterward, how can the writer give them enough time to run from one set to another and take their positions? He must write something in between, obviously, a bit of business that works smoothly and naturally into the continuity, to give them that precious time. And if Mary has to make a costume change immediately after Scene Two, it's obvious that the story must be constructed so that she does not appear in Scene Three.

These problems are not present in screen writing, because film can be made in "takes" and clipped together. But live television is continuous action. Once on, the play runs through.

In short, a television writer must not only be a creative story writer, he must also be a technician and mechanic.

As to the script itself, I believe in writing in as many camera directions as possible. True, the director may change them to suit his own interpretation. But more often than not, the camera treatment of the story by the writer is an important factor in telling the story, from a *story* point of view. A camera closeup, or angle, can give emphasis to a point, mood to a character.

The television script, at the time of this writing, takes the conventional form of pages split down the middle, with audio on one side, and video on the other. Some producers like audio on the left, video on the right, and vice versa. It doesn't matter too much, although some actors say that they memorize their lines better when the dialogue is on the left hand side of the page.

Perhaps it would be well, at this point, to illustrate the form with a typical scene from an actual television shooting script. This scene comes from one of the programs of the Barney Blake series produced by Wynn Wright, directed by David Lewis, with American Tobacco as the client. To those who have never seen a shooting script, it might be illuminating.

SOUND AND *AUDIO*	*VIDEO*
	Fade in CLOSEUP of Barney's typewriter as before, going at full speed.
MUSIC: (Mood theme)	
	Superimpose *ROLLER TITLES:* BARNEY BLAKE Police Reporter in "THE CURIOUS CORPSE" by Max Ehrlich
	Take out SUPERIMPOSITION
	Fade out CLOSEUP of typewriter

SOUND AND *AUDIO*	*VIDEO*
	Fade in CLOSEUP of radio-phonograph turntable, turning, playing record.
(Segue to fine classical recording)	
	Dolly back and pan for CLOSEUP of Denescu, sitting in Forsythe's living room.
(Denescu, holding cordial glass and listening to the music.)	
	Pan to TWO SHOT of Allan and Helen Forsythe on love seat near phono.
(Music ends.)	
	Take ALTERNATE TWO SHOT on Allan and Helen.
(Allan rises and crosses to the phonograph to turn it off.)	
	Pan with him
ALLAN: Well, Professor Denescu? Did you enjoy it?	
	Take MEDIUM SHOT of Denescu
DENESCU: Excellent, Doctor Forsythe! Most gratifying! (He rises) Thank you for letting me hear it!	
	Take MEDIUM SHOT on Allan

SOUND AND *AUDIO* — *VIDEO*

(Helen comes into the picture with Allan)

HELEN:
The pleasure is all ours, Professor! We're always making our friends listen to our records.

ALLAN: (Busy at the machine)
I only hope we haven't bored you.

(Denescu comes into the picture, back to camera.)

DENESCU:
Bored me?

Take
GROUP SHOT on Denescu.

DENESCU: (continuing)
On the contrary, my dear doctor, you and your charming wife have given me a perfect evening. Good food, good wine, good music and good friends. What more could a lonely bachelor ask for?

Take
MEDIUM GROUP SHOT

I drink to you . . . because I envy you!

(He drinks)

HELEN:
You envy us, Professor? Why?

DENESCU:
Because you have all this to share with one another . . . a home, full of warmth and love . . .

SOUND AND *AUDIO*	*VIDEO*
	Take GROUP SHOT on Denescu.
And what have I? A title, "Professor of Anatomy"—while for a home I have a cold, impersonal laboratory on the university campus. With whom do *I* live? Corpses! Cold, dead corpses and cold, half-dead medical students who *should* be corpses!	
SOUND: (Phone rings)	
	Take MEDIUM GROUP SHOT
ALLAN: (laughing) Those half-dead medical students grow up to be doctors like me, Professor, don't forget that. Excuse me, will you?	
(He crosses out. Helen turns with him)	
HELEN: Allan, not another night call!	
ALLAN: (off screen) I hope not!	
(Helen turns back to Denescu)	
HELEN: (despairingly) Almost every night!	
	Take MEDIUM CLOSE SHOT of Allan as he picks up phone at table near door.

SOUND AND *AUDIO*	*VIDEO*
ALLAN: Doctor Forsythe! . . . Yes. . . . I see. . . . All right, Mrs. Harris, I'll come right over. . . . Oh, just a few minutes. . . . Try to keep him quiet till I get there. . . . Good-by!	
(He hangs up and turns back to Helen.)	
	Pan
(Helen comes into the picture to join him.)	
HELEN: (unhappily) Must you go, darling?	
ALLAN: (nods)	
(Denescu saunters into the picture.)	
My apologies, Professor Denescu, but I've got to look in on this patient. I'm sorry. . . . !	
DENESCU: Nonsense, Doctor, I understand!	
	Take REVERSE MEDIUM GROUP SHOT on Allan.
ALLAN: Will you entertain our guest until I get back, Helen? I'll try to get back as soon as I can.	
HELEN: Of course, darling!	

SOUND AND *AUDIO*	*VIDEO*
(She kisses him lightly on the cheek.	
Together they walk to the door.	
	Pan with them.
Allan goes out and Helen closes the door after him. She turns to face Denescu, leaning against the door with a smile.)	
(Denescu comes into the picture and stands looking at her, with back to camera.)	
(Denescu raises his arms and she moves into them. They embrace and kiss, then Helen whispers, face to camera and close against his cheek.)	
Emil! Darling!	
	Fade out

A final word about television writers, and their organization.

The new television writer should acquaint himself with the Television Code of the National Association of Radio and Television Broadcasters, which came into effect on March 1, 1952. This code expresses broad, guiding principles for television programming and defines acceptable material.

The Television Writers Guild is one of the membership guilds of the Authors League of America.

In order to be eligible for an *active* membership, the writer must have had telecast at least one-half hour of script, either in a single show, several programs totaling thirty minutes, or twenty dramatic spots (commercials) adding up to at least one half-hour of time. The active member has a right to vote.

In order to be eligible for an *associate* membership, the writer must have written at least one-half hour or more of television material, and admission shall be upon recommendation of the Membership Committee. The associate member enjoys all the privileges of the active member, except the right to vote.

The Television Guild plans several activities in order to educate its membership to the needs and techniques of television. It plans the issuance of a market list, publishing the purchasers in the market for television material. In co-operation with other interested agencies, it plans craft meetings, and seminars where writers, directors, producers, camera men and other craftsmen will discuss the medium, exchange information. And of course, it will represent the television writers in their contract negotiations with the buying agencies.

As to the television writer's equity in his material, the following are the general policies of the Television Writers Guild in respect to agreements with producers, stations, and agencies:

1. Leasing of material, with no outright sales.
2. Maintenance of a continuing financial interest in the material, with additional payment for each reuse or a percentage arrangement for continuing use on film or kinescopic recording.
3. Contracts to be made for the existing number of stations, with additional stations requiring additional payment.
4. Copyright to be in the name of the author.
5. Where the writer has provided the idea or format, his interest in the package should be consistent with his contribution and in addition to his compensation as script writer.
6. Payment to author on acceptance of script or not later than ten days after telecast.
7. Kinescopic recording of material should specify one-time use on each station within specified time limit after original telecast. (30 days recommended.)
8. Author to receive simultaneous audio and video credit whenever the producer, director, or other craftsmen receives such credit; authorship credit on video or in publicity to be in equally favorable position, in equally large type, for the same number of times and for the same length of time on video as the credit to producer, director, or other craftsman.

The television writer today knows that, like the screen or radio writer, his name will probably be obscure to the public, although important in the industry. A novelist or a playwright can become famous overnight with a best seller or a hit play, and it may be that television will develop a few writers who may become nationally known.

Personally, though, I doubt it. Television writing will be production writing, on a week-to-week basis, following the radio tradition, and to a much lesser extent, the screen tradition.

How many radio writers could an average participant name on any quiz program? How many screen writers?

But the television writer will be an expert, in a highly specialized craft, and not the office girl with a typewriter and a ream of paper and an ambition to write continuity for the boss. He will come, for the most part, from other crafts, with their already existing contracts providing him with equity in the material he creates and writes.

And he proposes to keep that equity in his brain children, right from scratch.

36

The Origin of a Style and Passages from "*Their Finest Hour*"

WINSTON S. CHURCHILL

Former Prime Minister of Great Britain and her war leader, Winston Churchill has also won great stature as a literary figure.

Winston Churchill's statement of the origin of his style, given with the understatement which he uses always with such effectiveness, has pertinent advice for any writer who wishes to improve his own style. "I got into my bones the essential structure of the ordinary British sentence—which is a noble thing." Then, as he says, "I did not feel at any disadvantage."

The brief passages from his book, *Their Finest Hour,* illustrate Churchill's power to use his style for all high purposes: to communicate with vividness, with sincerity, with depth of feeling; to evoke a scene so directly that the reader must enter the experience; to stir emotion and always to hold in restraint the great force behind the words. He is master of the significant detail, the precise word, and the unexpected phrase. Any writer of any kind of prose, fiction and nonfiction, can learn from Churchill.

H. H.

The Origin of a Style

. . . by being so long in the lowest form (at Harrow), I gained an immense advantage over the cleverer boys. They all went on to learn Latin and Greek and splendid things like that. But I was taught English. We were considered such dunces that we could learn only English. Mr. Somervell—a most delightful man, to whom my debt is great—was charged with the duty of teaching the stupidest boys the most disregarded thing—namely, to write mere English. He knew how to do it. He taught it as no one else has ever taught it. Not only did we learn English parsing thoroughly, but we also practiced continually English analysis. Mr. Somervell had a system of his own. He took a fairly long sentence and broke it up into its components by means of black, red, blue, and green inks. Subject, verb, object: Relative Clauses, Conditional Clauses, Conjunctive and Disjunctive Clauses! Each had its colour and its bracket. It was a kind of drill. We did it almost daily. As I remained in the Third Fourth . . . three times as long as anyone else, I had three times as much of it. I learned it thoroughly. Thus I got into my bones the essential structure of the ordinary British sentence—which is a noble thing. And when in after years my school fellows who had won prizes and distinction for writing such beautiful Latin poetry and pithy Greek epigrams had to come down again to common English, to earn their living or make their way, I did not feel myself at any disadvantage. Naturally I am biased in favor of boys learning English; I would make them all learn English; and then I would let the clever ones learn Latin as an honour, and Greek as a treat. But the only thing I would whip them for is not knowing English. I would whip them hard for that.

From *Their Finest Hour*

ONE day after luncheon the Chancellor of the Exchequer, Kingsley Wood, came to see me on business at Number 10, and we heard a very heavy explosion take place across the river in South London. I took him to see what had happened. The bomb had fallen in Peckham. It was a very big one—probably a land mine. It had completely destroyed or gutted twenty or thirty small three-story houses and cleared a considerable space in this very poor district. Already little pathetic Union Jacks had been stuck up amid the ruins. When my car was recognized, the people came running from all quarters, and a crowd of more than a thousand was soon gathered. All these folk were in a high state of enthusiasm. They crowded around us, cheering and manifesting every sign of lively affection, wanting to touch and stroke my clothes. One would have thought that I had brought them some fine substantial benefit which would improve their lot in life. I was completely undermined, and wept. Ismay, who was with me, records that he heard an old woman say, "You see, he really cares. He's crying." They were tears not of sorrow but of wonder and admiration. "But see, look here," they said, and drew me to the centre of the ruins. There was an enormous crater, perhaps forty yards across and twenty feet deep. Cocked up at an angle on the very edge was an Anderson shelter, and we were greeted at its twisted doorway by a youngish man, his wife and three children, quite unharmed but obviously shell jarred. They had been there at the moment of the explosion. They could give no account of their experiences. But there they were, and proud of it. Their neighbors regarded them as enviable curiosities. When we got back into the car, a harsher mood swept over this haggard crowd. "Give it 'em back," they cried, and "Let *them* have it too." I undertook forthwith to see that their wishes were carried out; and this promise was certainly kept. . . . Certainly the enemy got it all back in good measure, pressed down and running over. Alas for poor humanity!

From *Their Finest Hour*

It seems incongruous to record a joke in such sombre scenes. But in war the soldier's harsh laugh is often a measure of inward compressed emotions. The party were digging out a bomb, and their prize man had gone down the pit to perform the delicate act of disconnection. Suddenly he shouted to be drawn up. Forward went his mates and pulled him out. They seized him by the shoulders and, dragging him along, all rushed off together for the fifty or sixty yards which were supposed to give a chance. They flung themselves upon the ground. But nothing happened. The prize man was seriously upset. He was blanched and breathless. They looked at him inquiringly. "My God," he said, "there was a bloody great rat!"

....

It did not matter where the blow struck, the nation was as sound as the sea is salt.

....

The reader will realize that all this clatter and storm was but an accompaniment to the cool processes by which our war effort was maintained and our policy and diplomacy conducted. Indeed, I must record that at the summit these injuries, failing to be mortal, were a positive stimulant to clarity of view, faithful comradeship and judicious action.

37

On Style

RUDOLF FLESCH

Born in Vienna in 1911, Rudolf Flesch came to the United States in 1938 and received his Ph.D. at Columbia in 1943. Author of *The Art of Plain Talk, The Art of Readable Writing, The Way to Write, How to Make Sense*, and *Why Johnny Can't Read*, he has been a free-lance "readability" researcher and consultant since 1946 and has taught writing at New York University.

Dr. Flesch's book, *The Art of Plain Talk*, has led many people to give up pretentious, elaborate and complicated language for simple, clear, and sometimes forceful expression. His book dealt with language in everyday life, the speech and writing of ministers, diplomats, lawyers, book reviewers, music critics, advertisers, and businessmen. In this article on style, Dr. Flesch turns to fiction.

His first point, on which he bases his argument, is this: the writer today writes for a vast reading audience, millions of readers who lack leisure, patience, and literary background, and who are unwilling to put any effort into reading. To communicate with these millions, writers have developed a simple, reportorial, almost anonymous style. In closing, Dr. Flesch suggests that the artist may have a moral obligation to make his work accessible to all of this great audience.

Perhaps the writer has a further obligation, both moral and aesthetic, which sets him free to develop his own style, a style which fits the experience he is trying to convey. He may hope to lift the reader above this anonymous level, to stretch his imagination, to excite him with new perceptions.

H. H.

On Style

MR. MALDERTON was a man whose whole scope of ideas was limited to Lloyd's, the Exchange, the India House, and the Bank. A few successful speculations had raised him from a situation of obscurity and comparative poverty, to a state of affluence. As frequently happens in such cases, the ideas of himself and his family became elevated to an extraordinary pitch as their means increased; they affected fashion, taste, and many other fooleries, in imitation of their betters, and had a very decided and becoming horror of anything which could, by possibility, be considered *low*. He was hospitable from ostentation, illiberal from ignorance, and prejudiced from conceit. Egotism and the love of display induced him to keep an excellent table: convenience, and a love of the good things of this life, ensured him plenty of guests. He liked to have clever men, or what he considered such, at his table, because it was a great thing to talk about; but he never could endure what he called "sharp fellows." Probably, he cherished this feeling out of compliment to his two sons, who gave their respected parent no uneasiness in that particular. The family were ambitious of forming acquaintances and connexions in some sphere of society superior to that in which they themselves moved; and one of the necessary consequences of this desire, added to their utter ignorance of the world beyond their own small circle, was that any one who could lay claim to an acquaintance with people of rank and title, had a sure passport to the table at Oak Lodge, Camberwell.

This is Dickens. Not one of his famous passages, to be sure, but representative, recognizable Dickens. There can be little doubt that it is good writing—and that it has style.

It would be tempting to analyze such a passage and find out just how and where it bears the personal stamp of the author. But I want to do something else. I want to start with the fact—for it *is* a fact—that the style of this passage is unmistakably out of date. If written today, it could not be called good writing.

Let's look at the words and sentences. Dickens writes "from a situation of obscurity" where a good professional writer today would simply say "from obscurity"; he writes "by possibility" for what today would simply be "possibly"; he uses long, periodic sentences; and he uses words like "affluence" and "their respected parents" that are hardly permissible even in humorous usage today.

What is the reason for these differences between the Victorian style and ours? Obviously, since writing is done for the sake of readers, the difference lies with the reading public. Compared with the millions of potential readers today, Dickens, though immensely popular, wrote for a limited audience. His readers took their time over his novels and, in fact, read them aloud. They enjoyed his leisurely method of telling and his polysyllabic twinkle. He could safely write about Mr. Malderton's being "hospitable from ostentation, illiberal from ignorance, and prejudiced from conceit," because he knew his readers would not begrudge him the effort needed in understanding these phrases.

The writer today writes for a vastly larger audience. On both sides of the Atlantic, many millions more have acquired the habit of reading. These added millions are a different kind of people. They don't have the literary background of Victorian ladies and gentlemen; they don't have their leisure and patience; they are unwilling to put more effort into reading than they would into watching a movie or listening to the radio. A reader of today, reading "hospitable from ostentation, illiberal from ignorance, and prejudiced from conceit" with his customary newspaper-reading speed, would stop, turn back, and reread—or, more probably, he would just read on and let the matter go.

So the Victorian style just isn't adequate today. But what style is? Let's look at a paragraph written in 1948 that performs roughly the same function as Dickens' description of Mr. Malderton's home and family:

> The Caffreys are substantial people in Wakefield. Mrs. Caffrey is the daughter of Grafton Kenyon, whose grandfather, William G. Kenyon, founded Kenyon's Department Store in 1856. It is the only department store in Wakefield. Caffrey works in the family store. He is thirty-five and fair-haired, and looks like a photogenic football player. When he was at Providence College, from which he graduated in 1936, he did play some football. The Caffreys, who have two children—a seven-year-old daughter named Carol and a four-year-old son named Kenyon—live in a pleasant twelve-room house of two and a half stories. It is painted white and has a well-kept lawn on three sides.

This happens to be from John McNulty's "Jackpot" story in *The New Yorker*. But it is irrelevant who wrote it. The passage certainly isn't recognizable McNulty; it isn't even recognizable *New Yorker*. In fact, the most significant thing about it is that it has no personal style at all. It could have been written by anyone among thousands of today's writers who have learned how to do a good reporting job. Its style is *the* accepted, mid-Twentieth-Century, "anonymous" style.

This style is not inferior to the personal styles developed by the great writers of the past. On the contrary: it is superior. It is superior because it can be learned, because it is more economical, and because it does its job by sticking to observable facts. Dickens uses a good many abstractions to tell his reader about Mr. Malderton's status in society. McNulty simply says that the Caffreys' house is painted white and has a well-kept lawn on three sides. On balance, I think, McNulty tells us more.

Comparison of the two passages shows the characteristics of what I called today's "anonymous" style. McNulty's fourteen-word sentences are about one-third shorter than Dickens'; he uses no complex words where simple words will do; and he strictly avoids expression of his own thoughts and sentiments. This is the crisp reportorial style hammered out by Hemingway and his followers, by *The New Yorker*, and by *Time*. It is admittedly journalistic writing—factual, simple, and idiomatic.

This journalistic writing is so respectable today that authors like Steinbeck or Thurber don't hesitate to occasionally sandwich a reporting job between their other literary work. They take pride in doing these menial literary tasks, and pride in writing the style that goes with them. Actually, what happened to writing is not too different from what happened to scientific invention and research. Fifty years ago our inventions came from individual geniuses like Edison; today most great inventions are made by anonymous researchers, following a fixed procedure.

To be sure, for the beginner the choice does not lie between his own personal style and the generally used reporter style. Usually, his problem is simply that of getting rid of bad writing and getting the hang of good writing. Ordinary people don't write like Dickens or Conrad or Henry James. What they write is more apt to resemble the following random sample from yesterday's paper:

> Although the music dramas of Wagner remain among the mainstays of the Metropolitan Opera Association's repertoire and concerts of the excerpts from them are rarer nowadays than was the case not so many years ago there is still much pleasure to be derived from such a concert when it is devised as intelligently as the one planned for the Philadelphia Orchestra in Carnegie Hall last night by Eugene Ormandy, but conducted by his associate, Alexander Hilsberg, because Mr. Ormandy was suffering from a virus infection.

This is ridiculously bad writing. In fact, it probably wasn't written at all, but hurriedly dictated. And yet, it is a fair sample of the kind of prose that surrounds us on all sides.

Anyone who wants to call himself a writer must first graduate from this kind of thing to being able to write "It is painted white and has a well-kept lawn on three sides." But after he has done that, should he proceed from there to fashion his own personal style?

Some people say he should. The English critic Cyril Connolly, for instance, recently quoted the following passage from Virginia Woolf:

> Considering how common illness is, how tremendous the spiritual change that it brings, how astonishing, when the lights of health go down, the undiscovered countries that are then disclosed, what wastes and deserts of the soul a slight attack of influenza brings to view, what precipices and lawns sprinkled with bright flowers a little rise of temperature reveals, what ancient and obdurate oaks are uprooted in us by the act of sickness, how we go down into the pit of death and feel the waters of annihilation close above our heads and wake thinking to find ourselves in the presence of the angels and the harpers when we have a tooth out and come to the surface in the dentist's armchair and confuse his "Rinse the mouth—rinse the mouth" with the greeting of the Deity stooping from the floor of Heaven to welcome us—when we think of this, as we are so frequently forced to think of it, it becomes strange indeed that illness has not taken its place with love and battle and jealousy among the prime themes of literature. Novels, one would have thought, would have been devoted to influenza; epic poems to typhoid; odes to pneumonia; lyrics to toothache. But no.

Mr. Connolly rightly admires the "long, effortless, masterly first sentence, eighteen book-page lines without a full stop." And he adds nostalgically: "Where will we find sentences like that one today?"

I admit that I cannot bring myself to feel the same kind of nostalgia. Long sentences are still being written today by some of our leading writers, but more often than not they seem rather like a kind of morbid growth. Opening William Faulkner's recent novel *Intruder in the Dust*, I read:

> It was just noon that Sunday morning when the sheriff reached the jail with Lucas Beauchamp though the whole town (the whole county too for that matter) had known since the night before that Lucas had killed a white man.
>
> He was there, waiting. . . .

It took me a second or two to realize that the word "he" referred neither to the white man nor to Lucas Beauchamp nor even to the sheriff, but to the boy from whose point of view the novel is written. After identifying the "he," I naturally looked for the boy's name. But Faulkner does not care for satisfying a reader's natural curiosity. The boy's name, Charles Mallison Jr., appears for the first time, quite incidentally and inconspicuously, in the following sentence on page 68:

> Because he had already passed that long ago when that something—whatever it was—had held him here five minutes ago looking back across the vast, the almost insuperable chasm between him and the old Negro murderer and saw, heard Lucas saying something to him not because he was himself, Charles Mallison junior, nor because he had eaten the plate of greens and warmed himself at the fire, but because he alone of all the white people Lucas would have a chance to speak to between now and the moment when he might be dragged out of the cell and down the steps at the end of a rope, would hear the mute unhoping urgency of the eyes.

Intruder in the Dust is a powerful novel and Faulkner, of course, has the right to fashion his own style for his own artistic purposes. In a way, this is an admirable achievement. But maybe the social function of the artist goes beyond that. Maybe he has a moral obligation to make his work accessible to all who could be enriched by it. If so, then Faulkner, and most other writers who use an intensely personal style, have gone too far in their literary artistry. By forgoing the humble, reportorial, "style-less" style, they have betrayed the great audience ready for the fruits of their imagination.

38

On the Difficulty of Dramatizing A Novel

HAROLD FREEDMAN

A graduate of Columbia University, Harold Freedman worked with the Washington Square Players while still an undergraduate. Within a short time after graduation he became an agent for dramatists and has been associated since that time in partnership with Carl Brandt as an agent also for the dramatization of novels. Among the playwrights he has represented for many years are Maxwell Anderson, Robert Ardrey, Philip Barry, S. N. Behrman, Mary Chase, Clifford Goldsmith, Sidney Howard, Arthur Laurents, Kenyon Nicholson, Clifford Odets, Paul Osborn, J. B. Priestley, Terence Rattigan, Robert E. Sherwood, Thornton Wilder, and Emlyn Williams. Among the recent novels which he has handled for dramatization are *On Borrowed Time, The Late George Apley,* and *Tales of the South Pacific.*

As Mr. Freedman says, the theater has its fascination for the novelist. After all, *The Late George Apley, Life With Father, On Borrowed Time, Rain,* and *Uncle Tom's Cabin,* have led successful double lives, first as fiction and then as drama. The writer's imagination begins to see his own novel in Act One, Two, and Three, and perhaps himself bowing out between the curtains in response to the first night audience shouting enthusiastically for the author. After all, he has written a novel and he has seen many plays. Why not make a play out of his book?

Mr. Freedman, from a long experience with the theater, suggests that the transformation is less simple than it seems. His comments will discourage some novelists (and save them time as well as distress). Other novelists, more stubborn or more stalwart, will heed Mr. Freedman's advice and either set out to learn a new technique or hope to annex a good collaborator.

Perhaps the most startling and thought-provoking single sentence in this article is that which states that Priestley and Maugham who are successful playwrights do not attempt to dramatize their own fiction! This is no accident, says Mr. Freedman.

H. H.

On the Difficulty of Dramatizing A Novel

THE theater has its fascination for the novelist just as the novel has for the playwright. What comes to the playwright as a welcome relief to express himself without intermediaries, appears, conversely, to the novelist as an opportunity to escape from the library and the bookstalls into the—to him—humanized excitement of rehearsals and the publicized glitter of the opening night. But there is a long and difficult road to travel before he can reach this goal and achieve the ultimate satisfaction—observing an audience enjoying his work.

First of all the writer who wishes to dramatize a novel must realize that he has inescapable collaborators. Anyone who has seen the same play on more than one occasion, especially if he has seen it in different cities on a tryout, must have felt vividly the magnetic current that flows between the actors themselves and the audience. What one night may seem a gay and charming comedy, may on another turn into a dull and boring dud. An over- or undersympathetic audience on an opening night, an "off" or an unusually brilliant performance, and you will hardly recognize the play you have seen only a few days before. The most astute of dramatic critics have on occasion reversed their opinions when they have seen the play a second time under more favorable circumstances.

This kind of collaboration can be a great help to the playwright if he knows how to use it. If the material of the novel is of such nature that the dramatist can count on the audience bringing into the theater a wealth of associations or emotional experience already linked with the material, he has a strong initial advantage. This will happen, for example, if the play concerns Abraham Lincoln, or, let us say, concerns a re-examination of the dreams we live by; but not if the play has Franz Josef for its hero, or deals with postwar conditions in England. Is it any wonder, then, that the best professional play reader will sometimes go wrong when his imagination fails to keep constantly before him these omnipresent collaborators? I have brought this up at the beginning because the difference between the contribution of the reader of a novel and the contribution of the audience at a play is the force which directs much of what I have to say. I hope this will become more apparent as I go on.

Writing for the theater is growing less rigid as it borrows from other media: the flash back and the quickly shifting scene from the motion picture, the informative or narrative statement from radio, the stream-of-consciousness expressionism from the novel. Playwrights are escaping from the confines of Ibsen to which audiences have for a long time been accustomed; they are going back to Sophocles and Shakespeare, Jonson and Sheridan, and even delving into the technique of the Chinese theater. With this looseness of form, they can make a play from almost any novel.

But even though there are no rigid rules, do not think, if you are to turn a novel into a good play, that you can dispense with the exacting discipline the medium demands. Those who have successfully broken out of the old confines are thoroughly aware of the craft of the great playwrights of the past. They have been anchored in tradition; to go ballooning, throwing out ballast all the way has proved the surest trip to failure and discouragement.

Certainly it is easier to make a play out of *Of Mice and Men* than out of *Lord Jim*. It is simpler to deal with a basic emotional conflict of character than with an intellectual abstraction. Although Shaw called Sherlock Holmes an incompetent bungler, he is better in the theater than Lupin whose analytical exhibitionism cannot compete with the familiar emotional responses which his more humane British counterpart evokes in the average audience.

And then, although in these days of confusion and bewilderment, killing or suicide seems to dramatists to be the inevitable denouement, I still urge you, even if you insist on embracing the tragic mask, not to ignore its comedic neighbor, showing a rift in the clouds where people may still get what they want through sanity and balance. Hanging on the other side of the curtain the mask of comedy is not only a symbol, it is another collaborator, always hovering over the audience, ready to co-operate with you in rousing it to easy laughter.

I might describe the methods followed by any individual dramatist in making a play out of a novel, but it would not be advisable to try to follow them. You cannot write another *Hamlet* merely because you have meticulously analyzed it. In that mysterious area of subconscious thought where the novel received its original impulse there is a point of departure with which the dramatist must become identified if he wishes to make a true dramatization of the book. Any first rate job should have its own creative originality. Sidney Howard, reading de Kruif's chapter on *Yellow Jack* with deep sympathy and comprehension of its spirit, wrote the play as a detective story.

But once this intuitive grasp is there, the creation must be the dramatist's own; it is usually easier for a newcomer to follow this path than for the novelist who must first retrace his steps and then re-create familiar material for a new medium. It is not just an accident that experienced writers like Priestley and Maugham do not attempt to dramatize their stories, although they have been very successful in their original writing for the theater.

The novelist who is fascinated by the idea of traveling alone in this new medium may find it a desert with many a mirage. He has heard that other people as well as the dramatist have a creative hand in making a play, but in his first enthusiasm he foresees no obstacles in them. He will be lucky, however, and accidentally lucky, if, before he is through, he has not reached a state of bewilderment, frustration and helpless frenzy. He has a vague idea of association with a benign manager who is to keep a wary eye over the proceedings, but he has had little warning of the endless discussions with the director and the actors in a realm where, for him, few signposts stand out. Only in that sunny perspective after the rare success can he sort out in retrospect the lessons he has learned.

That is, if he gets that far. Conrad, on the only occasion when he tried writing for the theater, arrived eager and expectant at his first rehearsal, hoping to hear his text sonorously and exactly spoken for his particular delight. He was startled to find the actors involved in deciding from what part of the stage a line could be most effectively delivered, whether sitting or standing, whether accompanied by business, whether delivered facing the audience or turned away from it, with this or that intonation, haltingly or tentatively expressed. All Conrad wanted to hear were his elliptical lines spoken by automatons, fluently. He fled the theater forever.

At times a novelist whose book has for one successful reason or another attracted the theater's attention, refuses to have it made into a play. No persuasion, no financial blandishment will move him; no promise of entering that environment which many novelists, as if to fend off this Circe, have satirized. He has a revulsion against a bowdlerization of his work, against a distortion of the nuances and of that delicate balance of thought, feeling, and philosophic comment—everything he has weighed so sensitively to give the novel his own special touch. He knows the theater, the way it resorts to vulgarization of values, and he cannot bear to see the character drawing over which he has labored with such pain reduced to a skeleton on which to hang the talents of an actor. Even if he makes his own dramatization, his work has moved into other hands—those of the director and the actors—and he no longer feels the same identification with it.

What then would be in store for him who is more adventurous, unjaundiced, and even optimistic? If he has perhaps at some time thought seriously of what his book would be like as a play, he may have the curiosity and enterprise to accept the challenge himself. His novel has many scenes of uninterrupted dialogue which he naturally thinks should fit in unaltered (or slightly cut down, as he has been warned against long speeches) into the completed play. His story pattern is there, for him to set up his situations. What he must do now, he assumes, is somehow to introduce his characters, who are described objectively in the novel, so that their relations to one another in the play are evoked successfully. Perhaps he has been told that their past should become clear as present issues develop. He is not aware that existent scenes which he pieces together with new dialogue do not quite convey the same values which gave the freshness and personal quality to his writing that made the novel so much admired; somehow as this proceeds rapidly and easily he feels that he has satisfactorily made his book into a play.

I am taking all this at its worst. No one would be more horrified than he to see this melange before an audience, which demands its own part in the proceedings, makes its own observations and judgments, rejecting sometimes what the characters say for what they do. Dialogue which lived and sparkled for the reader may be too explicit, too elaborate, too unevocative, when an audience listens. No matter how well dialogue reads, it must play well. Merely juggling around familiar material does not re-create it afresh for the theater. The text that is literary differs in all that matters to the theater from the terse phrase which evokes tension, the sharply spoken paradox which produces laughter.

Shall the novelist then turn his book over to the experienced dramatist rather than go through the agonies of making this unrewarding transformation himself? Or shall he try to work in collaboration with him? The answer depends upon the nature of his own dramatic instinct and upon the dramatist he is able to secure. Some dramatists can function only without the novelist at their elbow; however sensitive they may be to the novelist's desire to maintain the integrity of the many facets of his book, they feel the need for completely re-creating it. You have only to look at some of the faithful dramatizations of your favorite novels to conclude that even at the risk of being partially overshadowed you had better be chaperoned to Broadway by Pegasus, not by Dobbin.

If, however, you have a native dramatic instinct, and if your novel falls without too much difficulty into play form; if you do not have to twist your creative vision too strenuously; then you may find your best solution in working with a sympathetic dramatist. Even then you must be prepared for the most anguished readjustments. Favorite passages which are the highlights of the novel may never appear; and if they do, they may be so torn out of context or so twisted around as to have entirely different connotations. You will learn soon enough how subtlety must give way to what seems to you the obvious, an obviousness which in the hands of a fine actor may, to your surprise and delight, evoke in the audience a value as sensitive and as imaginative as the original;

you may finally perceive, however reluctantly, that you must be concerned with the immediate emotional response rather than refined cerebration. Wilde understood the theater; Huxley remains in the library. Dialogue which stimulates rumination rather than emotion is disturbing. The paradox which rouses thought rather than laughter is fatal.

The playwright working with a novelist may find himself running against the current of the novelist's thought and feeling. He must fuse in his own way for the purposes of the theater the revelation of character, the development of idea as the story and situations progress; he feels the necessity of building up to curtains, finding the single line which will convey the meaning for which the novelist has taken many pages; he uses the innumerable little tricks the theater has learned to get the audience to contribute its part. He knows he must not write what the audience will supply.

Under the persuasive but relentless demands of his collaborating dramatist the novelist reluctantly boils scenes down, desperately transforms pages of comment and philosophical reflection to a single line spotted at a critical moment. When the collaborator has written a scene that seems to the novelist unforgivably stark, and, incredulously, he sees this come to life on the stage, producing values entirely different from his own; when lines he wrote under duress gets laughs or produce tingling excitement, the novelist comes to a belated understanding of the reason for the dramatist's arguments and pleadings. He becomes suddenly aware of a new alignment of values, a new synthesis, a curious integration of values other than his own which has created something different but strangely similar to his own novel.

If in spite of all my warnings, you are still attracted by the challenge of doing the work alone, still curious to learn for yourself the difference in technique; if you are undaunted by the tribulations in store for you, I will try to give you a little of the customary advice. Find out what your essential conflict is. Make everything contribute to that. Eliminate everything from the novel which does not contribute to the conflict. Develop your characters as you present the conflict. Reveal them first to the audience and then to themselves. Discover the tricks of technique for impressing on the audience relevant facts, for centering its attention on the important issue, for acquainting it with whatever is to be kept secret from the various characters, etc. The actor knows ways to emphasize a point or to build to a climax; you should know these devices.

To sum up: what are the differences between the dialogue and structure of the play and the novel? Arthur Hopkins, in his fine book on stage direction, writes: "In the theater I do not want the emotion that rises out of thought, but thought that rises out of emotion." The novelist can reveal his characters to you through analytical comment. He can tell his reader all about them, he can describe their environment, the various factors which conditioned them. The dramatist must get his values from what his people say or do; and more from what they say or do than the way they say or do it. The contribution of the actor and the participation of the audience necessitate a certain pace and economy in the dialogue recognized by the capable dramatist who knows just what response he hopes to get.

The play moves on relentlessly watched by an audience whose mind is a blank sheet, receptive to whatever experience the dramatist wishes to put it through. The pace is a game played by him and the audience. He must never be ahead of the audience or behind it as the play goes on. As he nears the end, if he repeats what the audience already knows, if he fails to contribute the exact final development of event, idea, or character, he will let down the play in exact measure with the accumulated vitality and anticipation he has won. You will be forgiven if you dawdle a little when the curtain goes up; once you start to canter, the audience will be at a gallop by the time the first curtain goes down. However quiet things may seem to be on the stage, the mind of the audience will be racing. It will permit no side steps except those it can take in stride. When the curtain rises again the members of the audience bring all their previous involvement with the play to bear on the next act. Not for them the indirect approach of the novelist. A new set of characters, a new background must meet an impatient demand for its relationship to that emotional involvement stored up out there beyond the footlights. Tributaries will be welcome if they join the surging river but parallel streams are rejected. New lines of story or idea (possible in the novel) unrelated to the previous flow merely scatter the interest. "What is the line of the play?" asks the director as he seeks to find the centralizing thread which he knows the audience is waiting to grasp. If the audience can follow this thread with interest until the end of the play it will accept the play.

The dramatist must draw his thread out of the novel. It is not necessarily a story line. It may be a thematic line or a line of character development. It may be a line of all three: a combination of a developing story revealing characters to the audience and then to themselves, working out the theme in the process. This single line is something for the audience to follow; it holds the play together.

For the theater the transition from one point of development to another within a scene must have a logical progression. The same progression must appear from one scene to the next as the crescendo mounts. The actors feel immediately anything out of place or not properly attuned. They say, "It won't play!"

Finally I should like to try a little to lay one ghost that besets the novelist who decides to be his own dramatist. He has been told that above all he must have action on the stage. The daily reviews bewilder him with their insistence. "It was too talky—it had very little action—it was a conversation piece." What shall he do to avoid this deadliest of all epitaphs? He determines to do his play only in terms of physical movement, of physical conflict. At least he will have plenty of harsh words and violent denunciations. But action, my friend, as in Berkley's Idealism, is in the minds or emotions of the audience, not in the rough and tumble of the stage. If a scene presents a progression of relationship or a development of a situation; if the characters have advanced in their points of view at the end of a scene or if opposing points of view emerge, the play will then persuade the audience that it has action.

As I glance back through these admonitions I am reminded of an occasion when I once offered these fragments of advice to a young novelist who came to me about a dramatization he had just made of his own novel. I had brought to bear upon it all the principles I have offered you. "Here is a fellow," I said, "who has not hit it right, who does not yet know the difference between literary and dramatic dialogue, between the values necessary for a play as against the novel, but who has a genuine gift for high comedy. He just needs a little of my high flown instruction, a little knowledgeable finger wagging, to earn the plaudits of Atkinson, Barnes, Watts and John Mason Brown.

This fellow is not interested in pratt-falls and custard pies, but in brilliant verbal give and take suffused by the genuine comic spirit. This fellow really understands his Plautus and Aristophanes, his Sheridan and his Shaw."

But I was wrong. He wanted me only to tell him how the Marx or the Ritz Brothers would fit into the play, or how Sliding Billy Watson would write it. "Your pontifications," he wrote me, "are about as clear to me as the Quantum Theory. I am now getting some instruction from guys more on my own level, who are simply interested in a fast buck. They are not concerned with theories, but have told me just what changes to make. With their suggested revisions they assure me the play will be snapped up."

Having been put in my place, I could only wait and see. That was three years ago. I am still waiting.

39

The Psychology of the Artist

DR. BEATRICE HINKLE

Several years after receiving her medical degree from Cooper Medical College, now the medical department at Stanford University, Dr. Beatrice Hinkle came to New York where she now specializes in psychoanalysis. It was she who in 1908 opened at Cornell Medical College the first psycho-therapeutic clinic in America. Author of *The Re-Creating of the Individual* (1923), and numerous other works on psychoanalysis, she also translated *The Psychology of the Unconscious*, by C. G. Jung (1916), and *The Living and the Lifeless*, by Dirk Coster (1929).

Every writer, probably every creative artist, knows that he cannot always make use of all his power. He suffers from periods of drought, in which not even a trickle flows. He works at times doggedly, persistently, knowing that he is not tapping his full ability. Then suddenly, through no conscious act of his, he is in full command of his daemon (or his daemon is in full command of him!), he is writing as a whole man, carried along on a flood of creation.

Some writers describe this release as a second wind, like that in extreme physical fatigue or in great peril. That kind of release comes, say the doctors, from an excess of adrenalin. But the solution for artists who are suffering stagnation or a complete block is not as simple as a shot of gland essence. Psychiatrists say there is no single answer as there is no single cause for these blocks. Some psychiatrists regard these blocks lightly; perhaps you don't really want to write, they say, or perhaps you are tired.

Dr. Hinkle, through years of work with troubled men and women, has met artists of various kinds, and has come to certain conclusions about people with creative impulses. In her book *The Re-Creating of the Individual*, she gives a chapter to the psychology of the artist in which she suggests, to quote her words, "some insight into the special psychic processes on which all art production depends." Her comments on the creative personality might offer a basis for further work on how to handle it better.

H. H.

The Psychology of the Artist

THE study of the psychology of the artist has always been an alluring one, for his is the personality which reveals to us through definite forms the peculiarly human capacity of nonbiological creativeness. Through the technique of psychoanalysis it has been possible to gain some insight into the special psychic processes on which all art production depends regardless of its quality or character, and to study the impulses and mechanisms at work. Fundamentally the male artist approximates more to the psychology of woman, who, biologically speaking, is a purely creative being and whose personality has been as mysterious and unfathomable to the man as the artist has been to the average person.

In the previous chapter I emphasized the fact that woman is a being dominated by the creative urge and that no understanding of her as an individual can be gained unless the significance and effects of that great fact can be grasped. In the psychology of the artist we have the masculine counterpart of woman's creativeness. Both possess the same thing in common—an imperious urge toward the fulfillment of their destiny, which no difficulty of outer circumstance or environment can completely stifle. They are each dependent upon the other for the necessary fecundation to stimulate the creative processes to fruitful activity: for the woman, it is the objective sexual relation with the man which is necessary to start her creative product, the child: for the male artist, it is an adequate subjective relation with the woman which is necessary for the quickening of his creative product, be it poem, painting, or invention. Both the artist and the woman possess a particular

Reprinted from *Recreating the Individual* by permission of Dodd, Mead & Company.

relation to the unconscious and this living active process which dominates their organism, apart from its own upkeep and renewal in the service of self-preservation, must be recognized as a distinct factor producing a definite effect upon the psychology of these individuals and separating them from ordinary man.

Many students of human biology have called attention to the creative capacity as the peculiar possession of human beings in general. In a large sense this can be observed everywhere, and thus all people are potential artists. Certainly when any genuine creative work is produced, the mechanism of its production is always the same whether the producer is called an artist or not or whether he belongs to the artist type or not.

Nevertheless the artist has always been and still is a being somewhat apart from the rest of humanity, and is entitled to be considered in a class by himself. Although as an individual he will be found to fall into one or other of the psychological types already discussed, and to reveal in his art production this type characteristic, any adequate understanding of his psychological processes must take account of his special creative activity in the same way that woman's specific functioning must be reckoned with in any consideration of the individual woman.

The special psychic activity of the sexual libido in the artist, which distinguishes him from the biological woman, as well as from other men, produces a unique condition for which there is no parallel outside of the human organism. The specific fruit of this functioning has been the production of a humanly created world in contrast to and yet intimately interpenetrated by the world of nature. It follows that those individuals whose creative activity results in the bringing forth of these peculiarly human products—in contrast to the biological forms which man shares in common with all living creatures—must of necessity require a special study and consideration.

The artist in common with woman has always been looked upon a little suspiciously and curiously by that portion of mankind who consider themselves stable and solid and who represent the commonsense or rationally organized individuals. For the artist, again like the woman, possesses a reality of a different order from that of the ordinary man. His ego is entirely identified with his creative processes which for him constitute the entire meaning and purpose of his life. Hence his individual adaptation is made to this capacity just as the woman has adapted to her reality, which comprises all that concerns her function and her purpose.

He is known to be emotionally unstable, neurotic, and often appears mentally unbalanced or even psychotic. Genius and madness have from time immemorial been associated, and the lives of the creative artists and geniuses in all fields do reveal an overwhelming preponderance of erratic conduct, emotional stress and irrational reactions, coupled with definite psychic disturbances manifested in conflict, struggle and mental disorder.

It is these accompaniments of masculine creative activity that produced that amazing theory in the last century connecting genius with degeneracy. Because of the very evident resistance of the artist nature to the adaptation demanded by the outer collective reality which is the goal of so-called normal persons, he comes to be regarded as a degenerate on one side or as a superior being on the other.

When one looks back over human existence, however, it is very evident that all culture has developed through an *initial resistance against adaptation to the reality in which man finds himself.* This resistance acts as a stimulus to his inner impulse to action and to creation, thus causing him to shape and remake his environment to suit better his need and desire.

Through the impact of man upon the given objective reality, a constantly new and changing condition is created. Therefore the reality into which a child is born today is somewhat different in its adaptive demands from that in which his grandfather was born.

Nevertheless, although all new creation is dependent upon the same subjective process, this play directly upon the environment itself, indulged in by man in general since the beginning, is not the activity to which I refer, when I speak of the unique capacity of the artist. The artist is one whose efforts and interests are primarily occupied in creating a new and unique product, which is endowed by him with a distinct life of its own and which embodies his feelings and ideas in definite form. It is this surrogate form of life which we call art that he offers to the world as his contribution in place of himself as an ordinary adapted being.

The artist is the individual whose psychic processes are of a character which permit us to recognize that man has attained to a new and different kind of creative mechanism, one peculiar to himself even though based upon a purely biological process which he shares with all other animals. Although the artist rarely uses this power in connection with any self-creation, his product being something which is thrown off from himself, nevertheless in the capacity which he possesses there lie potentialities for the human race of which it has scarcely dreamed.

The mystics are the only ones who have gained a glimpse into what is possible when this same capacity is used primarily in the service of the individual himself instead of for the creation of art. And I do not include here the pseudo-mystics' hysterical experiences any more than the pseudo-artists' claims, both of which are so apt to obscure the entire subject and prevent any real understanding of a genuine inner human achievement.

In previous chapters in this book I have referred to the existence of a surplus libido over and above that used in the process of adaptation to reality. It resists adaptation and is actually incapable of such employment. The libido that becomes organized in the service of adaptation to the demands of external life and to the demands of biological maturity forms one portion, and that which cannot be utilized forms another. This is the basis for that dualism which characterizes human life. In the little child this surplus libido, because of his immaturity and the simple responsibilities demanded by necessity, is far in excess of the portion used in adaptation; it is unorganized and finds its expression in play which occupies most of his waking hours. This play is commonly of two definite forms; that which occupies itself in purely exteriorized motor activity, and that which finds its expression in the mental realm, creating phantasies, images and make-believe with the raw material of sense perceptions coupled with individual wishes. Although these two forms of play activity are frequently intermingled and pass into each other, nevertheless they are often found quite distinct and separate in different children and at different times in the same child.

The play of the child as he grows older, although still modeled upon his instinct activities, is associated now with the particular environment and culture which make up his external world of perception and outer stimuli. At first unconscious imitation plays the important role but soon the creative impulse is recognized at work in the new combinations and imaginative activity displayed in the use of the environmental factors. The transformation which they undergo may become eventually aesthetic creation or that more general aspect of creative activity in which invention and improvement upon the already existing conditions are the chief forms. This creative activity is of the same order as that visible everywhere in nature. It arises through a vital necessity inherent in the organism and is the impulse which brings man, of all the living beings on this planet, into the position of nature's rival. This is expressed in his ceaseless activity to subdue and conquer her and at the same time in his attempt to understand and co-operate with her; it is objectified in the world of culture which he has produced inside the natural world.

Ribot speaks of all aesthetic creation as dependent upon a luxurious need and refers to the theory that art has its origin in superfluous activity. But what is this superfluous activity?—just the energy that is not needed for the direct business of adaptation or that portion which cannot be adapted to the reality of the time. That amount which cannot be harnessed and domesticated but insists on its own form of activity rather than one which is offered ready made, is the energy used for the creation of art.

. . . .

For the artist most definitely lives in two worlds, the world of objective reality being colored and shadowed by the subjective world of the ideal and of phantasy. The latter is made real to him through his capacity for arresting it and fixing it in form. This technically developed skill and intellectual training is the objective maturity which he brings to the aid of his unique psychic processes. He thus raises them out of the mist of the unconscious into the light of consciousness and embodies them in concrete form. The fruit of his psychic activity is seen in those highest forms of human creation, art, religions, and philosophies.

The supreme artists are those who possess within themselves the functions and mechanisms of the creative activity in the right relation with each other, so that the mysterious inner union, which takes place in the unconscious at the moment when the artist feels himself possessed and lost in the mystic embrace, occurs as naturally and easily within him as the analogous act in the physical realm. For there is no doubt whatsoever that the fecundation which takes place as the preliminary act of all art creation is of the same character as that which precedes physical creation in the natural world. There are different forms of fertilization even in the organic world, besides the common one among the higher animals. There is a self-fertilization in which one creature possesses the complete mechanism through which the new creation takes place instead of its division between two separate individuals.

Also, there is a myth which tells of a time when human beings were physically androgynous and the sexes were not divided. Although the myth is translated, as always, into terms of physical reality, the artist, because of the spiritual process occurring within him through which his creations are produced, presents an analogy to this mythical human being complete in himself. Although this is a psychical reality instead of a physical one, it is nonetheless actual, in that it produces real effects. Like many other energic processes in nature, it can be intellectually grasped only through its manifestations.

. . . .

The creator does not create only for the pleasure of creating but . . . he also desires to subdue other minds. This can be called the secondary effect, having particularly to do with the creator's self-feeling or ego consciousness in relation to the herd.

. . . .

The attitude and reactions of artists toward their art children reveal an attitude similar to that which mothers in general possess toward their children. There is the same sensitivity to any criticism, the same possessive pride, the same devotion and love, with the accompanying anxiety and distress concerning them. . . . [Some] artists are really only mediums used by the unconscious processes, and their art children whether good or bad are entirely dependent upon their heredity and not upon the conscious personal contributions of their parents.

On the other hand we have the artists who invariably have brought to their creations the loving surrender of all they have and are; who suffer the pain of experience and submit to long distasteful discipline better to serve their creative purpose; whose gift consists not only in an unconscious mechanism . . . but in a complete dedication of their efforts and energies in all seriousness to their destiny. These are the artists for whom no effort is too much and no sacrifice too great that will contribute to their creations.

40

The Literary Life

AN ASSORTMENT OF NOTES AND COMMENT FROM *THE NEW YORKER*

The author of these notes on the stresses and strains of writing has asked that they appear anonymously; a request which the editors fulfill but do not condone. Since, however, his style is one of the purest and most characteristic of any aphoristic thinker since Thoreau, his admirers will in any case recognize the mind behind the mask. For those who do not know him, let this admirer merely suggest that you be not misled by the minutiae from which he starts. After all, every circle has a point for a center. The size of the circle is determined by the energy with which it is expanded, not by the magnificence of what it may or may not take off from. Our notetaker may start from a pebble but reach the horizon's rim.

E. J.

*The Literary Life**

An Assortment of Notes and Comment from *The New Yorker*

January 21, 1928

It was inevitable that we should finally run across that old college friend whose life ambition had been to write a novel that would cut deeply into the world of American letters. Sooner or later our path was bound to cross his, and we would again see the man who had gone forth from the campus to scotch literary bugaboos, to create new forms, new ideals. Well, it happened. We met him on the street. "What are you doing?" we inquired, stupidly. He cleared his throat. "I am writing advertising," he replied, "and I will give you a sock in the eye."

December 15, 1928

The pain which attends all literary composition is increased, in some cases, by the writer's knowing how much per word he will receive for his effort. We came upon a writer at his work recently, and were allowed to sit quietly by while he finished his stint. Quite casually he mentioned that he was getting fifty cents a word. A moment or two later his face became contorted with signs of an internal distress. With his hand poised above the machine, he seemed to be fighting something out with himself. Finally he turned to us. "Listen," he said, grimly, "do you hyphenate 'willy-nilly'?" We nodded, and saw him wince as he inserted the little mark, at a cost of half a dollar.

May 11, 1929

"Writing is not an occupation," writes Sherwood Anderson. "When it becomes an occupation a certain amateur spirit is gone out of it. Who wants to lose that?" Nobody does, replies this semipro, sitting here straining at his typewriter. Nobody does, yet few writers have the courage to buy a country newspaper, or even to quit a city writing job for anything at all. What Mr. Anderson says is pretty true. Some of the best writings of writers, it seems to us, were done before they actually thought of themselves as engaged in producing literature. Some of the best humor of humorists was produced before ever they heard the distant laughter of their multitudes. Probably what Mr. Anderson means, more specifically, is that life is apt to be translated most accurately by a person who sees it break through the mist at unexpected moments—a person who experiences sudden clear images. A writer, being conscientious, is always straining his eyes for this moment, peering ahead and around; consequently when the moment of revelation comes his eyes are poppy and tired and his sensitized mind has become fogged by the too-frequent half-stimuli of imagined sight. No figure is more pitiful to contemplate than a novelist with a thousand-dollar advance from a publishing house and a date when the manuscript is due. He knows he must invite his soul, but he is compelled to add: "And don't be late, soul!"

June 27, 1931

Most commentators have envied Mr. Coolidge his job, and so have we. We've envied him not so much his word rate as a certain quality of mind that ought to make writing easy. Not that we think he ever dashed off anything idly or hastily—we've heard it said, and we believe it true, that he took his daily paragraph seriously and gave a lot of time to its preparation. But he was, in our opinion, extraordinarily well equipped for turning out a daily paragraph, with a set of hardy New England convictions that would make writing a cinch. For instance, in a recent article, in the short space of two hundred words he touched on Spain's revolution, differences between Church and State in Italy, economic problems in England and Germany, the disturbance in France over Austro-German unity, uncertainty in Russia, the World War, the current depression, and the deficit in the national treasury. Then, casting about for a suitable sentence in conclusion, he wound up with this: "The forces of good are still superior to the forces of evil." To which he signed his name, Calvin Coolidge. A lot of commentators, ourself included, believe that the forces of good are superior to the forces of evil, but most of us work for editors who would send back such a sentence with the marginal notation: "So what?"

In general we think Mr. Coolidge took his job *too* seriously. Every writer of paragraphs or columns knows that his best stuff is apt to be not the finely chiselled piece, but the occasional flow of uncancelled clauses—the regurgitated spirit—words that run to paper swift as rain. Next year we want to see Cal stop counting words, and let himself go.

November 26, 1932

The State has queried us about an item on our last year's tax return —a deduction for traveling expenses. "Please show," the letter says, "why this is necessary and ordinary." We can't possibly show that. Things we do seldom seem particularly necessary, although some of the places we go seem rather ordinary. Why should New York State assume that the only deductible items are the necessary and ordinary expenditures? Were it not for certain phenomenal and ridiculous uses to which we put our private funds, we would not be making our living at all. People are not as rational, nor life as predictable, as the State thinks. There is something about people that compels them to do extraordinary and unnecessary things half the time; often their very restlessness brings them, indirectly, the income for which the State should be grateful—instead of quibbling.

No writer can foretell whether a specific expenditure (for travel or for anything else) is going to yield him a return. Sometimes he makes a killing by buying a nickel subway ride; again he may buy himself a trip around the world and not produce so much as a salable quatrain. It annoys us to discover that the State assumes that we are a race of bookkeepers, that every citizen has at his fingertips the myriad items of his costly little existence. How do we know what we spent last year? Were we to keep count, we'd not have a moment's time in which to earn the great sum from which New York State is getting fabulously wealthy.

July 8, 1933

Because of the way the income-tax law is drafted, the government in collecting its revenues unwittingly discriminates in favor of persons whose occupation is finance. Mr. Kahn, Mr. Morgan, paid no taxes during the bad years because their capital losses were tangible, ponderable, and were kept in a little book by a secretary or a lawyer. What about persons whose occupation is letters, and whose capital losses are unrecorded except on the memo-pad of the heart? What about a writer, we'll say, who finds himself obliged to write a certain amount of stuff during the course of a year, 94 percent of which he regards as inconsiderable, uninspired, and faintly trying to everybody? The money he gets from this, though it keeps him alive, gives him no illusion of gain; and his capital losses, though gigantic, are unreportable. There is no space allotted them on the blank. Or what about a poet who goes a whole year without thinking of so much as one good line? If he happens to be, so to speak, gainfully employed somewhere, he pays his little tax to the government, never mentioning the appalling loss of his lyric capital.

Under the rule by which Morgan and Kahn paid no taxes, we should like to ask the government to refund us 94 percent of the tax we paid in 1927, '28, '29, '30, '31, and '32; and further to request that there be immediately a space made on the income-tax form for the capital losses a writer sustains—either from writing something he doesn't want to write at all, or from failing to write something he wants terribly to write.

November 25, 1933

As the year goes into its dying phase, the thing that most distresses us is the paucity of our literary output. Other than these few rather precise little paragraphs, into which we pour the slow blood of our discontent, we never get around to writing anything at all, in a world when not to write is considered irregular. Though we brood a good deal about writing plays and books, and speak of it familiarly at lunch to our friends (as though we were in the middle of it), a careful search of our premises at the end of a year reveals no trace of a manuscript—merely a few notes on the inside flap of paper-match packs. When we look around and see the output of other writers we grow faint. Both President and Mrs. Roosevelt, to name only two other literary people, have published a book in the past year; and to realize that they, who are really busy, can do it, while we, who seldom have anything pressing on hand, cannot, is extremely discouraging. Literary jealousy is probably at the bottom of many of our anarchical impulses.

March 3, 1934

We encountered a writer this week who wanted our advice. He wanted to know whether he should give up his job teaching school and move to town, where he could meet other writers. "What do you want to meet other writers for?" we asked sharply. And he didn't know. "If you just want to know how they look," we continued, "they look terrible, particularly in the late evening in groups of three to seven, or in the morning singly. If you want to know what they talk about, they talk about themselves and the things they write." The writer thanked us and went back to his useful work of teaching school and writing, safe for a few months more, anyway, from the demoralizing effects of mingling with his craft.

After he had gone, we sat here wondering whether we had been justified in advising a writer to stay away from writers. The longer we pondered the matter, the surer we felt of our ground. In each other's company, writers tend to magnify the significance and difficulty of writing and to destroy its essential simplicity and directness. They also act up more than is necessary to preserve the tradition of temperament. The breakage is very high. In clusters, writers lack that nobleness and grace of character from which come nobleness and grace in art. They ruin tablecloths with lead pencils. Jealous as pigeons, they knife each other in the back and are sorry the next day. We doubt if the total output of writers, good and bad, justifies the enormous fuss and clatter they make out of the business of literature.

Another reason for advising anyone to stay away from the vortex of letters is the tactics of the procurers. An overwhelming number of all books, plays, articles, reviews, stories, poems, and pamphlets that are written in the course of a year originate not as the result of the author's urgency but of somebody else's persuasion or direction. The vestibule of the Muse is packed with solicitors. It seems to us that the great restlessness of publishers, agents, and idea men is degrading and a too great drain on the reservoirs of creation. Anybody who can spell is sought after these days by middlemen holding out sugar cookies.

Of course, mixing with literary people has its amusement value. Certainly there is no sight more engrossing than that of a writer getting ready to write something. We have known several writers who spent virtually their whole lives trying to get themselves into position to create. Something was always wrong: either they needed fewer people about, or they needed more people about, or a room higher up from the earth, or a room below ground. If they were in love, they couldn't write because the passion was too absorbing; if they were out of love, their pen stood still for want of love's urging. One writer once told us he had to be "right down on the ground where he could touch it" before he could create. We have always been mildly jealous of persons of this sort, who find in preparation for work a pleasant substitute for work itself, and whose whole skill is in making sun, moon, and stars conspire for one perfect moment of literary labor.

July 20, 1935

One of the discouraging things about literature as a profession is that it is not a profession at all and has no entrance requirements. To be a dentist, one must hold a degree from an academy; but to write a book, one need hold not so much as a bunch of violets. Anyone can join the ranks of us writers, leaving, for the moment, his own field—or sometimes not leaving it. There is a book out now, we notice, by Dr. Bissell B. Palmer, a surgeon dentist, who was last seen by us in an attitude of extreme extraction. He was using a chisel on us. As we lay there, gazing up into his eyes and wondering how long the novocaine would last, we never supposed that he was dreaming of a book. Which shows how little we know of what goes on in the heart of an extractionist!

October 26, 1935

There are few more pitiable objects than a writer, up and dressed in the morning, ready to write. If he be under compulsion to create something beautiful and immortal before ten minutes past two—an hour set by a methodical publisher—terror grips him and he begins to resort to as many ruses as a hunted fox. One of his favorite tricks is to pay a visit to a barber, in order to delay, by twenty minutes or so, the dreaded moment when he must push the clean sheet of paper in his typewriter and sit staring at it with wide, bloodshot eyes. A barber's chair is a writer's last sanctuary; if all else fails he stakes everything on a hot towel and an olive-oil shampoo, hoping that when the pores are opened up something will find its way into his head besides the warm oil, hoping that with the last aromatic pat of witch hazel against his cheek the blood will come, hoping that he will surprise the Muse in a bottle of Wildroot.

This pressure brought to bear on writers is no joke. The long arm of the printing press reaches out into the farthest nook and corner, sparing no one. Every noon sees insatiable publishers out pimping for the Muse, goading authors over the luncheon table, mentioning dates of publication, serial rights, trying to rig up a date between a writer and his secret self. Not even business people are allowed to mind their own business and remain uncreative. We know a zoologist who needed some mice for classroom demonstrations, and when he wrote to a mousery in Florida ordering specimens, he got back a letter asking him please to tell what he wanted the mice for, as "an editor has asked me to write an article entitled 'What in the world are they used for?'" The zoologist flew into a rage, and could hardly face his class.

April 24, 1937

Partly by stealth, partly by cunning, a doctor gained entrance to our middle ear last week, hoping to discover there the secret of the dizziness from which we suffer. He blew and he blew, setting up Eustachian williwaws of seeming great intensity. The ear must be the very vestibule of the mind, for as we sat there bracing ourself, it seemed as though all the great winds of the world were rattling at the door of the skull, and that the next squall would explode the partition and carry our Intellect away. We still have a ringing in the ear—a globule of Thought, caught in a sea puss; and we still yaw about when we try to hold a course through the streets. If they can't find anything wrong in our ear, we understand, they are going to look under our teeth, for traces of mice. And from there it's only a short jump to the tonsils themselves, where the Harpies live.

Physicians on the trail of a man's dizziness are explorers of a hardy sort. They are ready to go anywhere, on short notice, traveling light. They speak of "toxicity," and set out for the Yukon. Yet there are undoubtedly toxic secretions in a man which the medical fraternity know very little of. A writer, detecting signs of decay in his own stuff, secretes internal poisons which would make even a diseased tonsil sit up and take notice.

May 21, 1938

A call has gone out to writers to meet on Sunday in the cause of a Federal Bureau of Fine Arts. "In issuing this call," said the letter we received, "we are moved by a belief that it is the desire of all writers . . . to have the advance of culture accelerated, the base of art broadened, and the economic place of artists reasonably secure."

Here, in a sentence, is the issue. One must decide how he feels about the acceleration of culture before he can know whether he wants a Bureau of Fine Arts. It is as common to believe that culture should be accelerated as to believe that whooping cough should be retarded, yet we have never heard any devotee of the bureaucratic ideal make out a solid case for this proposed quickening. A Bureau of Fine Arts would indeed accelerate culture, in that it would provide public money for creative enterprise, and by so doing would make it easier for artists and writers to go on being artists and writers, as well as for persons who are not artists and writers to continue the happy pretence. Such a bureau would presumably have other effects symptomatic of acceleration. The radio, for example, has immensely accelerated culture in that it has brought to millions of people, in torrential measure, the distant and often adulterated sounds of art and life. But it is still an open question whether this mysterious electrical diffusion has been a blessing to man, who appears at the moment to be most unhappy about nearly everything.

Santayana, although he won't be at the meeting Sunday, is a writer whose views on the diffusion of culture we find instructive. "Great thoughts," he says, "require a great mind and pure beauties a profound sensibility. To attempt to give such things a wide currency is to be willing to denaturalize them in order to boast that they have been propagated. Culture is on the horns of this dilemma: if profound and noble it must remain rare, if common it must become mean. These alternatives can never be eluded until some purified and high-bred race succeeds the promiscuous bipeds that now blacken the planet."

Advocates of a bureaucratic culture, in wishing to establish artists more firmly in the national economy, argue that it is to a nation's advantage to make its creative souls more comfortable financially; but here we feel they are confusing an aesthetic ideal with a social one. When two persons are in need of food, there is always the embarrassing question whether to feed the talented one first, on the somewhat questionable grounds that he may live to provide beauty for the other one (who in the meanwhile may die of starvation, or laughter). This is essentially what the bureau proposes, and it is a proposal which naturally meets with very little opposition among writers and artists, who feel both hunger and beauty, and who can always use a little dough.

Sponsorship of the creative ideal by the government has many delightful delinquencies. It assumes, among other things, that art is recognizable in embryo—or at least recognizable enough to make it worth the public's while to pay for raising the baby. And it assumes that artists, like chickens, are responsive to proper diet. We sometimes wonder if they are. Housman, when they asked him what caused him to produce poems, said that as far as he could determine it was usually some rather inappropriate physical disability, such as a relaxed sore throat. This catarrhal theory of the creative life has always fascinated us, and it should give the government pause before setting aside too great a share of the public funds for improving the vigor of poets.

August 1, 1942

William Saroyan, the wingèd, has been talking things over with his draft board. He has given the board its choice of taking his body (and leaving his mind alone) or else deferring both body and mind so that he can go on writing in a civilian capacity. "If they want me as a person, as a body," he said, "the responsibility is theirs. However, I'll insist on one thing and that is that I be a soldier and no more, that I will not be required to write." This dream of divorcing the intellect from soldiering is common to many of us, although few of us manage to use the word "insist" with Mr. Saroyan's charming innocence. The fact is, the Army is the only organization in the world that can compel an independent writer to become a press agent or propagandist. This power which the Army wields is a very grave responsibility—in our opinion just as grave as the power to order a man into a military engagement from which he may not emerge whole. We are, in fact, deeply sympathetic with Mr. Saroyan's feelings in this matter. We would also love to be in his squad when the sergeant hands him a pen and orders him to make like a playwright.

October 10, 1942

Whit Burnett, editor of *Story Magazine*, is the first person, so far as we know, to work out the batting averages of living American writers —a move he made by way of preparing himself for editing an anthology. Thus, from a literary scene badly muddied up by the foul uncertainties of who was any good, now emerges a clear, concise picture carried to three decimal places. It is a big help to have this check list and to know that Thornton Wilder is batting .681, Hemingway

.805, and that Sandburg heads the bunch with .853, the No. 1 creative American. We in this office are interested, professionally, of course, and a staff meeting has been called to decide whether we will henceforth publish a writer's percentage after his name. What we sincerely hope is that the publication of these batting averages based on the actual vote of the people (Burnett didn't make it very clear who the people were, except that they were a "cross section") will put an end to the brawling which goes on between writers, who now and then become locked in mortal struggle over a fine point of literary supremacy. (You recall what happened when Max Eastman met Hemingway in a publisher's office.) There should be no occasion, any more, for physical violence. A heavy hitter like Hemingway can simply pull out the morning newspaper and point to the list with a broad sneer.

Perhaps the thing we liked best about the Burnett batting list was the inclusion, among living authors, of Clarence Day. That has our full approval.

January 2, 1943

We notice there's a book out called *How to Retire and Like It.* We haven't seen it, but it is certainly one of those books which are a living denial of their own theme. Writing a book is hard work, any way you look at it, and anybody who is doing that much work is not retired—he is up and around. The literary life is, in fact, the greatest hurdle for anyone who is racing toward the goal of ease and leisure. For those who come fresh to that life from some other sort of life, it is a tremendous stimulus and driving force, because of new excitements and checks from magazines and all that sort of thing; and for those who have always lived the life, there is no end to it short of the grave. A few people have been able to stop writing, but you can number them on the keys of your typewriter.

Imagine, if you can, what the literary life has done to Mrs. Louise Dickinson Rich, who wrote a book called *We Took to the Woods,* describing the pleasures of isolation. Her book is now a Book-of-the-Month Club selection, and although the author may still rise early and get breakfast with her mittens on, she unquestionably faces a long, grueling day indoors at a desk piled high with letters from wistful escapists, thwarted woodsmen, and publishers. We like to lie in our snug city bed at night and think of the Rich cottage in the Maine woods, with the snow drifting around the eaves and the letters accumulating in the living room, near Ralph's gum boots. Next summer, if our guess is any good, the road which goes by their camp will resound to the thud of sightseers and pioneers of one sort or another, and Mrs. Rich will sneak silently over the ridge with her portable and start the first chapter of the inevitable sequel, called *We Took to Our Heels.*

January 27, 1945

We were walking about Radio City the other day and a piece of paper fluttered down in front of us. We picked it up and found that it was a fragment of a radio script, containing this direction: "SOUND—Remote Homesick-making Toots on a Train Whistle." We threw the paper away but could not dislodge this image from our mind. High in the big R.C.A. Building, some writer, some toiling, ink-stained, coffee-drenched wretch had pecked this out on his typewriter, manufacturing pathos out of standard material—nostalgic toots on a train whistle. In due course an obedient sound man, nervously watching the script, had tooted his remote toots. These, it is safe to say, had been heard by thousands, perhaps millions, of people sitting in their homes and cottages in Cattatonk on the D.L.&W., in Pocatello on the Union Pacific, in the outskirts of Rahway and Leesburg and White River Junction and Gloversville and Little Rock, remote from Radio City. The noise of the radio in their parlors had drowned out the sound of the real train whistle that was tooting round the bend not far from the homes and cottages. (Never pick up a piece of paper.) We began to see how untrustworthy are radio's standard devices, how fragmentary the story they tell. This writer, high in his tower, had he once as a boy listened to the real thing and felt the real uneasiness? It may well have been a remote train whistle in some sleepy valley that stirred something deep inside him, bringing him up to the city, one more script writer to the tower, who then, hearing a different train, turns in upon himself and tries to toot himself back home.

May 19, 1945

We laid over in Hollywood one night last week between trains, to pay a call on a former easterner in his new setting. It was our first visit to the place, and we came away with no very distinct impression.

Except for its air of impermanence and the complete breakdown of its transportation facilities, Hollywood seemed indistinguishable from any other wealthy backwater. We remember arising early and standing on a zebra skin while shaving. We recall that the writers we encountered seemed in good health but that they kept looking behind them, like girls crossing a pasture. One of them confided to us that he had been on the same page for three days and saw no way of getting off it. Writers were working in pairs, or groups, and they seemed more like conspirators than interpreters. On the whole, Hollywood struck us as a difficult place in which to pursue the literary life, with pretty stenographers lounging around in slacks and with a mocking bird outside the window shouting, "Flap-doodle, fol-deroo, fol-deroo, kill it, kill it, kill it."

December 11, 1948

Before a book can be published in Czechoslovakia, the publisher must submit an outline of it to the government for approval. Accompanying the outline must be written opinions of "responsible literary critics, scientists, or writers." (We are quoting from a dispatch to the *Times.*) The question of who is a responsible critic or writer comes up in every country, of course. It must have come up here when the Algonquin Hotel advertised special week-end rates for "accredited writers." We often used to wonder just how the Algonquin arrived at the answer to the fascinating question of who is an accredited writer, and whether the desk clerk required of an applicant a rough draft of an impending novel. It seems to us that the Czech government is going to be in a spot, too. No true critic or writer is "responsible" in the political sense which this smelly edict implies, and in order to get the kind of censorship the government obviously wants, the government will need to go a step further and require that the critic himself be certified by a responsible party, and then a step beyond that and require that the responsible party be vouched for. This leads to infinity, and to no books. Which is probably the goal of the Czech government.

The matter of who is, and who isn't, a responsible writer or scientist reminds us of the famous phrase in Marxist doctrine—the phrase that is often quoted and that has won many people to Communism as a theory of life: "From each according to his ability; to each according to his needs." Even after you have contemplated the sheer beauty of this concept, you are left holding the sheer problem of accreditation: who is needy, who is able? Again the desk clerk looms—a shadowy man. And behind the clerk another clerk, for an accreditation checkup. And so it goes. Who shall be the man who has the authority to establish our innermost need, who shall be the one to approve the standard of achievement of which we are capable? Perhaps, as democracy assumes, every man is a writer, every man wholly needy, every man capable of unimaginable deeds. It isn't as beautiful to the ear as the Marxian phrase, maybe, but there's an idea there somewhere.